Private Listing

Boss Me

C.S. Berry

Cover Photo by Michelle Lancaster www.michellelancaster.com

Cover design by Lori Jackson https://www.lorijacksondesign.com/

Object Cover design by Opulent Design

Author Note

Dear Reader,

Welcome back! If you haven't read Private Listing: Watch Me and Private Listing: Bind Me, please be aware that this is a serial. There is no recap and if you haven't read the first two books, you will likely be lost unless you're looking for just the spicy stuff, which there is plenty.

Everyone else, I hope you're ready for this. Sorry, for the cliffy at the end of the last one. Private Listing started out as a serial and it became a four book series with additional content and edits. These books are meant to be read in order and there will be cliffhangers. Though this one is softer. Fair warning.

Don't worry. There is plenty of group spice, but beyond sex, she develops personal relationships with each of her guys.

PRIVATE LISTING is very much about consensual play.

While I tried to be as conscious of proper play within BDSM, please remember this is a fantasy. It does not follow all the rules. While everything might be possible, always go to a more trusted source for information than my book

I love connecting with my readers. You can find me at my Facebook group, C.S. Berry's Spicy Executive Suite. You can also follow me on Instagram, but I generally post about the stories that are ongoing on Kindle Vella (which may contain spoilers). While there are new scenes in the book, you can always continue in the Vella, in case you can't wait for the next book to release. The chapter numbers coordinate with the episode numbers.

For a list of content warnings or to join my newsletter, please visit my website csberry.com.

XOXOXO,
C.S. Berry

Chapter 77

In the Loop

Blake

Seth heads into his office after lunch, but Madison isn't with him. He wanted some time to help ease any aches she may have from all our fucking the past few days. It's my night to sleep with her. I'll have to get inventive, because no matter what she says, she needs a break from being fucked.

But we can still do things to relieve the need that seems constant between us. I smirk and listen for her to come up. I'm sure Seth gave her a time limit. Leaving her alone has us all worried, but maybe we're crowding her too much.

There's nowhere safer than our apartment. But it seems like every time we leave her alone something happens.

Besides, it's hard to leave her alone. I've never met such a natural submissive as Madison. She gives in so beautifully to our every desire. I need to make sure she's not just doing it to please us. That she enjoys it as much as she seems to.

A new email comes in from Theo, who's working at Taylor's. I wanted Hunter to be her stalker. It would have tied everything up in a nice bow. Maybe he would have gotten some prison time or at least an arrest on his record.

The guy is too damned cocky to creep in the background, though, like her stalker has. No, he had no issues going after her in the middle of the day with witnesses everywhere.

The sad reality is his father will probably not do much about it.

I glance at my open door. Her desk is still empty. How long has it been?

If she's much longer, I'll go hunting for her. But right now, I focus on answering Theo's email. He needs details from some files here, and I dig around on my computer to get him the information.

I should call my friend on the force to see if they've made any progress.

Madison screams. My heart stops as I race out of my office. Noah already has Madison curled against his chest. Trembling, she breathes deeply while he murmurs against her hair. Her shoulders shake and her hands clutch his shirt.

He meets my eyes and looks pointedly at Madison's desk.

Knowing she's being taken care of, I turn to the large white box and step closer. The whole interior is splotchy red. Inside is the dress she wore to dinner the other night. The night she played with Coop and Noah.

Now, it's torn almost to shreds, stained with red dye of some sort. And on top of it is photo after photo of her wearing it. Her on campus. Her in line for coffee. At the park. In the library. In class. In her apartment. In her bathroom, putting her hair up.

Fuck.

A slip of white paper on the floor catches my eye. I pick it up.

Shame about your dress, little one. You should take better care of your things. I know it was your favorite. That's why I bought one years ago to make sure you'd be able to wear it for me. Soon.

The elevator opens, but I'm busy looking through the contents of the box, using a pencil to sift through the remains of her dress. I don't want to destroy any evidence the police might be able to obtain.

"What's happening?" Coop asks, his voice urgent as he strides over to us.

"Is this a bad time?" another voice asks. "Maybe I should come back."

I lift my head and meet Patrick Beck's brown eyes. Patrick is our attorney. He's a few years older than us. A family man with a wife and two kids already. His shrewd gaze takes in the scene in front of him.

Coop glances in the box before moving to take Madison from Noah's arms. He kisses the top of her head and tucks her against him. "No, Patrick, stay. We need to finish the legal on the Haverside project today. Would you mind waiting in the conference room?"

Patrick's eyes linger with curiosity and interest on Madison in Coop's arms. But then he nods, his expression blank, and heads into the conference room. Noah follows him and shuts the door behind Patrick.

On the way back to us, Noah opens Seth's door and gestures to him before returning to Madison, rubbing his hand down her back.

"Where did this come from?" I ask.

"Delivered to the front desk. I picked it up after lunch," Madison says. Coop's chest muffles her words.

"I'll go check." Noah presses a kiss to the top of her head before heading to the elevator.

I pull a clean tissue from her desk and lift the photos out using it. There must be fifty pictures of her in that dress. Different days, different seasons. All candid. Some from a distance. Some close up. Fuck.

When I touch the dress with the tissue, it doesn't come away red. It's dry.

"We threw that dress away yesterday," Coop says, barely above a whisper. He grabs a tissue and hands it to Madison. She clutches it in her trembling hand as she finally looks over at me.

Her eyes are watery and her skin pale.

Coop looks like he wants to say more, but with Patrick here, we need to stay quiet. Even though he's our lawyer, he's an outsider. But he deals with all our legal, including our NDAs and consent contracts.

"What's happening?" Seth emerges from his office and takes a step toward Madison. Coop shakes his head and darts his gaze to the conference room door. We can't raise suspicion.

Patrick may know that we had the contracts drawn up, but he doesn't know if she signed them or what the status of our relationship is.

Seth's fingers clench like he wants to take Madison into his arms, but we need to maintain the lie that she's only with Coop. I'm fighting the urge to hold her as well. Taking a deep breath in, Seth stands beside me, searching the contents of the box.

"Patrick is in the conference room." Coop runs his hand over the nape of Madison's neck. Her cheek rests against his heart while she watches Seth and me with huge blue eyes.

"I'll call my friend. This is definitely escalating."

The note is almost threatening, but with such pleasant tones to it. Barely a threat at all, except for the red, shredded dress. It's like he cares about her. It's creepy as fuck, is what it is.

"Who would do this? I can't think of anyone who would hate me enough." Madison shivers against Coop.

"Old boyfriend? Someone who thought they deserved your attention and didn't get it? Maybe Valerie and her boyfriend trying to shake you up?" I don't even believe that one. It's too methodical. That doesn't seem to be Valerie and Jeff's MO. I sit on the edge of her desk next to the box. "This guy—"

"Or girl," Seth says. His blue eyes are hard as he shuffles through the photos, careful to use a tissue on the corners.

I nod. "You're right. This person has been following you for years without making this kind of contact." I pause. "Or has anything like this happened before?"

"Creepy boxes with a torn dress? Videos of me naked? Weird

texts?" Madison trembles and shakes her head. "No, nothing like that."

I glance toward the conference room. I swear I see a shadow under the door. Jerking my head toward it, I blow out a breath. "Let's put this away. We'll see what the police have to say about it."

Madison moves to help. Coop tips her chin up to make her look him in the eyes.

"Sweetheart, I'm going to grab your tablet and a laptop, and you're working downstairs for the rest of the afternoon." Coop meets my eyes. "Can you go down with her?"

I nod with my lips pressed flat. "Of course."

I still have some phone calls and some work I need to do, but nothing that can't be done downstairs. "Let me know when Noah gets back and what he's found out. I may need to have you downstairs when the police come."

Coop presses a gentle kiss to Madison's lips and then gently guides her toward me. Her wide blue eyes gaze up at me. I resist the urge to draw her into my arms and hold her until all of this goes away.

Fuck, this girl is under my skin, and I don't want to get her out from under it.

Coop

Rage shudders through me as Madison walks to the elevator with Blake. Someone is after her. They've gotten to her twice. Once while under our care. That's bullshit.

As they enter the elevator, her eyes meet mine. I give her a reassuring smile. As soon as the doors close, I drop my smile. For her, I could pretend anything, but right now, I want to destroy something. I want to set fire to the box and all its contents.

When Seth puts the items back in the box, something catches my attention.

"Wait." I step forward and reach for the pictures. Seth catches my hand and holds it. That urge to lash out fills me again. I close my eyes, unwilling to hurt one of my best friends.

"Use a tissue or a glove." Seth's words lack inflection. My eyes meet his, and I can see the same carefully banked rage blazing in them.

I'm not alone. My brothers are on the same page. We all want to protect Madison at any cost. He releases my hand. I grab a tissue and pick up her letter opener in my other hand.

Using the letter opener, I lift the dress to reveal another picture. My chest fills with a swarm of bees, buzzing and angry, aching to burst out and destroy everything in their wake.

"What the fuck." Seth reaches in and takes the picture.

It's our lobby and I'm kissing the shit out of Madison by our elevator. Was that Monday? It doesn't matter. This is proof the stalker knows about me and Madison. We already suspected he could have witnessed me fucking her in the file room. What else does he know?

How does he have this kind of access to us? Is it one of our employees? How could that be when she just started with us?

"There's more on the back." Seth's voice trembles with rage.

"What does it say?" But I already know. I can tell by Seth's voice and his stoic face. It's a threat against one of us.

"Don't play with the boys, little one, unless you want to find out what I do to keep what's mine."

I want to tear the picture from Seth's hands and rip it into little shreds. I want to find this bastard and teach him I'm not so easily cowed. That when faced with a fight, I don't back down. I fight to win. And Madison is mine.

Seth returns the picture to where we found it. "This stays between us. The police will find it, but Madison doesn't need to know."

"She doesn't need to know that this fucker is coming for us now?" I can't keep the rage from my tone. Fuck, I need to calm down. Our lawyer is here and I need to focus on work. I know this but my insides churn. I swipe a hand over my hair, wanting to dig my hands into it and pull to feel something besides this swirling hate in the pit of my stomach.

"No, she doesn't," Seth says with a finality that brooks no arguments.

I inhale. He's right. She's already scared. Her whole body trembled like a leaf against mine. I didn't want to let her go, but she needs to be protected. Blake would do anything for her, just like any of us.

The elevator dings and Noah steps out. He shakes his head. Nothing. This guy—or person—is a fucking ghost. They move in and out of our lives, leaving wreckage without leaving a fucking clue.

A noise comes from the conference room. A reminder I have work to take care of. Fuck.

"I've got to get back to work." I gesture to the closed door. If this stalker would come at us using a computer, I might be able to do something, but this is best handled by the police.

Seth releases his breath. "I'll let you know when the police come."

Noah grabs my shoulder and squeezes.

That dress. What we did with Madison that night. Does the stalker know we're the ones who ripped that dress from her body?

"Show Noah the picture." With that, I walk into the conference room.

Patrick looks up from his phone as I enter. "Everything okay?"

"Yeah." I resist the urge to run my fingers through my hair. It's tucked in my standard bun for work. "Just a personal issue."

"Anything I need to be read into?" Patrick raises his eyebrow. He's not just the company's attorney, but with my large trust and assets, I use him as my private attorney as well.

"Not at this point." We're dealing with this on our own. Of course, the police have everything we know about. We aren't stupid enough to keep this to ourselves. We have resources but they're limited. The police have more access, but we also know there's only so much time the police can spend on a case like this. There's no suspect and no evidence to point to a suspect. Yet.

Besides the two videos and the file room, the stalker hasn't really made their presence known to Madison until now. She has no clue who it might be. It's frustrating, but we have to wait and see what happens next. That's the power a stalker holds. They have access to you when you aren't even aware of them.

You always have to look over your shoulder. Waiting for their next move.

"You need me, I'm here." Patrick leans back in his chair and runs his hand through his neat blond hair. "The firm has access to whatever services you might require."

"Thank you." I'm aware of their services. We used them for all the background checks we've done. When Andrea went nuclear, they were the ones to press her back into her box. For a hefty sum of money, to her and to them for their services.

"Will you be at the benefit tomorrow?" he asks. This is small talk while I get set up and ready to work. It also gives me time to cool down and focus.

"Of course. Will you and Anna be there?" I log into the tablet I left in here.

"The firm has a table every year. We were lucky to find a babysitter for the night."

I've never met Patrick's children, but I know they're young. I make a noncommittal noise.

"Was that the new assistant?" Patrick jerks his head toward the door.

"Yes." I can't talk about her right now. The anger still boils within me.

Patrick clears his throat. "Are you involved with her?"

I glare at him, wondering what his motives are. He knows about the contracts. His office drew them up for us.

"Sorry, that just seemed emotional rather than physical." He holds up his hands in surrender. "Just protecting my assets. After all, we uncovered her debt in our background check. I hope she isn't taking advantage of you."

I bark out a sharp laugh. "No, Patrick. She isn't taking advantage of me. For her protection, to the outside world, we're seeing each other. Besides, the company pays her plenty to cover her personal debts, which she acquired while attending school. Not because of some gambling or shopping habit. She's sharp and works hard and deserves every penny she earns."

"It wouldn't be the first time a woman thought she caught a big fish." Patrick pulls out his files from his briefcase. "We just need to be careful."

Leighton. She came from old money, but she wanted the power of my name. Elizabeth Hartfield. That bitch thought she'd won the fucking jackpot, getting close to me through Seth. I'm used to being wanted for what I can offer. After all, I'm gorgeous and wealthy. I'm bound to attract certain types of women.

Patrick was the lawyer for Morrigan Technology Group when we had to handle Andrea and Rachel. His firm handled my family's needs for years, so he's familiar with my history from when he took over my family as a client. But comparing Madison to them is unthinkable.

"She's not like those other women." She's softer, fewer harsh edges. Every reaction with her is honest, not contrived. I believe her when she says she wants this experience with us.

Patrick nods. "I hope not. For your sake."

I don't need his worry. I just need Madison to be safe.

Chapter 78

Logging Hours

Madison

When a noise startles me awake, I bolt upright on the couch and the tablet slips to the floor with a clunk. Blake glances my way.

"You okay?" He rises from the chair.

"I'm good." As soon as my heart stops racing, I'll be better.

He stands anyway, abandoning his laptop. Reaching down, I pick up the tablet and set it on the coffee table before he sits next to me.

As he tucks a stray strand of hair behind my ear, his green eyes search mine.

"You could go lie down in my room if you want to sleep." His fingers curl around the nape of my neck, sending shivers coursing through my tense body.

"No, thank you." I have to pull myself together. "I have work to do."

Pressing his lips together, he nods and strokes his thumb along my jawline.

"Do you want to talk about what happened?" His voice is gruff.

"No." After screaming my head off, I shut down inside, letting them take care of me and shuffle me around between them. When

Blake and I came downstairs, he made me some hot tea and set me up on the couch to work.

His friend on the force came quicker than we expected. When he took the box as evidence, I had to explain there might be cum on it. And that they may find two different samples. I'm lucky I didn't explode into flames from embarrassment. He didn't even bat an eye and just said if they find any DNA on the dress he would contact us to come in and give samples.

We went through the pictures in the box to pinpoint when and where each one was taken to see if there was a pattern. Some of them were impossible for me to pin down. It was my favorite dress. I wore it a lot during college.

Blake took the officer aside and talked to him for a few minutes while I looked at my life as seen through the eyes of someone who wants to terrorize me. I still can't imagine who would want to do this. I didn't make a lot of friends during college. But I also didn't make enemies that I know of.

I had some unwanted attention from a professor and a few guys who asked me out and I told them no. But I couldn't tell you what those guys' names were now.

Before the officer left, he let me know the phone they'd taken into evidence for the Valerie and Jeff case received a lot of worried texts from a number labeled *Neighbor Robert*. He gave me a printout of the texts, which I set on the island and didn't even glance at. I had too much already swirling around my brain.

After that, we quietly went to work. Me on the couch and Blake at the dining room table. It must have all caught up with me because even as interested in working as I am, I fell asleep.

Blake's lips turn down at the corners, but he doesn't press me to talk about it.

What is there to talk about? Someone is creeping on my life and there's not a damned thing I can do about it. They can get to me anywhere. But hopefully not here.

Which will keep me a prisoner in this apartment. Not that it's a hardship when the other inmates keep me so well entertained.

"I could go with you and sit in bed while you laid down?" He draws his hand away from me, and I miss his warmth immediately.

"No. I don't want to sleep." I hold up the tablet.

He nods and stands. "We protect what's ours."

A burst of warmth floods my chest. Tears choke my throat. "Thank you."

He returns to his workspace and picks up his phone. I focus on the notes I was reading before I fell asleep. Falling asleep on the job is so unprofessional, but I'll make up the time even if I have to work into the night.

I'm not here for a free ride. I earn my keep. While I enjoy my bosses in more ways than just work, I need to keep learning and growing as an employee so someday I can run my own business. While I don't know exactly what I want to focus on, I know I don't want to be beholden to a boss or bosses for the rest of my life.

My life is my own and I want to live it that way. I don't want to coast through life as someone else's possession like my mother has. Sure, my father loves her, but he also makes her feel small sometimes because he works to support her.

As the sky darkens beyond the windows, I need to do something more active. My fingers still tremble, and every little noise sets my pulse racing. Figuring I'll work more after dinner, I go into the kitchen and pull out food to cook.

I'm cutting up vegetables to stir-fry when Noah comes in the door. His eyes immediately seek me out and he walks over to me. I set the knife down right before he pulls me into his arms and hugs me so tight and so close.

I wrap my arms around his waist and exhale against him. He's like this warm beacon in my life. When I'm in his arms, nothing can get to me. I inhale the crisp, woodsy scent of him, and some of the tension releases from my shoulders.

"How are you doing, kitten?" He presses his lips against the top of my head.

"Good."

At least, I am in this moment, with his arms around me. I could stay here forever.

Forever isn't part of our arrangement though. It may not be limited in time, but these guys will eventually grow tired of me and the drama I unknowingly brought with me. Maybe things won't be so easy sexually. Maybe having a stalker will drive them away. Or maybe I'll leave to start my own life and they'll continue on as if I was just a side note.

Just another assistant for the next one to wonder about.

My eyes burn for a second, but I squeeze them shut and draw away from Noah, forcing a smile to my lips. He tips my chin and kisses me softly. I could bask in the tenderness of this kiss for a lifetime and never get enough.

Pressing his forehead to mine, he draws in a breath. "I wish you were mine tonight."

I touch his cheek and whisper, "I'm always yours."

It won't matter how long I'm away from him. Noah is mine and I'm his. Maybe we won't be together but we'll always belong to each other.

He kisses me again. His dark eyes hold me still for a moment before he walks over to Blake. I sigh. While Noah is easy to fall for, I'm surprised how easy it's been to fall for all these guys. Every day with them I fall a little deeper, a little harder.

I barely hear Coop before his arms wrap around me from behind and he tugs me against his hard body. He leans down and whispers in my ear, "Curious how to get both of them into your bed tonight?"

A laugh escapes me. Noah and Blake glance over to me and Coop.

"I bet if you asked Seth nicely, he'd orchestrate a really low-key playtime for you." Coop's whispered words feed the desire that's always on simmer around these guys, even when the world seems against me.

I squeeze his arms and tilt my head back and to the side to look up at his blue eyes shining with laughter. "I don't think tonight is going to be that night."

He kisses the top of my head and squeezes me back against him. When his hard cock digs into my ass, my body softens in anticipation.

Addictive. That's what these guys are.

"I can't wait to show you off at the benefit." His words curl around me like warm smoke that could dissipate quickly. A flutter of nervous butterflies releases in my stomach.

"I hope I don't embarrass you. I've never been to anything like this before. How will I even know how to act?" It's not like there were a lot of formals growing up, and even fewer that I attended. In college, I kept to myself. I didn't join a sorority or go to any parties.

"You'll be fantastic, sweetheart." He kisses me behind the ear, then smacks my ass as he pulls away. "Make my dinner, woman."

As he backs away with that flirty smirk on his lips, I give him a genuine smile because, for a moment, he got me out of my head. Away from the trauma of opening that box and seeing all those pictures and the dress and the note. I turn back to the cutting board and pick up the knife.

"Hey." Seth steps in front of me and takes my face in his hands, squatting so our faces are on the same level. "Where'd you go, princess?"

I blink at him and focus on those beautiful dark blue eyes. "Nowhere."

He searches my eyes for a few heartbeats before his thumb sweeps over my lower lip. "Do you want me to finish making dinner?"

My hand hurts and my gaze falls to where it's clenched tightly around the knife handle over the cutting board. I release my grip and set it down. "I . . ."

I what? I'm losing it? I need to stay busy to keep my mind distracted, but that's not even helping. For years, someone has followed me and taken my picture, and I never noticed. How could I not notice the same person time after time?

I bought that dress a year before I moved in with Valerie. So that leaves someone in college or maybe someone who followed me here from my small town. Or maybe somewhere I interned early on or an old side job. It's not like I haven't met a ton of people in my short time here in New York.

Any of them could have decided I was theirs, but I didn't know it. How could I not know it?

I blink and I'm at the table. Fuck, what the hell is going on?

I focus on Coop.

"There she is. You worried us, sweetheart."

"You need to sleep, kitten."

"Eat first." Seth puts the stir-fry on the table in front of me. My stomach rumbles, reminding me I barely touched my lunch.

"Are you okay?" Blake takes my hand into his warm one and I nod automatically. "It's okay to zone out a little. You've been through a lot recently."

I take a deep breath before I meet his eyes. He's always searching. Does he ever find me?

"I'm good. Just a little tired from last night." I thread my fingers into his and draw on his warmth.

"Then we'll make it an early night." Blake takes my hand and doesn't release it as he dishes up some food for him and me.

I look around the table and smile at the guys to reassure them I'm fine. We had a late night, followed by an active morning and busy lunch, and then the box . . .

I don't let my mind sit on that again as I eat with the guys. They talk about work around me, and I try to focus and make note of what I'll need to work on tomorrow. I really should finish working tonight, too, but Blake is right. I need sleep.

"We won't have a meeting at the end of the day tomorrow." Seth's voice draws my attention. "We'll need time to get ready for the benefit. We'll take separate cars."

Ah yes, something else to dwell on. Two of my guys will be on actual dates and Blake will have his sister with him.

"When does your sister get in?" This is the easiest thing to focus on. Not on the burning pit of jealousy stirring inside.

"Kayla gets in tomorrow morning and will work until I pick her up." Blake squeezes my hand before he releases it to eat. "She's excited to meet you."

"Does she know about us?" I mean all of us.

"She'll think you're dating Coop. That will be easiest for now." Blake takes a sip of his drink.

I sigh. To the world, I'll be Coop's girlfriend, or his latest piece of ass. To these guys, I'll be the woman they come home to but can't tell the world about. Am I good with that? Being their secret? Falling in love with men who can never claim me fully?

"We won't stay until the end. After, we'll all come home." Seth takes a drink. For a second, my brain stalls on them bringing their dates home, but that's not what he means. He means they'll come home to me and our bed.

I don't know which would be worse—staying at home waiting for them, or watching my men with women who want them.

"No kissing or inappropriate touching?" I ask hesitantly. Again, who am I besides their employee and fuck buddy?

Seth's eyes meet mine. "Nothing besides them holding our arms and dancing."

Coop barks out a laugh. "Because Elizabeth won't try anything to get back into your bed? And who knows what type of conniving woman Noah is bringing? After all, his mother set him up."

I swallow the food in my mouth and it falls like a lump into my stomach. My guys are attractive and each quite the catch. I wouldn't blame these women for trying for more. But right now, they're mine, and I won't give that up without a fight.

"Seriously, Coop?" Noah shakes his head. "She's a fucking date. Not my choice for marriage or even to date seriously. I did this because Blake's bringing his sister, and as much as I love seeing Kayla, she won't draw heat off Madison dating you."

"We do have to appear to be on dates." Seth pushes back in his chair. His gaze holds mine. "But we'll all be coming home to you, princess. Don't think for a minute either of those women could get under our skin."

I nod. This is a fucked-up situation.

"Don't leave Coop's side." Blake picks up his plate and takes it to the kitchen sink. "We don't know who will be there. It's possible Valerie or Jeff could get in. While we put Hunter in the doghouse with his father, he'll still probably be there. And whoever your stalker is . . ."

"Whoever my stalker is will probably be there. He seems to be everywhere in my life. Even before I knew I had a stalker." I pick up my barely touched plate and take it to the sink, standing next to Blake. "I won't go anywhere alone except the ladies' room."

"No." Blake shakes his head.

"I'm not taking Coop to the bathroom with me." Yeah, that would go over well. We'd probably never make it back out. My cheeks flush with the heat rising in my body.

"When you go, Kayla will go with you." Blake acts like this is a done deal.

"Who's going to attack me in the bathroom?" I throw my hands up. I don't expect absolute privacy, but I don't need a babysitter either.

"Valerie." Seth's voice draws my attention to the others beside the island.

"Your stalker could be a woman, kitten." Noah's voice is quiet and practical.

"Whoever my stalker is has taken pictures and videos and intruded in my life enough." I straighten and meet each of their eyes. "Valerie and Jeff already took away most of my freedom. I just want things to go back to being normal and easy."

Blake draws me into his arms. "Things were probably never normal or easy."

I blow a strand of hair out of my face. He's right. Things have never been easy. This isn't easy, except being with them. That's easy. Letting them into my heart. That's easy.

Watching them on their dates with other women? I don't know how I'm going to handle that. But I know it won't be easy.

Chapter 79

Hanging by a Thread

Madison

"What's on your mind, tiger?" Blake puts his tablet beside the lamp.

After cleaning up the kitchen, Blake insisted on coming to bed. I said good night to the others and got long lingering kisses from all of them. I changed into PJs that were in a drawer in Blake's closet and settled in bed next to him with my tablet to finish reading some reports.

The words are blurring when Blake asks me that question. I set the tablet on the nightstand and rub my eyes. "Work. I'm behind. It feels like I'm always behind."

Before I started, the temp had done the bare minimum. Bringing everything up to my standards takes time. And then after the attack, I didn't work a full week. Shit like this keeps happening.

His arm wraps around my shoulder, drawing me into his side. I snuggle in against him, appreciating his spicy scent and warmth. See? Easy.

"Work will be there. You don't have any deadlines. If we need to work the weekend to catch up, we will." Blake rubs his hand down my side over my hip. "But for now, we need to get some sleep."

Fuck sleep. I straddle his lap, pressing my hands against his chest. "I'm not tired yet."

Raising an eyebrow, he smirks at me. "I'm under strict orders to let you rest."

Damn Seth. Usually I like his orders, but this one sucks. I pout.

Blake chuckles but his cock is hard between my legs.

"I'm fine," I assure him.

He rubs his fingers over my lips. When I take them into my mouth and glide my tongue along them, sucking on them the way I want to suck on his cock, his eyes darken. That's what I want to see.

"There might be a way to mutually satisfy each other without causing additional soreness," Blake concedes.

I pull his fingers out of my mouth and lean in to kiss him. As soon as our lips meet, he takes over. His tongue sweeps into my mouth. His hands pull my hips against his, rocking his thick, hard cock between my legs.

Damn, that feels good. I'll never get enough of these guys and what they can do to me.

"My room, my rules, tiger." He licks my lips as he pulls away.

"Yes, sir." A shiver of desire flows through me. Ready to play and be played with.

"Strip."

I reach for my camisole.

"Over there." He points to the floor beside the bed.

I slide off his lap and off the edge of the bed. Being efficient, I quickly dispose of all my clothes until I stand before him naked. My breasts rise and fall with every quick breath. I'm wet, ready, and waiting for his command.

Sitting against the headboard, he doesn't take off his boxers. His erection presses against the fabric, and my pussy tightens in anticipation. He pats the space between his legs. "Here. Face away from me on your hands and knees. Chest to the bed. Ass up. Legs spread."

I hurry to follow his commands, eager for the oblivion he can give me. To get out of my head and let him take control would be a blessing today. Everything lately seems to be out of my control, but giving in to Blake, that's my choice.

I choose to obey him. I choose to give him full access to my body. If I say the word, all this ends, but it's my choice to continue. My choice to surrender.

When my ass is in the air before him and my legs spread to present him with all of me, I shiver, aching for his touch.

His fingers trail down my thighs to my knees, making sparks flow through me. This afternoon was difficult, but having Blake play with me will make it all better for tonight. I'm safe in his bed.

"You need to ask permission to come, tiger." He grips my ass cheeks and spreads them apart. My pussy throbs with need.

"Yes, sir." I press my forehead to the mattress, waiting for him to touch my pussy. To do something besides look at it and my puckered hole.

"If you come before I give you permission, you'll get five spanks and won't get to suck my cock."

"That seems a little—"

He cuts my complaint off with a smack on my ass. "Don't talk back."

I bite my lip at the burn his palm leaves behind. He rubs my sore cheek, and wetness floods my pussy at the sting.

"What do you say, love?"

"Yes, sir." I push my hair back from my face, hoping he'll touch me now.

"You'll have to beg for it." His finger slides along my groin. So fucking close but not close enough. "And I'll decide whether you're worthy of it. Or not."

I whimper. Fuck. Every word he says just makes me wetter. I need him to touch me. To fuck me. With his tongue, his fingers, his cock. I don't care what, but I need something to touch my pussy. And soon.

"What did Seth do to you at lunch?" His fingers trail up the inside of my thighs only to skate down the backs instead of touching me where I want him.

"He used a warm dildo in my pussy and fucked my ass with his cock." I bite my lip as his fingers tease close before gliding away. My breath catches and releases. I want to take over. Tell him what I need and make him do it, but that's not Blake. Blake wants my surrender.

I release that desire and give myself over to him. He'll give me what I need.

"Still sore?" His fingers pause below my ass cheek.

"No, sir." I hold my breath, waiting for his touch.

When his fingers fall down my thighs, I huff out a breath.

"So impatient." His hand grabs my ass cheek, the one he smacked, and squeezes.

I suck in a harsh breath at the sizzle of pain along my taut nerves. "Please."

"What do you want, love? If you tell me, maybe I'll give it to you." Both his hands massage my ass, waiting for my answer.

"Fuck me, please." I rock against his touch, needing so much more.

He tsks me. "That's not very specific. Fuck what? With what? Do you want my cock in your mouth? My fingers in your ass? My tongue in your cunt? You're a smart girl, Madison. Use your words."

Every word out of his mouth just makes me want more. I tremble with desire. "Yes. All of it."

"Okay, love."

Relief pours through me. Finally, he's going to do more. His hands move down my thighs to my knees and I whimper in defeat. Then he grabs my legs and lifts my lower body up. I scramble to catch myself with my hands on his thighs.

"What—"

"Shh, love. Wrap your legs behind my neck." He guides my knees to his shoulders, and I work on putting my legs around his neck like

I'm sitting cross-legged in the air. Except with my pussy in his face and my face in his crotch.

I swallow as he adjusts me to just where he wants me, holding my hips level with his mouth. All the blood is rushing to my head, but I don't care as long as he puts his mouth to use on me.

"Pull my cock out." His warm breath teases my wet pussy. A warm rush of desire sizzles along my veins.

Hurrying, I lower his boxers and free his thick cock. My mouth waters, already anticipating tasting him on my tongue.

"You wanted it all, love, and I'm willing to provide." Blake's chuckle warms me. "Just remember, you have to ask to come."

I lick my lips at the drip of precum on his slit. "Yes, sir."

"You first, tiger." He shifts so his arm is around my hips and his other hand is free. His bicep bulges at the weight of me but his grip is firm. He won't drop me.

As I position him next to my lips, he eases his finger into my pussy. I let out a hiss, blowing on his tip.

"Just gathering some lube, love."

I lick the precum off his slit as he thrusts his finger in and out a couple times. My pussy clings to his finger and the pressure builds inside me.

"Any pain?" His lips are so close to my pussy that every breath winds me even higher.

"No, sir." I whimper.

"Good. Stop hesitating and take my cock in your mouth, or I'll stop playing with you."

"Yes, sir." I slide my mouth over him. It feels odd taking him upside down. I've done it before on the conference table, that first time with my head hanging off, but this feels different. All my blood feels like it's rushing to my head, making me a little dizzy.

"We don't have long before you'll have to come up for air, so suck me good, tiger."

I lick and suck his cock, taking him a little deeper at this angle. He pulls his fingers from my pussy and slides them back to my asshole. His mouth opens on my clit as his finger pushes into my puckered hole.

Holy fuck. My whole body lights up like a fucking Christmas tree at the stimulation. He's gentle with his fingers, but his mouth devours me, making me moan around his cock.

Blake shifts his mouth, and his tongue thrusts into my pussy in time with the finger sliding in and out of my ass. As keyed up as I already am, it won't take long for me to come.

We tease each other a little before Blake withdraws. I whimper at the loss of his touch.

"Pull off, love."

With a final suck, I retreat with a pop. My head feels all swimmy.

With a few smooth moves, I'm on my back with him hovering over me. My legs are still wrapped around his neck and his cock is in my face.

"You good, love?" His hot breath against my wet pussy makes me throb.

"Mm-hmm." I reach a hand up to stroke his cock, using my saliva to glide over him. Not having to hold myself up has its advantages.

"Relax. If you need me to stop, tap on my leg twice." Blake licks my clit and I shiver with aching need. "Repeat it."

"Tap twice to stop." Lifting my neck, I suck his head into my mouth.

"Fuck, I love your mouth." He lowers my hips to the bed and presses his mouth to my pussy. His tongue dives in as his finger presses back into my asshole. As he eases his hips down, I lower my head to the bed. Then his hips move, fucking my mouth as I suck and lick him.

His tongue and finger fuck me in the same rhythm as his cock until I'm a mass of want on the edge of explosion. But I need permission to come.

On the verge, I tap his leg twice and he lifts his cock out of my mouth, but he doesn't stop thrusting his tongue into my pussy. I bite my lip at the almost overwhelming urge to give in.

"May I come, sir?" My words are a harsh whisper as I keep myself from falling over the edge, holding back my climax. But his tongue is divine, and it's right there.

He stops what he's doing. "Are you ready to beg for it?"

Precum leaks out of his cock and drips on my lips. Licking it off, I hum to myself at the taste. I need more. I want it all.

"Please, Blake. Please make me come. Let me taste your cum and swallow it like your good girl. Please make me yours." I'm so wound up that just saying the words makes my pussy flutter and my ass tightens around his buried finger.

He blows his breath over my pussy, and I whimper at how close I am. I can't hold it back much longer.

"You can come after I do." He leans in and says against my pussy, "Not before, or you'll be punished."

Fuck. I don't know how much more I can take before I explode. His words make my belly quiver. It will be a challenge, but he has to be close too.

"Yes, sir." I take his cock in my hand and guide the tip to my mouth again. He thrusts inside me all at once. His cock in my mouth, his tongue in my pussy, and his finger in my ass. I'm barely holding the shattering pieces of myself together as I suck hard on him.

If he punishes me, I don't think he'll let me come again. And while this orgasm should be epic, I want to hold on to it. I want to do as he asks. I want to swallow him down while I shatter all around him.

Using my hands to stroke his cock and balls, I take him as deep as I can while he fucks my mouth. I release the tension holding me and focus on not coming from all the stimulation.

Just when I can't take it anymore and feel like I'm going to explode, he groans against my pussy as his cock thickens and unloads in my mouth. I swallow as my body shatters, falling into myself and giving myself over to the way he makes me feel. Tasting him, feeling him taste me. Fucking me so good that my climax keeps coming and coming as wave after wave crashes over me.

He shifts and sucks my clit. Colors burst behind my eyes in bright fireworks as my already primed body goes off like a rocket. He lifts his cock out of my mouth, and I cry out as I convulse around his finger buried in my ass.

His tongue laves at my clit, and tiny shudders ease me down onto the bed. I didn't even realize my hips lifted to meet his mouth.

"Good girl," he whispers before licking me again and drawing his finger out of me.

The aftershock ripples through my whole body, making me arch into his. He shifts to fall on his back beside me. My breathing is chaotic but I'm well satisfied.

I meet his green eyes, feeling so many things. Yes, that was about release, but it was also about surrendering to the way this man makes me feel. He protects me and comforts me. He's mine and I'm his.

The look in his eyes makes my insides buzz a little. It's filled with tenderness and desire.

His fingers trail over my breast, and little shudders trickle down me. I've been falling for Blake forever it feels like, but right now, it feels like maybe he's falling for me too. And for me, that's enough. "Thank you."

"Anytime, love."

I'll definitely take him up on that offer for as long as I can.

Chapter 80

Coffee Break

Blake

"Can you tell me something about you?" Madison asks. We're lying side by side, head to toe. Both of our breathing is still ragged as we come down from our orgasms.

I slide my boxers the rest of the way off and shift back to the head of the bed. Arranging the blankets, I cover both of us before I draw her back against my front. She snuggles into me as I wrap my arms around her, holding her close.

I'm glad I have her in my arms tonight. Safe. The stalker didn't come near her today, but who knows what kind of access he has? Or when he'll make his next move?

Fuck. I concentrate on the woman in my arms.

"What do you want to know?" I'm not exactly an open book, but I've also never had a lover want more than what I can give her in bed. I've never had someone like Madison in my life. My chest aches when she hurts.

"Tell me about your scar." Her fingers link with mine as she relaxes into me even more. Her words are a little sleepy. Will she even stay awake to hear the whole story?

"In college I tried my own thing. Tried to be with people besides the guys." I glance down at Madison's face. "Are you asleep?"

"No, just resting my eyes," she murmurs and turns in my arms. "Please tell me."

Her head rests on my shoulder as her arm and leg drape over me, holding me close. Fitting like a missing puzzle piece. I stroke my hand down her back. She's so lovely.

"I tried out for the rowing team. Intramural. The university's team is one of the top in the country, so that'd never happen for a novice like me." I pause, and she trails her hand along my side. "We got up at a ridiculous time every morning to hit the water. For months, we practiced for our first competition."

"Mmm. What happened?" She yawns.

"Everything was going great. We were actually doing well, but a guy in another scull made an error, and they ended up colliding with us. Our scull capsized and we all fell overboard. My head hit the edge of the scull, knocking me out. I sank like a fucking stone and sliced my shoulder on the rocks of the riverbed. The pain snapped me awake. I swam to the surface." I lift her hand and guide it through my hair to find the scar left behind.

"That had to be terrifying." Her fingers trace over it like she's trying to memorize and heal it.

"It was. But not as terrifying as Seth when he met me at the hospital. The cut was deep and needed stitches."

In college, it made sense to have Seth as our emergency contact. I don't think we even had a discussion about it. It just seemed right. He knows what to do in a crisis and keeps a level head. But this time he was rattled.

She trails her fingers down to the ridge on my shoulder. "He was scared?"

"When he got called, they wouldn't tell him what happened on the phone. He thought I'd died. He made me swear I wouldn't do anything that stupid again. Even though none of it was my fault, he said I should have known better than to go out for an intramural sport."

"Why?" She lifts her head, resting it on my chest to meet my eyes. Curiosity burns in hers.

"Because when you play with professionals, they're professionals. When you play with novices trying to be professionals, you get stitches." The words Seth said that day stayed with me. It's easy to recite them back to her now. I brush her hair back out of her face and draw in a breath. "He didn't want me to get hurt because he'd always had a future planned that included all of us. Without any one of us, Morrigan Technology Group might have failed or would have had unnecessary growing pains. We're better together as a unit. We could've had careers of our own, but somehow, when we work together things shine."

She gives me a sloppy, tired grin. "I agree. I like you all together and separately."

I chuckle as she returns to resting her head on my chest. "We like you with us."

She snuggles against me. No woman has held me the way she does. As if I'm her lifeline. Her anchor in the storm.

The tension releases from her as she slips into sleep. My heart throbs. It's been building over the weeks, but my heart aches with how much I like her in my bed and my arms.

I brush her hair out of her face, and she releases her breath. I've never slept with someone like her. She wants to sleep on me, not just beside me. Madison trusts me. She relies on me. She might actually like me. I'd be foolish not to give her my heart in return.

I just don't know if I still have much heart to give. I don't know if I can trust her the way she trusts me. I'm trying. I want her to be different, but part of me still fears that she'll turn on us, just like the others.

Until then, I'll be hers in whatever way my heart will let me.

Madison

This morning is different. I don't wake flooded with desire and longing, halfway to an orgasm, but to a gentle kiss and a good morning. Blake holds out his hand and I take it.

He leads me into the bathroom and we shower together. We soap each other, but it's almost comforting as he takes time to wash every inch of me down to my toes. When we finish, he wraps me in a towel, kisses me like he won't see me for a while, and sends me off to get ready for work.

When I walk into my closet, my clothes for the day hang ready for me, complete with underwear this time. I run my fingers down the skirt. Seth chose this for me. I love that he takes this decision off my plate and that it brings him pleasure.

Once I'm dressed and ready for the workday, I discover I've made it out to breakfast before anyone else. It's a little surprising. Normally Coop and Seth are already up and about, but Noah and Coop were as exhausted as I was yesterday. After I put on the coffee to brew, I make myself an egg and toast.

Footsteps walk up behind me while I'm buttering my toast. The clean and crisp scent of Coop's cologne alerts me before his arms wrap around my waist and tug me back into him.

"Good morning, girlfriend. Ready for our date tonight?"

I hold a piece of toast over my shoulder to him. He bites down and tears a piece off it. "I'm sure I can find something to wear."

He finishes chewing, then leans in and kisses the back of my jaw. "I plan on making my own marks on this gorgeous neck tonight."

He trails kisses down my neck, sending shivers coursing through me. I grab the counter as my knees weaken.

"Keep it in your pants until tonight." Seth's voice fills the room.

Coop scrapes his teeth against my neck before stepping to the coffeepot. My body trembles.

"You used to be such fun, boss. It feels like just yesterday when you had Madison naked, down on her knees, sucking your cock for breakfast." He snaps his fingers. "Wait, that *was* yesterday."

Seth shrugs. "She needs time off from us to get her work done."

I glance at my phone for the time and set my plate down on the island. I need to eat quickly.

"You can't just work the woman to the bone without giving her a little bone." Coop slides into the seat next to me with his coffee. He gives me a flirtatious wink and snatches a piece of toast from my plate.

My cheeks grow warm as he devours the toast and then sucks each of his fingers into his mouth.

Seth places another piece that he just buttered on my plate as he glares at Coop.

Coop gives both of us a smile and kisses me before heading to the door.

"See you upstairs, sweetheart," he calls out.

The door shuts. Seth shakes his head as he finishes making his breakfast. The sheet of paper I ignored yesterday draws my attention. I pull over the printout the police officer left.

ROBERT:

Everything okay? Do you need anything?

ROBERT:

I'm worried and hope you're doing well.

ROBERT:

You're always welcome at my place if things don't work out.

ROBERT:

Haven't seen Valerie, but hope you come home soon.

ROBERT:

I think I found something.

ROBERT:

Let me know if you're okay.

They go on like that for a while, but my gaze keeps straying to his message, *I think I found something*. What is that supposed to mean?

Seth sits next to me and looks over at the texts. "Your neighbor?"

I nod, setting the paper to the side. "He's always been nice. A little socially inept, but who isn't?" I shrug and shovel the rest of the eggs into my mouth.

"He doesn't appear to be the stalker, but be careful. We have eyes on him just in case." Seth catches my hand as I push back to leave the island. I meet his eyes. "Any encouragement might set him off."

"He's really fine. He says he found something and wants to know I'm all right." I lean in and press my lips to Seth's. He catches my neck with his hand before I can draw away and deepens the kiss. My insides flame to life.

He presses his forehead against mine and releases a breath. "I just want you to be safe."

"I'll text him and that's it." I search his eyes for any more worry.

He kisses my forehead before releasing my neck. "You should ask Hope to help you get ready. Tell her I said she can come up before the end of the day and she'll still get paid."

I grin as I grab my plate. "That sounds great."

After cleaning my dishes, I hurry upstairs to start the coffee brewing and empty the dishwasher. I'm putting the last cup away when I hear footsteps. I turn and see Coop heading into the break room.

"We keep running into each other." He closes in on me and traps me against the counter. His eyebrow rises. "I have a five-minute coffee break."

I brush some imaginary lint from his shoulder before lifting my gaze to his heated one.

"What do you hope to accomplish in five minutes?"

His mouth closes in on mine but stops just shy of touching. A little noise of frustration leaves me, and he chuckles. "You want to come, my little whore?"

Tingles race up and down my spine. His light blue eyes search mine.

"Are you offering?" I cock my eyebrow at him.

"Always, sweetheart." His soft lips capture mine as his hand slips under my skirt. His fingers trail up my thigh and stop at my panties. He whispers against my lips, "If I had my way, you'd never wear panties."

His fingers slip under and thrust up into me. My lips part on a gasp and he takes advantage, capturing my mouth again and tangling his tongue with mine as he finger fucks me against the counter.

His other hand grabs my loose hair and tugs my head back. When he trails his kisses away from my lips, he whispers, "Keep quiet or I'll bend you over that table and fuck you until you scream."

I'm not sure that would be a punishment. He kisses down my neck until he gets to the spot where my neck and shoulder meet, teasing the sensitive skin with his teeth and tongue while his thumb massages my clit.

The office disappears as my world focuses on this stolen moment with Coop.

"You're blocking the coffee." Blake sounds like we're just in the way and Coop doesn't have his fingers inside me and his mouth on my neck.

I open my eyes and all I see is the top of Coop's head and the ceiling. "Sorry?"

Coop licks up the side of my throat and brings his mouth back to hover over mine. Our eyes lock as he continues to thrust his fingers in and out. "Don't worry, Blake. Our girl is almost there. As long as she doesn't cry out, we'll be done. Of course, even if she does cry out, I'll be fucking her on the table, so we'll be out of your way."

The flames build higher with each word.

"Take your time. I have a call I'm not in any hurry to get to." The chair legs scrape the floor as he takes a seat. Fuck, I love an audience. Something I've never had before these guys. I love audience participation even more.

"I can feel that needy cunt fluttering around my fingers like a good slut." Coop's words brush my lips. "We both know you want to be pounded this morning. Your cunt needs a thick, hot cock in it all times of the day. Cry out and let's start the morning coming."

Blake chuckles like Coop told a joke. "She doesn't need a cock. My tongue worked just fine last night."

I bite my lip as Coop works me a little faster, a little harder. His fingers pumping in and out as his thumb rubs my clit firmer. He licks the seam of my lips. My breath rushes out of me. His blue eyes are alight with the challenge.

"You know," Noah says, "I'm not opposed to starting every morning finding Madison being fucked. I just hope that one of these mornings I'll be part of it."

Noah's words kick me even higher.

"That made her soaking wet." Coop gazes down at me, still holding me locked in this battle. Every touch and word makes me want to whimper, to curse, to moan. "She's probably remembering both of us in her hungry little cunt, stretching her out, making her scream her release."

The memory of that is too much. My pussy tightens around his fingers as my vision goes black. I couldn't stop from crying out if I tried. The orgasm is so intense, shattering through me like a wrecking ball.

"That's it, my little whore, get nice and wet for me to fuck you."

My fingers clench in his shirt as my body buckles from the tension and release. Coop drags his fingers out of me, sending an aftershock rippling through me. He lifts me and carries me over to the table Blake is sitting at.

"Turn around." He sets me down, waiting for me to follow his instructions.

Instead, I look up at him and straighten to my full height with my heels. I still only come up to his nose. My insides are still Jell-O from the orgasm, but I know what these guys like. "I have work to get to."

He smirks. "You definitely have work to do, sweetheart."

He spins me and presses my chest down onto the table with one hand on my back while his other flips my skirt up and yanks my panties to the side. "You have three cocks to take."

My eyes meet Blake's and he reaches out to brush some of the hair off my cheek. The move is gentle, almost tender compared to the violence of Coop's hand pressing me down. Fuck, I want it all, gentle, tender touches combined with rough fucking that leaves me sore and open for the next cock.

I want gentle lovemaking and hard fucking. Submission and control. Bound and free. I want whatever they give me. All the fucking time.

Coop's cock thrusts into me. Deep and hard. Fuck, that feels good. I widen my legs as he pumps into me. It's only been a little over a day since I had one of them in my pussy, but it was definitely too long. He fills me and stretches me with every thrust.

My mouth falls open as my climax builds again, making me squirm beneath him as he works hard and fast at filling me. His hand slips around my hip, and the minute he touches my clit, I go off like a rocket.

My moan fills the break room, thick and needy. Coop thrusts deep and groans in chorus with me as he fills me with his cum. My pussy convulses around his throbbing cock. He pulls out, and Noah slots his cock against my entrance before thrusting in with one push of his hips.

I let out a gasp.

"Feel good, tiger?" Blake opens his pants and strokes his cock, waiting his turn.

I lick my lips. "Mm-hmm."

I'm ready for more. Noah sucks on something and then I feel pressure on my puckered hole as he presses his wet fingers deep into me. I cry out as I come again. He thrusts his fingers in and out of my ass in the same cadence as his cock works my pussy, keeping me spiraling into pleasure.

When Noah groans his release, Blake stands. Every twitch of

Noah's cock inside me as he fills me with his cum makes my insides throbs.

"Good girl, kitten." He pulls out and Blake thrusts his thick cock into me.

Blake grabs both my hips and fucks me hard and fast. My already sensitive body gives it up to him in record time. Black edges my vision as I cry out, shattering around his cock. I sag against the table even as he keeps fucking me, and aftershocks rake through my body.

"Fuck, love. I missed this pussy." He thrusts in deep and spills his seed inside me.

When he pulls out, another cock presses against my entrance, sinking deep.

"Seth," I breathe out.

"You're going to be late for work, princess." He thrusts slow and steady. His fingers slide to my pulsing clit.

"I'm already at work, boss." The words fall out of me as I come on his cock. I can't even think straight right now, all blissed-out on orgasmic chemicals.

"You're being a distraction again." The fingers of his other hand squeeze my ass cheek.

I moan. "You like me that way."

He chuckles. "You're not wrong. How's your cunt today?"

"So fucking good." The words rise as another orgasm overwhelms me. I drag Seth into his release and he fills me with his cum. His cock is deep inside me, throbbing as my pussy flutters around him.

He draws out of me. A warm, wet washcloth is pressed over my pussy.

"We need to keep this pussy in good shape, babe." Coop's words are edged with a laugh. "The others might not get to steal you away during the benefit, but I will."

My pussy throbs weakly as he cleans me up and straightens my panties. Noah helps right me and my clothes before kissing me lightly. "Good morning, kitten."

My cheeks flame red. It's a really good morning. "Morning, Noah."

His dark eyes glow down at me. "This weekend I want to try all of us. A few different ways."

"Okay." I'll let them do whatever they want to me. I've proven that over and over. I want them as much as they want me.

He gives me a smile as his hand cups my cheek. "You make me feel like I could take on the world for you."

My heart pounds as it expands like a balloon in my chest. I cover his hand with mine. The words *I love you* press on my tongue to get out, but now isn't the time. Not when I've just been fucked by all of them.

I'm not sure I'll ever find the right time to tell him. Or any of them.

Chapter 81

Reach Out

Madison

Hope sends me an excited text with multiple exclamation points when I tell her I want her to help me get ready for the banquet. I'm still smiling at her text when Seth comes out of his office.

His eyes soften when he takes in my smile. I smile a little bigger and shift in my seat, still thinking about them all taking me in the break room this morning. Definitely worth the wait.

"What time should I tell Hope to meet me?" I wait with my phone, ready to text her.

"Noon." He stops beside my desk.

Whoa, wait.

I furrow my brow and set my phone down. "That's ridiculous. I don't need that long to get ready. I'm already behind on work—"

"That will be here tomorrow when we have to be down here working. And we'll want to have you close." Seth tips my chin up. "You have hair and nail appointments before your makeup appointment. Tim will drive you and stay with you. Your dress and everything you need for it is ready in your closet."

"I could just do my own hair," I mutter. I've never been pampered before and don't need to start now. Everything Seth does spoils me, but he doesn't have to waste his money on me. While it's nice to be doted on, the attention and care he gives me will make it that much harder when they finally let me go.

"This isn't a normal date. You'll be expected to look a certain way to be on the arm of Cooper Graham. People will be scrutinizing your every move." Seth brushes his thumb over my cheek, drawing a line along my jaw. "By the time the stylists finish with you, you'll be divine and flawless."

My stomach churns. I'll never be flawless. I also worry about the scrutiny and letting the guys down. But I'll try for him and the others.

Then I remember he came over here before I asked my question.

"Did you need something else?" I clear my throat.

He releases a breath and takes his hand from my face. "William Adams called to apologize again. He wants to make it up to you and us."

"Okay?" How does he want to make it up to me? His son cornered me and tried to assault me multiple times. Firing the asshole would be enough. Just acknowledging Hunter has a problem is enough. But I'm not sure that will happen.

"Add him on our calendar next Monday for lunch . . ." Seth pauses.

I have a sinking feeling in my stomach. "And?"

"Hunter will join us to formally apologize."

I want to rail and throw things. Pitch the biggest fit in the history of fits. Do I want to sit down and listen to the man who would have assaulted me tell me he's sorry because his dad forced him to? Hell no.

Swallowing down all that fury, I nod. This is part of being a future business leader. Sometimes you have to let people apologize even if they're faking it. Because that asshole is only sorry that he got caught. "Of course."

Seth clears his throat and I look up into his hard eyes. I'm not the only one struggling with this decision. "If it weren't for William, I would say fuck it, but he's a good man and a customer. Hunter is a dick, but we can't punish William for that."

"I know. It's fine. I understand." Even though my stomach is currently trying to turn itself inside out. I never want to be in the same room as that asshole again, but that's not my decision. This is a business and I have to be professional.

Seth kisses the top of my head. "Enjoy your afternoon, princess. I can't wait to see you tonight."

He heads to the elevator and disappears inside. Tonight. When he'll have another woman on his arm. Someone he once dated. Someone he once loved.

I don't know how I'm going to make it through tonight, watching Noah and Seth with other women. They have to make it look good for the press and the people attending. Will they make it look so real even I can't tell they're faking it?

Pushing it out of my mind, I pick up my phone and text Hope the details that we'll be taking half the day off to get pampered. She sends back a million emojis with even more exclamation points. It's enough to let me release the Hunter drama for now. And the worry about the other women tonight.

Smiling, I shake my head. I have a friend. My heart feels warm and content.

I glance at the piece of paper with Robert's phone number and texts. He tried to be my friend. Maybe not the type of friend I wanted, but he was nice to me when a lot of people weren't. I should just get it over with.

ME:

Sorry, this is Madison. Valerie texted on my old phone and the police have it.

Just got your messages.

I'm doing well and enjoying my new job.

You said you found something?

I set my phone off to the side, determined to get some work done today before I have to take off. My pulse thrums, nervous to know if he found my grandma's bracelet or something else. Maybe whatever he found isn't even mine. But the movers might have dropped something.

It's an hour later when my phone buzzes. Not thinking, I lift it to view the incoming text.

ROBERT:

Glad you're good.

Found some jewelry in the hallway. Thought it might be yours.

A bracelet you've worn.

My heart rushes. My grandma's bracelet? I thought I'd lost it.

ME:

Can you drop it off in the lobby of the Morrigan Technology Group building please?

ROBERT:

. . .

I blow out a breath. I just want my life back and that bracelet is part of me. It's part of my history. Grandma gave it to me when I was little, and I've always kept it with me. I've lost so much already. While the guys make my cage feel comfortable, I'm still trapped by the lurking fear of the stalker and Valerie.

ROBERT:

I don't feel comfortable leaving it with a stranger.

Okay, that's reasonable. Right? He's not the stalker. Or at least he's not on the suspect list anymore, so it should be fine. It will be in public with everyone around. Nothing to worry about.

ME:

> Okay. Text me when you get to the lobby on Monday. I'll come down and get it from you.

ROBERT:

> Okay.

> It'll be good to see you.

> If you need anything, I'm here for you.

I set the phone down. Yes, some things Robert says creep me out a little. But unlike Hunter, Robert has been nothing but kind to me. I can't see him creeping into my apartment and filming me without my knowledge. Or terrorizing me in a dark office building.

He's always wanted to give me things and help me. He's just a little odd. There's nothing nefarious about that.

HOPE:

> Is it time yet?

I grin at her text and glance at the time. Yup, it's time for whatever Seth has planned for me.

"I still can't believe you're dating Cooper." Hope takes a bite of salad while watching me with her huge blue eyes. We sit across from each other at a restaurant.

"Yeah." I smile as I push my salad around on the plate. My nerves about tonight are getting to me and my stomach feels queasy. What if I blow this? What if it's obvious the guys are all with me? What if one of them likes their date more than me?

What if I prove to them I can't handle any of this?

"The whole floor is abuzz with you and him kissing in the lobby on Monday. Some girls are sad he's off the market, while others are just mean bitches. A couple of women claim it won't last. But I know you and him will go the distance. You look so perfect together."

There's that damned word again. Perfection isn't attainable. Not for me at least.

"Mmm." She finishes her bite and takes a drink of water. "Courtney says you're not special just because you're fucking him. She's so bitchy."

"Why does she hate me so much?" I'm curious if Hope actually knows any of the backstory. Because Courtney hasn't liked me from day one.

"She was close friends with Andrea, their previous assistant. Courtney used to be pretty decent before Andrea was walked out. After that, she got real bitchy about the bosses, like they were at fault somehow for Andrea's issues." Hope sets her fork down and leans closer. "Seriously, Andrea was a bitch, and I'm sure whatever they accused her of, she did."

I take a bite to keep in the information I have. How she tried to blackmail them. I can't really discuss it anyway.

Hope glances around covertly like we're being watched. Except for Tim the driver, no one pays us any attention. He sits at the bar with us in his sights. When her gaze comes back to me, she says, "What really pissed her off was they didn't pick her for their assistant."

I cough around my food and swallow hard. Did she interview? Did she know the conditions of employment? Grabbing my glass, I drink some water to help wash it down.

"You okay?" Hope looks like she's about to get up and give me the Heimlich maneuver.

I wave her off. "I'm good. What do you mean?"

Hope takes a deep breath and leans forward. "Courtney applied after Andrea left, and again after Rachel left. She bragged to anyone who would listen that they would definitely pick her, but then they didn't."

"So she's angry I got the job she wanted?"

Hope shrugs. "That's all I can guess. She also flirts like crazy with Cooper."

My insides churn, hot and tumultuous. "So she wants my job and my man?"

"Pretty much." Hope smiles. "I wouldn't worry about it though. Cooper doesn't give her the time of day, and she's not half as capable as you are."

I'd knocked Courtney's name off the suspects list. Really, I never put her on it. The notes feel so sexual, but it could be a woman.

"Do you think she might be the one stalking me?" I whisper.

Hope's fork clatters on her plate as her mouth opens in surprise. "She does want what you have."

But everything the stalker seems to do pushes me into the guys' arms instead of tearing me away. The video in the shower. The terrorizing in the file room. The dress.

Fuck, the dress.

"She didn't know me before." I shake my head, once again eliminating her from the pool of suspects.

"What do you mean?"

I sigh and tell Hope about the box with the dress and the pictures. I leave out how the dress got ruined in the first place, of course.

"That's fucked-up. And so creepy." Hope pushes her empty plate away. "The police know?"

I nod, stirring my food with my fork. I ate a little, but my stomach just can't take any more. "Blake has a friend on the force who's been notified. He took it in as evidence in case we ever figure out who it is."

"They'll find out who's doing this." Hope seems confident and gives me a smile. "Now, we have some appointments to transform you into Cinderella."

I'm sure they'll make me look good tonight, and I can't wait to find out what Seth chose for me to wear.

Shaking off the doom coating me, I smile. "We both get to have our hair and nails done. And a massage."

"Man, am I glad I was nice to you." Hope grins. "I bet Courtney is kicking herself for being a bitch right about now."

"Let's hope so." I just hope tonight is the night my stalker takes off.

Chapter 82

Formal Occasion

Coop

I straighten my cuffs and make sure my cuff links are secure. The others have already left to pick up their dates, leaving just Madison and me in the apartment. And Hope.

Without Hope, we might not make it to the benefit. Which would be so sad. I smirk in the mirror. Spending hours alone with Madison doesn't seem like a bad idea. But that isn't the deal. Tonight is about being seen as a couple.

This wasn't the way our arrangement was supposed to go. I should have some hot woman who wants to sleep with a billionaire on my arm tonight. I wouldn't have fucked her, but Madison should be on Noah's arm.

They fit together. I'm just the creeper on their relationship. And yet, she welcomes me with open arms and soft smiles that make my heart feel odd.

While I've dated before, I haven't been exclusive with anyone since Leighton. At least not in the public eye. Leighton's family and mine wanted a connection through marriage. She was cold and condescending and knew how to behave in the spotlight.

No one in their right mind would imagine me dating someone like Madison. She's soft, nice, and good. Everything I'm not.

Hope opens the door to Madison's room and I look up, unable to stop myself. My heart thumps as I wait for Madison to walk in. I crave her in a way I've never craved another woman. I straighten to my full height as her heels click on the wood floor.

Her head is down as if watching her every step in those diamond-laden heels. Her golden hair falls in soft waves around her face. The gold silk dress clings to her curves, gently revealing her breasts, the dip of her waist, and the swell of her hips. The trumpet skirt flares out around her legs, swirling around her calves.

When she lifts her blue eyes to mine, my breath catches in my chest. Fuck, she's gorgeous. And mine. The overwhelming need to claim her stirs inside me.

My feet move until I'm standing in front of her. Her eyebrows rise and she gives a nervous laugh.

"Do I look okay?" She smooths her hands down her dress.

Carefully, I wrap my hand around the back of her neck and draw her close to me. My lips brush her ear as I whisper, "You look so fucking gorgeous. If Hope weren't here, I'd fuck you until you passed out from coming so hard."

"You look very handsome yourself," she murmurs.

I draw back and her cheeks are pink. Her blue eyes are dilated. Her lips part, and if it wouldn't fuck up her makeup, I'd claim her mouth, showing her exactly how I feel. I need to possess her tonight. Prove that I can be the man she sees when she looks at me.

Hope clears her throat. "So, we need to get going if you guys are going to arrive on time." She pulls out her phone. "I want to get a picture of the two of you first."

"Best to get a picture now, because that lipstick is going to be ruined by the end of the night." I step back and hold my arm out like the gentleman I'm not but was trained to be.

Madison places her hand on my arm and turns to face Hope.

Hope smiles as she takes a few pictures. I can't stop my gaze from drifting back to Madison. She's captivating.

Finally, she turns those blue eyes on me and smiles. "You know, all these pictures will be shown on social media."

"They'll show how enraptured I am with your beauty." I take her hand and raise it to press a kiss to each of her knuckles.

"Holy crap, that's hot. Okay, I'm under strict orders to not leave you two alone until we reach the car, so . . ." Hope fans her face before shooing us to the door.

I chuckle darkly as we follow her.

"I'd like to make it to the benefit in the same condition I am now," Madison whispers to me.

I nod. "Fine, but once we arrive, all bets are off."

Madison's cheeks flush as we all enter the elevator car. I wrap my arm around her waist and rest my hand over her hip. Hope's face flushes pink as she stares at the elevator numbers above the door like they are the most interesting thing here.

"We had an enjoyable afternoon." Hope's voice is a little higher pitch as she tries to ignore my thumb moving over Madison's hip. "Please tell Seth I appreciate the time off with Madison."

"I'll let him know." I'll also let him know we don't need a babysitter. I can behave myself. Usually.

Madison's neck and shoulders are bare, with silky ties running from the top of her breasts to cross between her shoulder blades. The back dips down to her midback. I plan to use that to my advantage in whatever dark corners I can find in the museum. I doubt she could wear a bra with this. Which makes me wonder if she did as Noah asked and left off her panties too. My fingers rub her hip, but I can't tell.

Diamonds grace her neck and drip from her ears. I picked some from my family's collection. Seth mentioned buying her some, but when I saw the dress, I knew the perfect set to go with it. Something also told me Madison wouldn't accept gifts of diamonds.

She's always so careful with the clothes Seth buys her and also a little nervous in them, like they just don't fit correctly. Of course, they fit her to perfection, but she just isn't used to what we have to offer. Or taking gifts from us.

So different from the other women who only want what I can give them.

I lift her fingers to my lips again as the elevator reaches the garage. Madison watches me through hooded eyes as I kiss each one.

"I think I'll seduce you slowly tonight, my dear."

Hope coughs and rushes out of the elevator toward Tim and the limo waiting for us.

Madison lifts her hungry gaze to mine. "Slowly?"

She pulls away from me and walks toward the limo. Her hips sway hypnotically as the fabric glides around her. Fuck, I'm going to be hard and uncomfortable all night until I can find a place to satisfy our urges.

When Madison reaches Hope, they hug each other and Hope passes Madison a small clutch purse, shimmering in gold and diamonds.

"Have fun tonight. Text me later." Hope waves as she heads over to her car.

"I will. Thank you for going with me today." Madison waves back eagerly, a little bit of her slipping through all the elegance dripping off her.

My heart jerks hard against my chest. She stops at the car door and looks over her shoulder at me with an expression that asks if I'm coming. Hopefully, within the next hour, we both will be.

"Ma'am." Tim opens the door for her.

She gives him a grateful smile and shakes her head. "Call me Madison."

I swear he gets a little pink as he almost does an *aw shucks* movement while she lowers herself into the car, carefully arranging her skirt around her. After he closes the door, I pat him on the shoulder. She's a force to be reckoned with, and she's all mine—at least until we get home tonight.

Tim coughs and we round the car together. "You're a lucky man, Coop."

I smile and nod. "I know I am."

I slide into the back of the limo as Tim gets in the driver's seat.

He clears his throat again. "I'm supposed to lock the partition down. Boss's orders."

Madison's laughter fills the car and my chest.

"You know I don't mind an audience, right?" My gaze flicks to Tim's in the rearview mirror, and he just shakes his head.

Madison takes my hand in her lap. "We can behave for the twenty minutes to the event."

Her gaze trails over me, and she reaches up to tease her fingers through my loose hair.

"Not if you keep looking at me like that." I sigh. I won't do anything in the car on the way to the event. She looks gorgeous, and I don't want to ruin her entrance for a quickie in the back of the limo.

"I like your hair down." She rubs the ends between her fingers.

"It's easier pulled back for the day." I catch a golden strand between my fingers. "As you should know."

She smiles. Her lips are a killer glossy red that will hopefully be smeared on my collar by the end of the night. My dry cleaner will charge me more for the cleaning, and I'll happily pay it.

"Are you excited?" I trail my fingers over the strap holding up her dress. She shivers beneath my touch.

"Excited, nervous. They're the same thing, right?" She takes a breath and smiles.

I shake my head. "You have nothing to worry about. Blake's sister will be with you when we're not. You should never be alone, and no one will get near you with us there."

Her smile softens as her eyes meet mine. "I meant about being your girlfriend for the night. I don't want to disappoint or embarrass you."

My fingers tease the nape of her neck as I search her eyes. "You won't embarrass me, and you could never disappoint me."

"I'm not fancy or rich—"

"Or snobby or pampered." I kiss her bare shoulder and talk between kisses as I kiss her shoulder up to her neck. "You are intelligent, caring, giving, and down to earth. Beautiful, lovely, exquisite."

I kiss beneath her jaw, and she releases a shaky breath. Her floral scent weaves its spell around me, making my cock ache with need.

"I couldn't ask for a better girlfriend." I draw back and meet her eyes, letting her see that I'm not just blowing smoke up her ass. Honestly, she could do a lot better than me.

Her cheeks flush and her gaze darts up to the rearview mirror. She pouts slightly.

"This museum has many nooks and crannies," I whisper. "I'm going to fuck you in every single one."

Her body shivers as her blue eyes meet mine. "What happened to seducing me slowly?"

I chuckle and dip down to kiss her breastbone above the diamonds. "This is slowly. If I had my way, I'd be deep inside you already. That red lipstick smeared all over my cock. And you would have shattered for me multiple times."

Her breath releases harshly against my lips, and for a second I consider leaning in and taking them. Sliding my hand beneath that silky fabric and finding the softest part of her, slick with her arousal.

I raise an eyebrow and give her a wolfish grin before I retreat. "You're stunning and everyone will want you. They'll be envious of me for having you."

She takes the necklace between her fingers and rubs the diamond pendant. "I only want you four."

"And tonight, you'll have all four of us, once this is over and done."

Her eyes sparkle as they meet mine.

"That doesn't mean I won't take advantage of having you to myself in the meantime."

Madison

I press my thighs together at the ache Coop causes. He left his hair loose tonight and it falls to his shoulders in a dark, silky curtain. His usual clean and crisp scent fills my head with indecent thoughts about him and me and what we could do if that partition were in place.

He smirks as he brings my hand to his lips again. Kissing, licking, and teasing my fingers. He's dressed in a tuxedo that fits him like it was specifically designed for his body. I have no doubt it was.

My pulse picks up again. Fuck. This is the world Coop grew up in. I feel like I'm playing dress-up in someone else's clothes. Like this is a huge game of pretend and everyone will realize I'm not supposed to be here.

Coop drags his teeth across my wrist, and my mind goes blank as my body pulses with need. I want to crawl onto his lap and let him have his way with me. But I also don't want to show up to the benefit looking ravished.

The car comes to a stop, and Coop's blue eyes find mine.

"You ready, sweetheart?"

Swallowing, I look out the window at the museum steps. Cameras flash and people are everywhere. I open my clutch and pull out the small mirror. My hand trembles slightly as I check my earrings, my necklace, my makeup.

Coop pushes my hand holding the mirror down. "You look stunning, Madison. You're ready."

When his door opens, he slides out and I take a deep breath. I can do this.

Chapter 83

Manage the Optics

Noah

The car stops in front of a three-story brownstone on a quiet street. This is the address Sara Morris sent me in the many texts we exchanged. I hate doing this. She seems so eager and excited about our "date," and I just want to snuggle on the couch with Madison while we read.

The driver puts the car in park. With a heavy sigh, I get out and walk to the door. Ringing the doorbell, I glance around. The noise of the city seems far off on this street. It's quiet and nice.

The door opens, and a little girl of about six years old looks up at me with a shy smile.

"Are you here for my mommy?" She grins up at me with her hands clasped behind her back. "Are you going to be my new daddy?"

My mouth drops open. What the hell?

"Caitlyn, go find Mom." A slender hand grabs the door, and the little girl giggles before running off. The voice yells after her, "And you aren't supposed to answer the door."

The door opens more, revealing a petite woman with strawberry blond hair pulled into an updo. Her dress is black with simple lines that follow her slender body down to black heels. I lift my gaze to her pixie-like face with fine features and big green eyes.

She smiles. "Sorry about that. My sister Caitlyn is a little demon spawn who gets away with murder since she was completely unplanned and unexpected. I'm Sara, and you're the unlucky guy who has to take me to the benefit."

I clear my throat. "Unlucky?"

"Look, I know your mother set this up. So did mine." Stepping out onto the stoop, she closes the door softly behind her. She lifts her gaze to me. "Let's just have a good time and check this off the setup list for the next few months."

"I honestly don't know what to say to that." I run my hand through my blond hair, probably messing up my attempt at styling.

Her sweet strawberry scent rushes over me as she turns to lock the door. She glances at me over her shoulder and smiles conspiratorially again. "You want to date me as much as I want to date you—"

"I—"

"Which is not at all." She turns to face me. Her hands fall on her hips and her chin tips up. "I need to be seen in public on the arm of the right guy." She gestures to me. "And I assume you need a female companion of your own to show off for whatever reason."

I step back and give her another once-over. This seems like a trap. "You seemed interested in your texts."

"Trust me, you didn't." She laughs. It's light and a little delightful. "Don't worry, Romeo. I have no interest in attaching myself to you in any way besides tonight. Maybe a few follow-up dates to keep my mother from insisting I get with this guy or the other. But you and me probably won't work long-term."

"Should I feel insulted?" I'm not sure what's happening right now. My mother would be furious if she found out my date wasn't as interested as she thought. That makes me smile.

She takes my arm and tugs me toward the car. "Not insulted. We're just both in this for the same reason. To get someone off our backs. Mine happens to be my mother. Maybe yours is your mother, or maybe it's to hide something, but I'm not interested in that."

"You aren't?" When we get to the car, I open the door and hold out my hand to help her in.

She winks at me. "I'm not."

I close her door and look up at the evening sky. This is going to be a trip. I get in on the other side and the driver takes off.

"Okay, so when we get there, I'll laugh and flirt and act like you're the best guy in the world. And you'll act like I'm the only woman you can think about." She smooths the fabric of her dress down. "In about a week, we can go out to a romantic dinner and that will give me about two months of my mother not caring what or who I do."

She smiles, looking rather pleased with herself.

"What if I had shown up wanting an actual date?" I'm more curious than anything.

She frowns and blows her bangs. "You aren't, right?"

"I have someone," I say carefully.

Her shoulders drop, and she smiles again. "Whew, for a minute, I was worried I read you wrong. I think you and I are going to be good friends, Noah." She taps on her lip and narrows her eyes. "Only friends."

"Works for me." I smile and actually look forward to tonight. The anxiety from before lifts. I promised Madison I'd play with her tonight, and it's looking like that might be more of a possibility.

"I hope you don't mind, but I'm going to cling to you in there like you're my last chance to get a man." She looks through her lashes at me.

I raise an eyebrow, wondering if this whole thing is one big con to get me to lower my guard around her.

She straightens her skirt and looks out the window. "I might be trying to make someone jealous."

She bites her lip but doesn't turn toward me.

"And this someone will be at the event?" The lines start to connect.

She nods and looks at her hands in her lap. "I didn't want to go alone and have him think I'm undesirable."

"No one would think that." It's a statement of fact. She's gorgeous. In a different way than Madison, but still beautiful. If I didn't have Madison, I might be interested. Maybe.

Her green eyes flick up to me before dropping back down. "Thanks, but he doesn't see me like that."

"Let me see if I have this correct." I pause and wait for her to lift her eyes to mine again. "You want me to go to the benefit with you to make another man jealous and date you for a while to get your mother off your back?"

"Yes." She doesn't even blink.

Fuck it, if she can be honest so can I.

"I'm taking you because I need to be seen with someone publicly, and my mother will also be happy if I'm dating someone." I'm careful to leave Madison out of it. But if she's observant, Sara might figure it out. I'll have to keep myself in check tonight.

"Sounds right." She takes a deep breath. "What do you think? Can we pull this off?"

"This jealous person won't be a problem, right?" I raise my eyebrow. We already have a lot to look out for tonight. If I have to add worrying about a stranger wanting to deck me to the list, I might need to set some guidelines.

She laughs bitterly. "Probably not. I could probably screw someone right in front of him and he wouldn't blink."

Fuck. "Then why?"

She sighs and looks out the window. Her fingers toy with the diamond on her necklace. "Maybe seeing someone interested in me will make him see *me* and not the girl he knows."

I've been the one no one noticed for most of my life. Living in the shadow of Coop, Seth, and Blake. They protected me, but next to them, I've always been younger and less desirable.

Until Madison. My chest warms. She desires me. Sure, she wants them too, but she seeks me out. We're part of the same puzzle. We belong together.

"Sounds like we have a deal." I reach out and take her hand, squeezing it lightly.

Her green eyes spark with life and she grins. "This is going to be epic."

***

Seth

Doing things for the good of the business has been my strategy since before we began MTG. This is just another one of those things I have to get through. An evening with my ex Elizabeth Hartfield. The car parks outside her mother's mansion.

I straighten my bow tie as I get out and head for her door. Nerves fly through me. My intentions are obvious, but what are hers? Does she expect us to get back together? Is this another run for Coop?

Fuck, why did I agree to this in the first place?

It seemed like a good option at the time. I don't have any feelings for her, and it would be a good start to our business relationship.

I ring the doorbell and knock. When the door opens, Elizabeth stands there, and I'm reminded of when we first met. Even though it's been nine years, she hasn't changed. Sleek dark hair falls to her bare shoulders. Her dark eyes are captivating.

Her red dress highlights her pale complexion and dark features. She's still gorgeous, but she doesn't stir my desire like Madison does. She also wouldn't be up for playing like Madison and I do.

"Good evening, Seth." She steps back and gestures for me to come in.

I draw in a breath before walking into the foyer. Their house is large, the marble entryway is just the beginning. When I was younger, I was in awe of all this. But it's another type of cage and just as hard to escape from.

"Are you ready to go?" I straighten my cuffs and glance at her, trying not to appear as impatient as I feel.

She smiles and walks to the study off to the side. "I thought we might have a quick drink before leaving. I know how much you always loved the study."

"The car is waiting for us." I gesture to the door, even as the clink of glasses sounds.

Fuck it. I follow her into the dark study. Old books combine with leather for a delicious scent. We fucked in here on multiple occasions. She liked it because she felt like she was sticking it to her mother. I liked the idea of getting caught.

"I got in some scotch that I think you'll like." She stands at the bar cart, pouring alcohol into two glasses. She sets the bottle down and picks them up. "I know we ended dreadfully before—"

"You tried to fuck my best friend." No inflection. No feeling. Just dead words.

Her smile falters as she turns, but she finds it again. "I was young and stupid. I'm just glad we can find common ground to start again."

We won't be starting anything but a business relationship between our companies. After the initial setup, I'll be happy to never see her again.

She holds the glass out to me and meets my eyes. Her smile falters a little at whatever she sees, then recovers.

Taking the offered glass, I lift it to my nose, inhaling the complex flavors. "I agreed to take you to this benefit because I needed a date."

Her smile softens as she holds her glass in both her hands. "It's so hard to juggle running a business and dating. It surprised Mother you were still available."

Sipping her drink, she looks through her lashes at me. She thinks I'm available, and that's what we want the rest of society to think. I throw back the scotch, ready to be done with this whole mess. I brush past her and set the empty glass on the cart.

"We should go now." I walk out to the foyer, cursing myself for thinking this might be a good idea. She used me. She tried to use Cooper. I thought I was past it, but the pit of my stomach still burns.

The sounds of her setting her glass down and picking up her clutch reach me. "Of course. Whatever you say."

She stops beside me and waits until I meet her eyes. "Like always."

Fuck that noise. Sure, she knows some of my sexual preferences, but not all of them. And I wouldn't fuck her now if she were the only woman available. Moving to the door, I open it for her. She breezes past me and waits for me to close the door behind us.

"I really would like to get to know who you are now, Seth." She blows out a breath. "I fucked things up royally in the past. I don't expect us to pick up with how we were—"

"That would never happen." I offer her my arm.

She places her hand on my arm and grips it tight. "We had something good. And while we can't have that back, maybe we can find something new? Maybe you can learn to trust me again?"

I grunt a noncommittal response as I lead her to the car and open the door for her. I never should have trusted her in the first place.

Chapter 84

Rivals

Blake

"Are we seriously the first ones here?" Kayla whispers loudly as we make our way into the museum. She holds my arm like she's afraid to get lost in the crowds of people filling the massive room.

"I'm not sure why you're surprised." I glance at my phone and check the positions of the cars bringing the others. People in fancy dresses and tuxedos fill the museum's foyer as everyone wants to be the first to see who's here. The benefit proceeds go to a shelter for homeless children. But mostly, it's somewhere to be seen by the rest of New York society.

"I kind of thought we'd all come together. At least Cooper." When she sighs, I roll my eyes. She's had a crush on Coop since she was twelve.

"He's dating Madison." Five times so far I've told her that tonight.

She frowns. "Yes, but he's still really nice to look at. He's just so pretty."

"I'll tell him you said that."

She hits my arm. "No, you won't."

"Trust me. Coop knows he's pretty already." A tray of champagne goes by, and I raise my hand to stop the waiter. I grab two and hand one to my sister. "He's serious about this one, so don't make any problems."

She arches her eyebrow and sips her champagne. "Is Coop serious about anything? Well, besides business, even then . . ." She sips again and peers up at me. "Is she pretty?"

"Gorgeous," I acknowledge. I can't wait to see Madison all dressed up. Or to help her undress when we get home. I want to strip her down to just the diamonds on her feet and neck. Fuck, just thinking about her makes my cock twitch.

"You sure you don't have a crush on Coop's woman?" Kayla chuckles like that would be hilarious. She had me buy her a new gown for tonight, a silver A-line dress that caught her eye when she went to dinner last night. Her heels bring her head to the height of my nose.

"I'm sure." . . . that my cock will be inside Madison before this night is over. But until then, we're all supposed to be on high alert. The stalker could be here, or even Val and Jeff. This is an open event. Not to mention Hunter. I can't forget his rage at her telling his father about his misbehavior.

He may not be her stalker, but he's definitely not a fan. The fucker thinks she owes him something.

"Stay close to Madison tonight. If she goes to the bathroom, you go with her." There's just too many factors we can't control in an environment like this.

"Do you want me to hold her hand while she pees too?" Kayla finishes her champagne and sets the flute on a tray. "I understand my duties, big brother. She's had threats and you take that shit seriously. I won't let you down."

Kayla had a stalker in high school. It never escalated because we smoked the stalker out. The girl got in a lot of trouble for it. But with all the shit that girl put her through, Kayla takes stalking seriously. It made her wary and cautious.

"Thank you." I glance into her green eyes, so similar to mine. "I really appreciate you doing this for us."

"Mmm. I'm mostly doing it to see Coop in a tuxedo. Have you checked out his ass? He's fine, with a long I."

"Fuck, Kayla." I shake my head, but she just laughs at me. The energy in the room shifts, and there's an electric buzz rippling through the crowd. "Speaking of the ass."

Coop strides in looking distinguished in his tuxedo, but he's not the one that draws my gaze. Madison is divine. Gold from head to toe with glittering diamonds accenting her natural sparkle.

"Holy fuck, Blake. I might have the hots for Coop's girl. She's gorgeous. They're way too pretty together."

Kayla's words make me swallow my tongue.

I'm not usually into watching like Seth, but Coop and Madison fucking is spectacular. Two beautiful bodies moving together like works of art. I could watch them fuck for hours and not get bored.

As long as I get my fair share of Madison.

Coop spots me and whispers something in Madison's ear. She turns and her blue eyes lock on mine. Fuck, I'm lost. There's no way what I feel for her isn't written all over my face. She smiles at me like she's missed me in the few hours we haven't seen each other.

Each stride of her heels brings her closer to me and thumps in time with my heart.

"Holy fuck, Coop, I didn't believe someone could be as pretty as you, but damn." Kayla bites her knuckle as she checks out Madison. "Just so you know, Madison, if you ever decide to give up on men, I'm always available."

"Fuck, Kayla." I shake my head. "First you want Coop, now you want Madison?"

She grins. "What can I say? I like what I like. If you two are ever looking for a unicorn . . ." Kayla points both her fingers at herself with a huge grin.

Coop laughs, but Madison looks a little confused.

"If Blake wouldn't rip my dick off"—Coop winks at me before smiling at my sister—"I would totally take you up on that offer."

Kayla preens and smacks my arm. "You're blocking my mojo."

I hold out my hand and gesture. "Madison, Kayla. Kayla, Madison. I'm sorry Kayla's not really house-trained."

Madison reaches out her hand, but Kayla comes forward and hugs her, grabbing Madison's ass. Madison's startled eyes meet mine and I shrug. Kayla's not really controllable if you don't give her strict boundaries.

Knowing how submissive Madison can be, I could see Kayla trotting all over those lines.

"All right. Release my girl." Coop steps forward.

Kayla grins and raises an eyebrow. "Okay."

She releases Madison and hugs Coop, grabbing his ass too.

"Kayla." I shake my head.

She steps back and grins at both of them. "Gotta have something to dream about in my lonely hotel room tonight."

"You could dream about your girlfriend," I suggest.

Kayla's smile softens. "Yeah, Bea is the best."

Coop tucks Madison in beside him. "Where are the others?"

I glance at my phone. "Noah's about five minutes out. Seth's about ten."

Madison's fingers toy with her necklace as she glances to the door nervously. None of us knows what to expect with Noah's date. But Seth's date almost destroyed our brotherhood. He may forgive her for business reasons, but Coop won't. I'm not sure I'm completely on board if this is what it takes to get Stiner Enterprises' business.

Coop grabs some champagne flutes from a passing tray and hands them out.

"So you get to work with these guys." Kayla moves to stand next to Madison. "How's that going for you?"

Madison's gaze flicks to mine briefly before landing on Coop's. "I'm learning a lot about the business. It's enjoyable and hard work."

Her cheeks flush. The memory of watching her eyes while she

got fucked this morning on the break room table flows through my mind.

"She's a quick learner." I release my breath.

Madison smiles as she meets my gaze. Is she remembering too? Or maybe she's remembering last night when I ate her pussy. Our eyes are locked. Coop steps between us, breaking up what was probably too much eye fucking.

"I'm just lucky I locked her down before any of the others could." Coop's voice is smug.

Yeah, by fucking her in the file room and getting caught hugging her by Hope. Real fucking lucky.

Kayla laughs. "Pretty sure it's frowned upon to bang your assistant."

Madison bites her lip and her brow furrows.

Kayla sees her expression and backpedals. "I'm just joking. Sorry, my mouth gets away from me sometimes."

"It's okay. I know it's not a normal situation, but I like Coop."

Madison looks at Coop with her soft eyes, and something hot twists inside me. Fuck, is that jealousy?

"Yeah, and he's also Cooper Graham. Fuck the rules. He's hot." Kayla acts like Coop and I aren't right here. "If he were my boss, I'd fuck him."

Coop shakes his head and raises an eyebrow at me. I shrug. Kayla's never been controllable. I definitely can't start now.

Madison

The room is full of people. The initial stir when I walked in with Coop has died down. At first, it was intimidating walking in on his arm. But most of the eyes were on him, and I can't help but understand why. He's gorgeous on a normal day, but put him in a tuxedo and ovaries explode right and left.

I wouldn't be surprised if some of the ladies present dragged their own men off to dark corners and fantasized they were the one with Cooper Graham.

Blake's sister is also a little shocking. Especially considering how Blake is. I'm not exactly sure what a "unicorn" is in her world, but something tells me she wants both Coop and me. I've actually never been with a woman before, but I'm definitely too wrapped up in my guys to even consider it.

"I was just teasing earlier," she confides to me, leaning in so the guys don't overhear. "Not about you and Coop being straight fire, but about the unicorn thing. I'm with someone right now, but as soon as that falls through, I'm all yours."

My cheeks heat again. "I don't—"

She laughs, loud and bold and infectious. "Sweetie, trust me. You're missing out." Her gaze strays to Coop and she purses her lips. "Maybe not in your case. Is he as good in bed as I think he is?"

My mouth opens and closes. I don't think I should discuss any of my men's talents with Blake's sister. The hairs on the back of my neck stand on end and I turn.

Noah's dark eyes meet mine, and my breath catches in my throat. His blond hair is unruly as normal, falling into his eyes. For a second, it feels like there's no one else here. My gaze takes in his tuxedo, which defines his solid chest and narrow waist and hips.

The air rushes in around me again as I notice the petite redhead on his arm. She's gorgeous and all smiles as her gaze takes in the room. She clings to his arm like she's just won the lottery of men.

She's not wrong.

Something dark and hot winds in my stomach. I thought I was ready to see him with a woman on his arm, but I don't think I'll ever be ready to see someone look at him like that. Coop's arm wraps around my waist possessively, and he dips his head to whisper in my ear. "He's still yours."

I drop my gaze from the two of them and then lift it to meet Coop's. He squeezes my hip. Sighing, I smile at him to let him know

I'm okay. Noah has to be convincing, has to make it look like he's dating this woman. It's all an act.

It's me he wants to fuck. Not her.

They stop in front of us, and my gaze is drawn to Noah's again.

"You look amazing, Madison," he says softly before clearing his throat and looking at his waiting date. "Madison, Cooper, this is Sara."

Sara smiles and it's like the whole room lights up. She holds out her hand to me. "It's so nice to meet you."

I take her hand and shake it briefly. "It's nice to meet you."

Coop takes her hand and lifts it to press a kiss to her knuckles. "A pleasure."

She giggles lightly and blushes. "And you."

Noah's eyes search mine. I take a deep breath and give him a smile I don't entirely feel. She and Coop talk, but I can't hear a thing over the pounding of my heart. She's perfectly poised and seems like just the type of woman Noah should be with. My heart squeezes.

Right now, the guys are mine, but I can't keep them. At some point, what we have will end, and they'll find women they can really be with. Someone like Sara, who doesn't come with all the baggage I have. Someone who fits in this world of diamonds and champagne.

Noah looks like he's going to reach for me, but Coop turns me away from him.

"This is our other partner, Blake, and his sister, Kayla." Coop's voice finally penetrates the roaring in my ears.

"Aren't you a doll?" Kayla takes Sara's hand. "Wherever did you find her, Noah?"

Noah clears his throat and glances quickly at me before turning back to Kayla. "Our mothers set us up."

Kayla laughs, drawing attention from the surrounding partygoers. "A setup? That's like my favorite trope for a rom-com."

Sara smiles politely and looks up at Noah with dreamy eyes. "I hope so."

Catching the waiter with a drink tray, Noah grabs two. He passes one of them to Sara and takes a drink. Coop rubs my hip and meets my eyes. He gives me a reassuring smile as I take a sip of my champagne.

The noise in the room dims and I turn to the door. Seth and Elizabeth walk in like they own the place. They pause in the entryway as they take in the room. If ever there was a power couple, those two would be the definition of it. Two titans of industry combining.

Perfection.

I lift my glass to take another sip, but my flute is empty. Coop takes it from me and sets it on a passing tray.

"Excuse us." Coop draws me away from the crowd and off to the side. My heels echo in the hallway as he leads me around another corner. "Breathe, sweetheart."

I suck a breath into my starved lungs. Fuck, I hadn't even realized I was holding it.

He pulls me tight into his arms and presses my head against his chest. "They don't want those women. They want you. Only you."

"But I'm not long-term." I lift my gaze to his. "I can't show up with all of you on my arm to something like this. Even if we could continue as we are, I would be their dirty little secret."

A rush of something awful fills me.

"Those women are perfect. They fit into the mold you guys need. I don't." I shake my head.

"Fuck that."

Chapter 85

Evergreen

Madison

"Fuck that."

My gaze jerks up to Coop's at the venom in his voice. He drags me down the hallway away from the crowd.

"Coop, we should go back. I'm fine. Really."

When he finally stops, he ignores my words and turns me to face an enormous mirror with an ornate gilded frame. The hallway is quiet, and I can just hear the crowd from the benefit. The mirror towers over both of us, filling the wall.

He draws my back against his front. Every touch feels molten against my skin. His hand slides across my waist, holding me firmly in place. "Look at yourself."

I meet his eyes in the mirror and give him a glare. Obviously I'm attractive since the guys want me. But that's not the point. I'm not perfect. I'm flawed and come with baggage most guys wouldn't be willing to deal with.

The guys are busy men who just require someone to take care of their needs. I can do that. I can be that for them. But long-term? Even if the stars aligned and all of us could be together without any cares in the world, I still wouldn't fit their perfect mold.

"I know what I look like, Coop."

"Do you?" His voice is low and rough in my ear. His words spin a web I want to get captured in. "Because you aren't seeing what I see."

"What do you see?" I flick my gaze over my reflection. The dress and jewelry are stunning. The makeup artist and hair stylist did a fantastic job. But even with me styled to be a perfect image of myself, I have never felt more beautiful than when I'm laid bare before these men and they devour me.

But it's not my reflection that keeps drawing my gaze. It's his. He's gorgeous. His dark hair brushes the shoulders of his tux. Tonight I can tell he belongs in this world of decadence and richness. Fuck, he looks like he created this world.

When I meet his fierce light blue eyes, they tug at something primal in me. Something wanton that only needs his touch to survive.

His fingers grip my chin and tip it up. The noise of the crowd is lower here. His words are soft. "There's strength in the column of your neck." His other hand draws light lines down it, making tingles course through my veins. "Even with it damaged, you held yourself like a queen. I've been waiting for weeks to mark this neck with my mouth and teeth, claiming it as mine. It's a shame I had to wait so long."

I tremble against him, for him. My insides are on fire, wanting his words, craving his touch.

His fingers toy with the diamond necklace. "These clothes and these jewels make you uncomfortable, but you aren't playing dress-up, sweetheart. You *own* everything that touches your body. It radiates out from you. They only sparkle because of your light."

"The diamonds are yours." I don't want them to think I need all this. I don't. Strip me of the diamonds and the gorgeous clothing, and I'm still who I've always been. Just Madison, a smart girl from the farmlands who managed to make it out. I want to create my own wealth and buy myself all these gorgeous things.

The only thing I want from them is them.

"But tonight you shine brighter than them, goddess. If Hope hadn't been there, I would have taken you into the bedroom and worshipped every inch of you." His fingers tangle in the diamonds. "These are just rocks. Beautiful, very expensive rocks. But you are divine."

His hand slides down the strap of my dress and beneath the silk to cup my bare breast. I gasp as flames lick at me. When I try to turn my head to see if anyone can see us, he holds my chin still and presses against me. What would happen if someone saw? Would we get kicked out? He rubs his thumb over my tightening tip, making my thighs clench together as need trembles through me.

"Your breasts make me want to spend hours touching, sucking, licking them. The sounds you make when I take them in my mouth make my cock harder than it's ever been. They drive me to distraction."

I swallow at the desire welling within me. My knees feel weak, and I'm grateful he's holding me up.

"I want to mark every inch of your body so everyone knows it's mine." His lips brush against my shoulder. Sparks cascade inside me as I let out a shuddering breath. He massages my breast and rolls my nipple between his fingers.

"Coop," I breathe out. We're in the middle of a hallway at a very public event, but he's turning me on to the point where I won't care if anyone sees us. As long as he fulfills the dark promise in his eyes.

My hands grasp his hips behind mine, holding on to the one concrete thing in this world.

"Do you see it yet, goddess?" he whispers against my ear. "Do you see why I fall at your feet to worship you? How I don't care if anyone witnesses me dying at your altar?"

I shiver against him again. His hand keeps my chin still, forcing me to watch as he strokes my breast beneath my dress. I'm on fire. So wet and ready for him. Aching need pulses between my legs.

"I could spend years worshipping this body and never get enough of you." He draws his hand out of my dress and I whimper, wanting it back. Afraid he'll leave me like this. A trembling mass of need. "Shh, goddess, let me make you soar."

His mouth latches onto the spot where my neck and shoulder meet. I forget everything around us as I watch his hand lower in the mirror. My dress slides against my legs slowly as he lifts it, just enough to allow his hand to slide underneath. Each ripple of silk against my legs is another teasing stroke from him.

He touches my bare thigh and fire rages inside me, blocking everything out except his breath against my skin.

"Let me worship you." His words douse the flames with kerosene, stoking it higher, letting me burn. His fingers leave sparks in their wake as they make their way to my center.

"Coop," I whisper, closing my eyes.

His fingers pause. "Look at yourself, goddess. See what I see."

I open my eyes as his fingers tease my clit.

"Fuck." Coop's breath grazes my bare neck. "I hoped you wouldn't wear panties."

I pant out a breath. "Lines."

"Watch." His command makes my eyes lock on us in the mirror. He's curled around me as he sucks, licks, and bites on my shoulder. His hand shifts beneath my skirt, and his thick fingers slide into me.

I gasp and meet my own eyes in the mirror. My cheeks are flushed as he strokes in and out of me, rubbing my clit with his thumb, winding me so tight. I can't turn my head with the grip he has. My lips part as I roll my hips with him.

"That's it, goddess. Answer my prayers."

His dark voice tips me over the edge as I ride his hand. Biting my lip to keep from crying out, I whimper as my orgasm shatters me.

"Beautiful," he whispers. I meet his eyes in the mirror. They're dark with restrained desire. "Do you see it now?"

His fingers stroke within me, sending a wave of aftershocks through me.

"I see it," I whisper as the look on his face holds me captivated, drunk on my desire for him.

Noah

When Coop rushes Madison away, I almost go after them. She went pale when Seth walked in with Elizabeth. She was already upset when I showed up with Sara. All I wanted to do was draw her into my arms and hold her. Remind her this is an act.

I actually move in the direction they vanished, but Sara's hand on my arm stops me.

Blake's eyes meet mine, and I know he feels the urge too. But neither of us makes a move as Seth and Elizabeth join us. We're here with other women to keep the gossip mill quiet. To everyone else, Coop and Madison are dating.

"Good evening." Seth glances in the direction Coop and Madison disappeared with a frown tugging on his lips.

We make the introductions. Even Kayla seems intimidated by Elizabeth. I don't blame her. Elizabeth is hard and there's a shrewdness in her eyes that's difficult to miss. She smiles softly up at Seth who doesn't even meet her eyes.

"Cocktails last for another fifteen minutes," Blake says to fill the awkward silence.

A waiter stops with a tray full of champagne flutes. We all take fresh drinks.

"Is everything all right with Coop and Madison?" Seth downs his glass of champagne as if he's been in the desert for days.

"Is there anything *wrong* with Coop and Madison, because to me they're fucking perfect." Kayla fans herself. "I mean, you all look very nice, and I'd take any of you. Well, except you, Blake. Ew."

"Thankfully you do have a limit," Blake mutters.

I take a sip of champagne before meeting Seth's eyes. I glance at

Elizabeth and raise my eyebrows. Seeing them together is what made Madison take off. He sighs. It was the wrong move to bring Elizabeth. Yes, it was easy and should have been a nonthreat to Madison, but Elizabeth clings to Seth like she's never going to let go.

I'm worried she's going to become another problem we'll have to deal with.

"How do you all know each other?" Sara asks.

"We grew up together and own Morrigan Technology Group." Seth shifts on his feet, moving slightly away from Elizabeth. She shifts with him, undeterred. Her hand remains wrapped around his arm possessively.

Sara glances at me with a smile. "That's amazing. I always thought it would be nice to have friends to work with."

"Do you work?" Blake glances toward the hallway Coop and Madison disappeared down. Fuck, he needs to knock that shit off. These women will either think he's into Madison or Coop. I don't know which would be worse.

Sara laughs brightly. "No, I'm still in college for another year. Finishing my masters, though I'm considering getting my doctorate to teach. But I might stop and find a job for a while before continuing my education."

"What are you studying?" Kayla asks. Her eyes watch all of us like a hawk. A few years younger than Blake, she's known us since we were kids. She might catch on to our concern, but maybe she'll think it's for Coop.

"Accounting."

That draws my attention. Sara smiles.

"You didn't mention that." Did she? In all the texts we sent back and forth? I knew she was in graduate school, but how could I not know her major?

"Funny, I thought I did." Sara shrugs. "Don't worry, I'm not after your job."

The women chuckle slightly.

Seth releases a breath and his shoulders loosen. I turn to see Coop and Madison making their way through the crowd. Madison's cheeks are flushed with color, and Coop holds her close to him.

She looks breathtaking tonight. Every inch of her makes me want to drag her into a dark corner and ravish her. But the only one who might get away with that is Coop. Hell, he might have already.

"Sorry, we needed a minute." Coop grins down at her when they finally join us.

Madison turns a deeper shade of pink, but at least she has more color than before. I also notice the red spot on her shoulder. I meet Coop's gaze, and he shrugs and gives me a smirk. Fucker.

"I love your dress." Sara draws Madison's attention. "I wish I had your height to carry it off."

"You look lovely. Heels help." Madison's smile seems a little more relaxed and natural.

Sara tightens her hand on my arm. "I'd need Noah to help me walk in heels like those."

Madison's smile freezes as she glances at me. It's a brief flick of her eyes. Not enough time for me to reassure her I'm all hers. That Sara doesn't really want me that way. I'm hoping to tell her at some point tonight.

"They take some practice," Madison acknowledges.

"I'm afraid gold would wash me out." Elizabeth takes a sip of her champagne. "It looks lovely on you though, dear."

"Thank you. I love your dress." Madison meets Elizabeth's gaze but avoids Seth's.

His lips tighten. He won't let that slide, but Madison's nervous. And she should be, this evening is only beginning.

The bell chimes, telling us it's time to move into the dining room.

"I hope the food is good. I'm starving," Kayla says as we walk together to our table.

"I'm sure they thought of you when creating the menu." Blake chuckles.

As we walk in, I step beside Madison and brush the backs of my fingers against hers. She inhales, but otherwise doesn't make any other outward sign of our touch. It settles something inside me, and I hope it does the same for her.

We have a long night ahead of us, but when we get home, she'll be mine.

Chapter 86

Food Chain

Blake

As we find our table, I feel someone watching us. I turn my head and catch Hunter glaring at Madison. He's two tables away, next to his father. A woman sits next to him with a smile plastered on her face.

When I shift to put myself between him and Madison, he meets my eyes. His rage is palpable. Bet he hoped Daddy would never learn of his penchant for antagonizing the female staff. He better not have any plans of revenge against our girl because I won't stand for it.

His eyes narrow, but then he turns to talk to the woman like nothing happened.

Fuck that asshole.

A hand brushes my back, and I know it's Madison's. Taking a breath, I turn to gaze down at her.

Thank you, she mouths.

I nod slightly. I may not be able to claim her, but I will do everything in my power to protect her. No matter the consequences.

Sara sits next to Madison, while Elizabeth is across from her next to Kayla. I move to take my seat. This evening was always going to be fucked-up. But Seth bringing Elizabeth just feeds a whole history of resentment.

"We didn't really have time to catch up during our lunch meeting." Elizabeth smiles like she isn't the devil incarnate. It might have worked in college, but we all know better now.

"You knew the guys in college?" Madison drapes her napkin over her lap as the waiter sets a salad in front of her. Her blue eyes focus on Elizabeth. Madison knows that already, but she's making conversation.

"Yes." Elizabeth smiles and tries to put her hand over Seth's on the table. When he moves it before she can take it, she reaches for her glass instead like that was always her intention. Her smile doesn't falter. "Seth and I dated. Of course, you know how tight-knit the guys are, so I got to know all of them."

The way she says *tight-knit* makes my stomach clench. Has Elizabeth heard the rumors? After Andrea left, things were tense for a while. A rumor spread that we didn't just work together, but that we fucked together too. Not everyone paid attention to it, but we lost some clients who felt it was morally repugnant.

I said good riddance, but Seth helped us regain our reputation. We each dated separate women for a while. With us out and about, the gossip died down. That got old quick though.

Pulling out of my thoughts, I clue back into the conversation.

"We work well together." Madison takes a bite of salad.

Chuckling, Coop grabs his drink and leans back in his chair.

Elizabeth's brown eyes flick to Coop. "How have you been?"

He raises an eyebrow at her as if she is an insignificant blight. He slides his hand into Madison's and places their joined hands on the table.

Elizabeth swallows as her gaze locks on their hands. She clears her throat. "I've watched your company growth. It's been impressive. It's good to see the four of you are still together."

"No thanks to you." Coop raises his glass in a mock toast to her and takes a drink.

"Wait." Kayla stops eating her salad and looks around the table. Her gaze stops on Elizabeth. "Aren't you the chick in college who tried to get with Coop while you were dating Seth?" She snaps her fingers. "I thought your name sounded familiar. Coop was with someone else, even."

Elizabeth flinches. "We all do stupid things when we're young." Her eyes focus on Madison, like Madison will understand. "I made a terrible mistake back then."

"Wow, you've got some huge lady balls to sit at this table and think everything is going to be fine and dandy." Kayla laughs. "Even I know you don't come between these guys."

"Kayla." I put some dominance in my tone to make her shut up. Her runaway mouth will lead to nothing but trouble. She doesn't even flinch.

"Maybe it's not lady balls, maybe it wasn't your choice to be here. Maybe Mommy is rich as Midas and holds the purse strings tight? Am I close? Seth might have been handsome, intelligent, and a good guy in college, but now . . ." Kayla leans back in her chair. "He's come into his own and maybe Mommy thinks you should test the waters. It doesn't take balls when money's on the line, does it?"

Elizabeth flushes red. I can't tell if it's embarrassment or anger. "Excuse me, but I need to use the restroom."

Elizabeth rises and heads to the bathroom.

Sara lets out a low whistle. "Wow. Man, am I glad my mom is relentless. I mean, usually I tell her *no way* on blind dates, but that was worth the price of admission."

Madison's brow furrows as she looks at Sara. "Kayla embarrassed her."

Sara takes a bite of her salad, then says, "Yeah, but when you've been around these people long enough, you learn to see the vipers before they strike. Kayla isn't a viper. She's a snake hunter."

She winks at Kayla, who preens.

"You need to keep this one, Noah." Kayla laughs. "I like her."

I shake my head. Madison looks between the two women. She seems confused as she glances at Noah.

"Okay, before she gets back." Kayla looks around the table and stops on Seth. "Why on earth would you bring that woman? You're better than that."

"Jesus, Kayla." I drop my head to my hand and take a deep breath. "I should have just gotten a regular date to this thing."

"Probably." Kayla chuckles. "But you know you love me."

She's right. She's my little sister and annoys the fuck out of me, but she's also my fiercest protector when I need one.

"Stiner is looking for a new cybersecurity firm." Seth sets his fork down, and his gaze lingers on Madison. "With as busy as work has been, I didn't have time to go looking for a date or mislead some woman that this means something more than it is, so when her mother suggested I take her . . ."

"You thought, why the fuck not?" Kayla raises an eyebrow. "That's fucked-up, man."

"You're not wrong." Coop leans back in his chair.

Seth glares at Coop, but Coop has a point. Elizabeth was a wedge in our brotherhood, and she doesn't deserve to sit at the same table as Madison. Definitely not as a placeholder.

"So let me see if I'm following this." Sara straightens in her seat and points her fork at Seth. "You used to date that woman in college until she tried to sleep with"—her fork swings to Coop—"you. And then you two broke up?"

"Yes," Seth sighs.

"And now, you're playing nice for your business connections?" Sara sets her fork on her plate.

"Yes."

She blows out a breath. "Damn, this is juicy stuff. I thought I had it bad, but damn."

Noah clears his throat. "I think it's best if we don't bring up anything more about this when Elizabeth gets back. While you might find it diverting, the clients that will follow Stiner are significant. This is a business dinner after all."

"Of course." Smiling at him like he hung the moon, Sara puts her hand over his. "I know how to behave at a business dinner."

Madison's gaze falls on their joined hands. Her face goes pale, but Coop must have touched her under the table because her eyes swing to his. He gives her a smile full of promise that has her melting.

Once again, my stomach flares with heat. I don't know what the fuck is happening with me. She's ours, not his. But everyone around us assumes she's only his. It wouldn't matter if I marked her and knew it was mine. They would all think it's his.

When Elizabeth comes back to the table, Seth stands to hold her chair for her. She gives him a grateful smile that he doesn't return.

I don't know how we're going to make it through this night.

Madison

The dinner conversation is a lot more tame after the drama. I actually felt a little bad for Elizabeth. If someone picked me apart and brought up something embarrassing I did when I was younger, I would have crumbled. Coop would have lifted me back up, but Elizabeth is in enemy territory here.

Sara and Noah talk about books they've read. Every soft laugh from her makes my stomach churn. Dinner should be delicious, but it tastes like sand in my mouth. Coop touches my thigh softly beneath the table, drawing my attention back to him.

He leans into my ear and whispers, "Do I need to show you again, goddess?"

My cheeks grow warm as his heated gaze meets mine. There's a promise in those eyes. One I'm not sure he could ever keep. He desires me, but of all of them, I don't think he could ever love me.

That makes me want to hold my heart away from him because I know he could do the most damage to it. Just by never returning my love.

His hand grasps the back of my neck, and his mouth claims mine. It's so easy to fall into him. To let him lift me up. Our tongues tangle, and I taste the scotch he's been drinking with dinner and a hint of mint. For a minute the world fades around us, and it's only the two of us again.

"I hope they have ice cream for dessert, because I need to cool down." Kayla's voice breaks through the fog of desire, and I pull away from Coop.

At least as far as he lets me. He raises an eyebrow before his thumb comes up and smooths below my lip.

Blake clears his throat and Coop releases me. When I reach for my glass, I meet Blake's eyes. There's a possessive light in them that keys me up, reminding me of the time at Taylor's when he dragged me into the office and later spanked me for every number of past lovers I still had in my phone.

I drag in a breath and take a large gulp of cold water.

Elizabeth glares at me until she notices my attention on her. Her face softens into a smile. While I don't want her humiliated at the table, I can't help but wonder what she's up to. What angle she's trying to pursue. Is she after Seth? Or maybe Coop still?

I set my glass down. "If you'll excuse me?"

When I stand, Kayla stands and says, "What a coincidence."

"I could powder my nose." Sara stands and brushes her hand on Noah's shoulder. "See you in a few."

I clench my fingers but smile as we all three make our way to the bathroom. Fortunately, we seem to have made it there before the rush and three stalls are actually empty. When I sit, I release a breath.

I didn't realize how difficult this night was going to be. I rub my temples.

Seeing other women claim my men. Not being able to do anything, not even a look that might reveal a longing for more.

"Noah's nice, huh?" Sara's voice comes through the stall next to me.

Noah's everything. "Yes, he is."

"But wow, Cooper's hot. Good job."

I'm not usually a bathroom talker, so I let out an acknowledging sound.

"Could you imagine being in a Cooper and Madison sandwich though?" Kayla's voice is loud.

My eyes widen and I release a huff of breath. I'll need to learn more about Blake's sister next time Blake and I are alone. I'm definitely not interested in being in any "sandwich" unless it's between two of my men.

Sara laughs. "You aren't very shy, are you, Kayla?"

"Not a single bone in my body." The toilet next to mine flushes and the door squeaks open. Kayla's voice moves farther away. "Though I think Madison might be a little shy."

The sink runs. Not with my guys I'm not, but I don't want to accidentally slip up. Especially around these women.

"Not particularly," I say.

"She's just quiet," Sara offers.

Both our toilets flush at the same time. We open our doors and head to the sinks.

Kayla steps next to me and I almost shrug back.

"Chill. I just want you to know that Blake told me about your situation, and I completely understand."

I swallow. Blake said Kayla would stay with me on bathroom runs, so I assume she means the stalker.

She sighs and leans against the sink. "I had one in high school. A chick, if you can believe it. Makes sense though. She saw all this and got obsessive on my ass." Her gaze takes me in. "I could see why someone would want to haunt your steps."

Definitely the stalker. Not my other situation that includes all my bosses. "It's been a little traumatizing."

"Damn, you have a stalker?" Sara closes in on us and says it softly enough that no one else will hear.

"Yeah, and he sent her a cut-up dress coated in red with pics of her over the years wearing it." Kayla's eyes widen for effect. "Blake also mentioned videos, but he wouldn't tell me what was in them."

Both their green eyes land on me. I step away and dry my hands. Yeah, I'm not going there. "They weren't friendly videos."

"That's so messed up." Sara shakes her head. "If you need someone in town, let me give you my number. Seriously, you might need somewhere no one would expect you to go."

I squint my eyes at her. "Why are you being so nice?"

She straightens. She can't be any taller than Hope, but she seems just as fierce. "We have to stick together in this business world. I know we don't know each other very well, but there have been times I wish someone would have reached out to me. So . . ."

She shrugs her delicate shoulders and holds out her hand for my phone. I take it out of my purse and hand it to her.

"Oh, I'm getting in on this. I think Blake is seeing someone on the down-low, but he refuses to tell me about it." Kayla reaches for my phone when Sara finishes.

Heat rises in my cheeks. "I wouldn't know about Blake's life outside of work."

Kayla laughs. "Yeah, right. You all live together. I mean if I were you, I'd be too busy with Coop to notice. So if you don't notice anything, I wouldn't blame you."

"I don't know who I would choose among those guys." Sara gazes off dreamily. "I mean, Noah is definitely a keeper, but there's something about each of them that revs my engine."

I raise an eyebrow at how close she is to the truth.

"Ew, Blake's my brother. Seth is like a brother too." Kayla leads the way back out to the ballroom. "I hope you two don't mind slow dancing with a chick, because I won't be dancing with my brother."

Sara giggles. "Get enough wine in me and I'll slow dance with just about anyone."

"I love a challenge." Kayla locks arms with Sara before turning to me. "Come on, I know you like the cock, but live a little. Chicks can be fun too."

Kayla winks at me before grabbing my arm to pull me with them. This is too weird, but I think I just made new friends. As long as Sara doesn't end up dating Noah. My chest tightens. At least, not for real.

Chapter 87

Think Outside the Box

Madison

On the way back from the bathroom, a woman tugs her date to a stop in front of me.

"Madison?"

Instinctively I take a step back, but Kayla's hold on my arm stops me. The woman steps closer, and I recognize Anna Beck, a woman I used to babysit for during my freshman year. Relief splashes through me and I smile.

"Anna, it's good to see you. How are Lily and Elijah?"

Anna pulls the man into her side as she faces us. "They're great. They definitely miss you. Patrick, you remember Madison, right, darling?"

Patrick's brown eyes meet mine briefly before he returns to searching the room. His blond hair is slicked back. "Of course, dear."

He doesn't seem to recognize me.

Anna shakes her head. Her auburn curls bounce around her face as she smiles. "He doesn't keep up with who watches our kids. I thought maybe you'd made an impression when he asked if the new nanny was someone else."

"It's okay." I really didn't know her husband very well. I spent most of my time with the children or studying.

Kayla tugs on my arm when the music plays. She and Sara hang back a little, chatting.

"You must be done with your studies by now. You were so determined. Where did you end up?" Anna looks like she could stand here and talk to me for days.

"I'm with Morrigan Technology Group." Much as I want to go with Kayla, I don't want to be rude. After all, Anna and her husband gave me a job that let me study while earning money.

"Darling, did you hear Madison? Isn't that one of your clients?" She turns back to me. "I can never keep them straight."

Patrick turns to her, and his gaze flicks over me dismissively. "Yes, they are."

"Patrick." Coop joins us and takes my hand from Kayla. He says softly, "I've got her from here."

Kayla gives him a pout and throws me a wink before she and Sara head back to the table.

"Coop." Patrick holds out his hand. His full attention turns to us then. His gaze falls to our linked hands before he gives me a curious look. "Is this your assistant?"

"Oh, my." Anna flushes with color. "You definitely landed a good one, Madison dear."

"I'm the lucky one." Coop presses a kiss to the top of my head.

"I wish she'd stayed our babysitter." Anna shakes her head. "It's so hard to find someone who takes good care of our children. Madison excelled at it."

Patrick makes an indifferent noise. He doesn't seem to like me that much, but he interacted with me very little when I was the babysitter. He'd save me cookies or treats and give them to me when he drove me home on the rare occasion he made it home first, or Anna couldn't drive me. It was sweet, but almost like an afterthought. Not that he kept it specifically for me.

"She's an excellent assistant. Apparently, she's good at everything she does." Coop tugs me in close to him and strokes his hand over my hip.

"Did you get the signature on that contract?" Patrick asks.

"Now, darling, you promised. No work tonight." Anna grins and takes Patrick's hand. "We don't get out much, so he's not allowed billable time on date night."

"That's a good policy." Coop squeezes me. "We need to return to our table. The speeches will begin soon. It was good to see both of you."

"Tell Lily and Elijah I said hi and that I miss them." I give her a smile. Those kids were the best.

"I will." Anna smiles. "Don't stay a stranger. We should do lunch sometime."

"I'd like that."

Anna was always nice to me. Never treated me like the help.

"Talk Monday, Coop," Patrick bites out.

Coop leads me back toward the table. His brow furrows like he's thinking through something.

"What's on your mind?" I tilt my head as I look up at him.

He stares over my shoulder toward Patrick and Anna. "How long did you babysit for them?"

I glance their way. They stopped at another couple and Anna talks animatedly while Patrick looks bored.

"About a year. It was good money, but then I got internships to help cover bills and get experience." I lift my gaze to Coop's. "Why?"

"You met Patrick during that time? He knew your name? You talked to him?"

"Occasionally. Mostly I dealt with Anna. Sometimes Patrick would get home first or take me home." I step closer to Coop. "What is it?"

"He didn't seem to know you when we did the background check. When he was in the office and the dress came in, he acted like didn't recognize you."

A shiver races down my spine. I didn't even know he was there that day. That box is etched in my brain, but I shake it off. "I'm not surprised. Anna had to remind him who I was just now. To him, I was the help and that's all."

"Hmm." His hand falls on my lower back. "Something is nagging at me."

I let him stew as we weave our way back to our table. Dessert has arrived and it's a chocolate cheesecake. Coop helps me into my seat before the lights dim and the speaker begins. His hand curls around my thigh and strokes my leg under the table.

I can't focus on what the presenters say. As I eat my dessert, Coop strokes the inside of my thigh, getting closer and closer to my aching center. The lure of a darkened corner where he could play with me more beckons me.

My eyes lock with Seth's and I bite my lip. His focus drops to my mouth. Heat sparks in his eyes and I hope no one else notices, because I want him to watch me. I want Seth to tell Coop and me what to do until we shatter.

It won't happen here though. Not with Seth at least. I lean in to Coop and press my lips to his ear.

"Coop?" His name is barely a breath, but he slides his hand higher. "Please."

The audience breaks out in applause. Coop turns his darkened light blue eyes to mine. Whatever he sees is enough. When everyone rises to applaud whoever did what, Coop takes my hand and draws me away from the table. I glance back and meet Seth's hungry eyes.

If we were home, I would reach out my hand and ask him to join us. But my gaze skips to Elizabeth clapping next to him, and my chest tightens. I close my eyes as I turn away from him.

Coop tucks me into his side as we make our way through the tables. A familiar face flashes into my view. For a second, I can't place where I know him, but then it registers. My literature professor, Mr. Jimi Alan. I flinch a little as he flashes me a sloppy smile, like he's had one too many.

He made it obvious that he wouldn't mind helping me with some personal, one-on-one tutoring. I had an A in his class, but he kept offering. I try to find him in the crowd again.

But Coop pulls me through a door. This must be an employee-only area. It's a long hallway with carts and racks along the sides.

"Are we supposed to be back here?" I whisper.

"Not here." Coop leads me down the hallway until we reach another door. Opening it, he ushers me through.

"Where are we going?" The door shuts behind us. We're in a part of the museum that is dimly lit and clearly not part of the actual event. The clinking of silverware and glasses no longer fills the air. Just silence and the light clicking of my heels on the marble floor surround us.

"My family donated the money for this wing. A lot of the furniture and artwork came from our personal collection."

My eyes widen as I take in the grandeur of the items. From gorgeously carved wooden tables topped with marble to priceless vases, the amount of wealth in this hallway staggers me. We had a few "antiques" at our house, but nothing on this scale. Ours were plain in comparison.

Coop slows and turns me to face a painting of a nude woman. She faces away from us, stretched out on a chaise. Tucking me against his front, he rests his chin on my shoulder. "My grandmother had this commissioned."

I lean against him as my eyes travel over the curves and dips of the woman's body. It's a beautiful painting. "It's lovely."

"Pretty sure the woman was my grandmother's lover." Coop presses his hard cock against my ass. "I'd commission an artist to paint you like that, if you wanted."

"That seems a little excessive." My eyes flick to the painting. It really is gorgeous. Though I can't imagine having a nude painting of me in existence.

"Maybe I'll have it hung in a museum in your honor. Would you like that, goddess?" He takes my hand and draws me deeper into the room. His smile is mischievous, and his heated gaze strokes over my body, making awareness prick at my skin. "People through the ages gazing at your delightful body, taking pleasure in the artful curves and precise strokes of the artist's brush?"

I laugh and it fills the room. "You wouldn't keep it for yourself? So you have something to remember me by?"

"Why would I keep it? When I have the real thing to warm my cock?" He pulls me into his arms. His gaze falls to my lips and my heart skips a little.

I can't even think about the future, but the guys will move on from me. All that we'll have left is our memories of our time spent together. My throat thickens and I clear it to loosen the lump lodged there.

I need more memories. So many more to squirrel away for a future that just seems bleak without them.

"Will you dance with me tonight, Coop?"

Kayla brought it up earlier, and I hadn't thought about dancing. Worrying about the guys' dates and the stalker had me so stressed out, I didn't even think about the actual benefit. I want nothing more than for Coop to sweep me into his arms and lead me around the dance floor.

He spins me out suddenly before spinning me back in. I release a surprised laugh. My insides grow warm and fuzzy as he dips me over his arm and holds me suspended in the air. He has me under his full control and can choose to either lift me back up or drop me.

"Do you want to dance, goddess?"

Not taking my gaze from his, I nod. "I would love to."

He lifts me slowly and presses me back until a marble column stops us.

"I'd love to dance with you," he says.

I see the twinkle in his eyes before his mouth claims mine. Our tongues dance as his fingers drag my skirt up. This isn't some darkened corner. This is the middle of a room, where anyone can walk in. Where security could find us.

What happens when we get kicked out?

"Coop." I shift my lips from his. He continues to kiss down my throat, leaving sparks in his wake. I squeeze his shoulders. "We can't do this here."

"That's the good thing about being me." He slides his tongue along the necklace before easing my dress off my breast. I flick my gaze to the right and left, positive that someone will find us.

His eyes capture mine as his fingertip trails over my nipple. Seeing the hunger in his eyes, I forget why I'm even arguing with him. His hunger calls to me, traps me. I crave his mouth on my body.

"Money provides me a lot of finer things." He punctuates each word with kisses trailing over my breast. My nipple is painfully hard, waiting for his touch. My breast feels heavy. "One of those things is fucking you in a room where you can see what my wealth can afford."

"I don't care about your money." As his mouth encloses my nipple, I gasp and arch into him. Too quickly, he lifts from me slightly and blows lightly over where his lips were. I whimper with need.

His darkened eyes hold mine captive.

"No, you don't, do you?" His voice has a sense of wonder to it. "You just want my cock deep inside you." Gathering my skirt, Coop lifts my leg to the side, opening me up to him. "But I won't come in your pussy or ass. As much as I want my cum dripping from your cunt to remind you who you belong to, I don't want to ruin your beautiful dress."

I catch his jaw in my hand and hold his eyes. "Are you going to make me come or not?"

"Such a needy cunt you have, my little whore." His fingers tease my inner thigh, so close to where I ache for him. My legs tremble. Needing whatever he'll do to me, not caring if this is on security cameras. I trust Coop to take care of me in all ways.

He leans in slowly until his mouth is just a hair's breadth from mine.

"I'll fuck you until you come, sweetheart, but then you're going to suck me off with those gorgeous red lips of yours." His every word makes me throb.

"Yes, please."

His finger trails over my clit.

A gasp catches in my throat as desire bursts like champagne bubbles through me. "Coop."

"So fucking wet for me." He chuckles darkly before capturing my lips. My body arches against him, wanting more, needing more. Trying to take everything he has to give.

Breaking the kiss, he leans his forehead against mine. Our breath is the only sound in this empty hall full of ghosts of the past.

"Take out my cock like a good little whore."

I bite my lip while my eyes search his. My hands find his belt and pull it loose. My fingers fumble in my hurry to undo his pants and have him inside of me. Filling me. Fucking me.

My hands finally release him from his boxer briefs. When my fingers graze his hard cock, we both moan.

"Fuck, sweetheart. I've wanted my cock buried inside you since you came out of your bedroom." His eyes hold mine as I stroke his cock while his finger teases my clit with soft touches.

"So fuck me, Coop." I suck his lower lip into my mouth.

He shifts closer, and I rub the tip of his cock along my clit until it presses against my entrance. His voice is rough when he says, "Look at me when I fuck you."

As soon as I lift my gaze to meet his, he thrusts deep inside me. My gasp fades into a moan as he slides out and thrusts back in. His hands lift my ass, and as he uses the column to help hold me, I wrap my leg around him. My hands cradle his jaw, feeling the roughness of his stubble.

Our eyes lock on each other as our hips move together. We've been together so many times before, but something feels more intimate this time. Our breath and the thrust of his cock into my wet pussy are the only sounds in this quiet hall. The only thing I have to hold on to is that look in his eyes that says I'm his. Suddenly, my heart feels like it's ready to leap.

"Fuck, Madison." He leans his forehead against mine, and his hand slips between us to tease my clit. "I need you to come. I can't hold back much longer."

His words, his touch, his cock work together to overwhelm me. I grab his hair. My whole body tenses as the damn bursts and my orgasm crashes over me.

"That's it, goddess. Come for me." He captures my mouth as I cry out.

It's too much. My pussy convulses around his thick cock, trying to draw him deeper, wanting to feel him come inside me. He pulls out before I'm ready and sets me on my feet.

I meet his eyes as I lower to my knees before him. With no hesitation, I take him into my mouth, tasting myself on him. Our eyes lock as I take him deep into my throat. His thumb caresses my cheek softly as I bob on him.

His hair falls around his face like some god of pleasure for me to worship.

"Fuck, you're such a good little whore. Slide your fingers deep into your greedy cunt and feel it pulsing around them as I come in your throat."

I slide my fingers inside and moan as aftershocks ripple around them. Coop grabs the back of my neck and makes me take him deep as he groans his release. I swallow every bit of his salty cum as I convulse around my fingers. He pulls out of my mouth, then tucks his cock back into his pants and sinks to his knees with me.

Our eyes lock again, and his are filled with a tenderness that makes my heart pound a little fiercer in my chest.

Taking my wrist, he draws my fingers out of my pussy and takes them into his mouth, sucking the taste of me off them.

"Fuck, I love the way you taste." He grabs my neck and claims my mouth with his. I wrap my arms around his neck and lose myself to the feel of his tongue against mine.

I don't think I can hold my heart away from any of my guys. Because in this moment, I can feel it opening to Coop.

While I'm terrified to give my heart to this man, I can't help myself.

He lifts his mouth and rests his forehead against mine. Our eyes lock again and hope wells inside me.

"I—"

The echo of a door closing cuts him off.

Chapter 88

Speculation

Seth

"I've always loved coming to events like this." Elizabeth leans closer to me. We're still at the table even though the speaker is finished.

I resist the urge to pull away. It's one night. I can get through this even if her being here makes my flesh crawl. It was a snap decision that I've been regretting since.

Instead, I can't stop myself from watching the door Coop and Madison disappeared through.

We all know she might be in danger tonight. Anyone can access this benefit. Her stalker—even her roommate—could be here, waiting for an opportunity to strike.

Elizabeth's fingers land on my jacket sleeve, forcing my attention back to her. I sigh. Not the woman I want to focus on, but I have to.

"You remember that one night? My sorority had a formal. We snuck out of the party. Kind of like your assistant just did with Cooper." Elizabeth's tone is nonchalant, but everything she says is calculated.

There's nothing subtle about her, even if she's trying to be. She's made it clear she wants to pick up where we left off, but even if Madison didn't exist, that would never happen.

I turn to meet her eyes. She smiles like the memory takes her back to a better time, but it's not real. Nothing about Elizabeth is real. It never was.

"You fucked me up against a wall. Made me beg you for my release."

I glance over at the others, but they're all deep in their own conversations. Thankfully. "What's your point?"

"We were good together once upon a time." She shrugs and releases a delicate laugh. Her calculating gaze lingers on the same doorway I'm working on ignoring for now. "I imagine this is new for Cooper and that's why he's so attentive to her. It probably won't last long though. What happens when Cooper dumps your assistant?"

I narrow my gaze at her. "What's your point, Elizabeth?"

"How is that girl going to deal with being dumped by Cooper Graham?" She smiles and smooths her napkin on her lap. "You might lose a perfectly adequate assistant by letting her fuck one of her bosses. You probably should work out a fraternization policy to avoid things like that."

"I appreciate your concern." It's nearly impossible to focus on Elizabeth's ridiculous maneuvering while worrying about the stalker and other threats looming here. I turn to look at the hidden door again. They shouldn't be gone this long. What if they've run into trouble? We almost let Madison down that first night.

"But girls like your assistant are a dime a dozen." Elizabeth sounds smug. "What is she? Twenty-five? Twenty-four?"

"What's your obsession with our assistant?" Tension winds inside me. I don't want to discuss Madison with Elizabeth. Fuck, I don't even want to be here with Elizabeth, but if it helps safeguard Madison's reputation, it's worth it. At least that's what I keep telling myself.

"He can't be serious about her. She's definitely not his type and she doesn't have the pedigree needed to be the wife of Cooper Graham. She looks like she's barely out of college."

Why is she so focused on Madison and Coop? What does she have to gain from this line of questioning? What is she digging for? Because if she's looking to return to where we were, she's never going to find a way to do that.

I may have been naive about her when I was in college, but I'm familiar with her and her type of woman now. She wants something she can weaponize. The real question is, to use against who? Whatever it is, I need to be careful with what I show her.

"She is." I glance at Elizabeth. I'm not sure where all this speculation is coming from. "Madison was top of her class and graduated with a master's in four years while having multiple internships that provided her with a variety of experience. Just because she doesn't have a legacy behind her doesn't mean she's not invaluable. And Coop saw that in her."

Elizabeth laughs lightly. "It figures Coop would want the twenty-two-year-old. When he's fifty, he'll still want twenty-year-olds."

"So what if he does?"

She makes a little noise of disbelief.

I'm beginning to think we need to send someone after them. To make sure nothing has happened. For a moment, Elizabeth sips her drink and remains quiet.

Elizabeth clears her throat. "They make quite the striking pair."

Fuck, why did I bring her to this?

"Yes, they do." You'd have to be blind to not see how beautiful they are together.

"I bet they'd be gorgeous to *watch*."

Everything stills around me. My gaze returns to Elizabeth's as she takes a sip of her drink, looking at me like she's caught on to something. The reality is she knows nothing and can't prove anything. We barely dove into my kinks when we were a couple.

That's pushing too far though and it's time to shut her down.

"Are you implying something, Elizabeth? If so, come out and say it." I pause. "I'm not the one who tried to cheat. I'm not the one who left our bed and went after your best friend."

She flinches at the reminder. Like we'll ever be able to put that behind us. She tore at something fundamental. She wanted him while she was sleeping with me. Fuck this catty bitch. I can't wait to get rid of her. This is the last time I give her any piece of me.

I give her my full attention, giving her what she thinks she wants. "Why does your mother suddenly feel I'm worthy of your time now?"

Elizabeth smiles like I'm actually interested in her. "It's not hard to see that you've changed, Seth. You've made a name for yourself. Built a business. You're a known quantity. Unlike when we were in college."

Her reasoning, while cold, is rational at least.

This is my fault for inviting this snake back into my life. For inviting her when I could have taken anyone else. Balancing Elizabeth's ego and the need to keep Madison safe is nearly impossible. Fortunately, I'm not the only one watching out for Madison. I catch Blake's eyes and nod toward where Coop and Madison disappeared. His eyes narrow and he gives me a subtle nod. We can't go after them right now, but we'll need to if they aren't back soon.

Coop better know what he's doing.

It's definitely time for a change of subject and to bring this back to a work dinner, instead of whatever fantasy Elizabeth wants to live out. We're done. Business is the only thing we'll ever have between us.

There are few things Elizabeth likes better than talking about herself.

"Tell me about your role at Stiner." Maybe listening to her drone on will make the time go faster. And Madison and Coop will return before I know it.

———

Coop

"Fuck." Madison's eyes widen as she fixes the strap on her dress.

Both of our gazes search the direction the door slam came from. Shit. I stand and reach down a hand to help Madison to her feet. She takes a moment to make sure she's covered, while I can't take my focus off the empty hallway.

Is someone coming or did they leave? How much did they see? No one has appeared, but the two of us are alone in a part of the museum that's supposed to be closed off. The guys will kill me for putting Madison in danger.

If it was security, they would have shown themselves by now.

Madison's hands are on my pants. I glance down. She's doing up my belt and straightening my clothes. Quietly taking care that we're put together. Her golden hair falls around her face.

Fuck. This woman cracks the wall around my heart. I have to be careful not to let her in. I'm not someone anyone stays for without wanting something in return. But when her worried blue eyes lift to mine, all I want to do is draw her into my arms and protect her from anything that might harm her.

The only people who haven't left me are Seth, Noah, and Blake. They're my family. My brothers. When I've given small parts of my heart to others, they've just thrown it back in my face.

I find out it's not me they wanted. It's what I could offer them. Wealth, status, security.

"Maybe they didn't come this far?" Madison slides her hands through my hair, grooming me.

That feels too nice. I don't think anyone has finger combed my hair in a long time. "We should head back to the benefit."

She nods and steps back. "How do I look?"

Like a goddess who just got fucked probably isn't what she wants to hear. I tuck her hair behind her ear and my chest fills with warmth. I smooth a thumb under her lips to clean up her lipstick until she can reapply.

Her lips part and her eyes darken. My cock twitches in response. Without thinking, I close the distance between us. Her fingers clutch my lapels as I hover over her lips. She lets out a little whimper of need.

Closing my eyes, I touch my forehead to hers and breathe in her floral scent. Just for a moment, to savor her. I release the tension in my shoulders and draw her hips against mine.

"We should go back now," she whispers.

I open my eyes and press my lips quickly to hers before drawing away. Taking her hand, I lead her back the way we came, scanning the area for anyone lurking. The employee hallway is still empty as we walk through it to the door that leads to the benefit.

Nothing unusual stands out to me. No evidence of someone waiting to pounce on us. Everything seems normal. The door muffles the music and voices as we approach the final door.

"Should we tell the others?" Madison stops before we reach it.

"We don't know that anyone saw us." I draw in a breath and look down the hall. "It could have been a security guard walking through the area near the door."

Her eyes narrow on me. We're both thinking it. It could have been her stalker or any number of creeps. I tug her into my arms and hug her, pressing a kiss to her hair.

She softens against me and my heart skips.

Drawing away from her warmth, I open the door and the sound of the benefit flows over us, full force. The lights are dimmed, and people are everywhere. On the dance floor. Clustered in groups talking. Sitting at tables.

I'm tempted to pull Madison back into the quiet hallways of the museum and say fuck it to socializing. But this serves a purpose. We need to be seen in public.

Wrapping her hand around my arm, I lead us back to our table. Seth, Blake, Noah, and Elizabeth sit there. No one speaks. I glance at the dance floor and see Sara and Kayla.

I pull out Madison's chair and she lowers gracefully to sit. Leaning down, I say in her ear, "I'll get us drinks. Don't leave the table without someone."

She touches my cheek and smiles softly. "Thank you."

My heart thumps hard in my chest. Fuck.

When Noah's gaze meets mine, he gives me a small nod to let me know he'll watch out for her. I need some distance. A chance to shore up my walls again.

The bar is on the other side of the dance floor. As I move through the crowds, some people lift a hand to get my attention and call me over, but I just wave and continue on my mission. No one else is at the bar when I arrive.

"Scotch neat and a white wine, please."

The bartender nods, and I turn to look over the room. What if someone saw me and Madison? What difference would it make?

"Cooper?" The familiar voice crawls up my spine as I turn.

"Leighton." My tone is flat. I should have known she'd be here. We've run into each other throughout the years since our breakup because of our social circles.

She smiles as she approaches me. Her brown hair is cut in a chin-length bob. As she closes the distance, her blue eyes assess me. Her black gown clings to her curves. Once upon a time, I thought I'd marry this woman.

"Coop, it's been too long." Leighton comes in and kisses both my cheeks. Her thumb comes up to rub her lipstick away.

Not long enough. I step away from her and her hand drops. "How are you this evening?"

At the other end of the bar, a woman distracts the bartender from finishing my drinks.

"I've been well." She's perfectly poised and doesn't fiddle with her necklace like Madison does. The table is far enough away that hopefully she can't see me talking to Leighton. The women the others brought have already caused Madison enough pain for the evening.

Leighton steps closer than would normally be appropriate and reaches out to pluck some imaginary lint from my tux jacket. Her cloying perfume wafts over me. In college, I loved the smell. Now it's a toxic scent I don't want near me.

"Elizabeth Hartfield is here with Seth," I break the news to her.

She flinches at the name.

"Would you like to come talk with her?" I smile like I think they're best friends who need to catch up. "She's apparently on an apology tour, so if you'd like to get yours—"

"I wish I could, but my date is waiting for me." She looks over her shoulder and a few feet away, a man stands next to the wall watching us. He doesn't appear bothered by her closeness to me.

"That's too bad."

The bartender sets my drinks beside me. I give him a smile as I pick them up. "It was something bumping into you."

Leighton steps closer and my patience runs thin.

"She's not the only one who needs to apologize." She looks up at me through her lashes as her fingers run over my lapel. "We could still be good together, Cooper. We make sense. Your family approves of me."

I step back. "I'm seeing someone. And the only family that matters to me are Seth, Blake, and Noah. You know, the clingers, as you called them."

Her cheeks flush pink, and she has the decency to look slightly chastised. She wanted to take me away from them. From the only people who cared more about me than what I could do for them. Fuck her.

"If you'll excuse me, I need to get back to my fiancée." I don't know what came over me or why I used that word.

But seeing Leighton's eyes flash with envy and jealousy makes whatever fallout worth it. I give her a slight nod before turning and walking back toward the table.

That's going to piss off a lot of people.

Madison

My fingers smooth over the diamond necklace as I wait for Coop. I can't exactly talk freely to the guys with Elizabeth sitting at the table. Noah moves to Sara's chair.

"Are you enjoying your evening?" He leans in to be heard over the music.

I want to turn and capture his lips. To find out if he's still mine, but I keep my face forward. "It's been good so far."

Tonight, I belong to only Coop and Noah belongs to his date.

His fingers touch my knee and I jerk to face him. No one should be able to see his hand under the table, but it's still possible. His dark eyes meet mine, and for a second, I'm lost. I want to lean in and kiss him, blow our world up and watch it burn, if only for a taste.

He leans in so our cheeks brush lightly before his mouth is beside my ear. "You look stunning tonight. I can't wait to get you home."

My breath catches, and I glance over at Seth and Elizabeth. Elizabeth's eyes are shrewd as she watches me and Noah. I don't know what type of reach she has, but I know she wants Seth back.

I laugh like Noah just told me a joke and move back away from the temptation of his warmth. "That's so funny."

I press on his shoulder like I'm just touching him in passing but push him back a little to remind him we're not alone.

Noah swallows but smiles at me like we're just coworkers. His fingers make small circles on my knee. "Are you going to dance tonight?"

My cheeks flush as I remember dancing with Coop in the empty room. "I hope so."

"You'll have to save one for me."

Fuck, it's hard to resist being close to Noah. I want him to hold me in his arms while we sway to the music. But I also know how I feel will be all over my face, and that's not a good thing.

"You should dance with your date." I force a smile to my lips.

He leans in, but I hold him back. He's my weakness. "She's—"

"Your date, so you should dance with her. I'm sure Coop will keep me occupied."

A flare of heat flashes in his eyes. His lips curve into a smile, but it doesn't reach his eyes. "I'm sure he will."

Coop chuckles behind me as he hands me my wineglass with a wink. "I've occupied her twice tonight."

My cheeks burn. He didn't exactly say that quietly. Elizabeth cocks her eyebrow at me like I'm beneath her. Coop sits beside me and draws my chair closer to him. The music shifts to a slow song. Kayla and Sara make their way back to the table.

Seth clears his throat. Elizabeth turns hopeful eyes on him with a smile, but he isn't looking at her. His watchful gaze is on Coop. "Maybe you should ask Madison to dance."

My gaze meets Seth's. He gives me a nearly imperceptible nod to just go along with it. Coop tosses back his scotch and stands again with his hand down to me.

"We need to discuss something, and I promised you a dance."

I drink some of my wine before taking his hand. Noah clutches my thigh for a second before his hand slips away. He turns as Sara approaches the table.

Suddenly, I can't wait to be gone. I don't need to hear Noah asking her to dance. I'm sure Sara is a wonderful woman. Maybe she might even be perfect for Noah. But that doesn't mean he's not mine.

Coop leads me to the dance floor and takes me into his arms. My insides buzz with warmth at his closeness. I'm sure Coop would be the last one to formally claim a woman like he's doing with me. But he actually seems to be enjoying himself.

And I enjoy his attention.

"Keep looking at me like that, sweetheart, and we'll be finding another dark corner." He smirks.

I shake my head. "I think people will get suspicious if we keep disappearing."

Coop lowers his head like he's going to say something when a large man bumps into his back. His brow furrows as he turns us to see who ran into him.

"Pardon me." Heath Duncan gives us both a huge grin as he moves his partner into step beside us. She's barely half his size with a curvy body, blond hair, and brown eyes. Her sparkly blue dress has a slit up the side. "You remember Becca, right?"

My eyes widen, recalling the phone call. Coop fucked me during that phone call, and when he mentioned he was seeing someone, Heath asked if it was Becca.

Coop laughs. "Always a pleasure."

Becca grins at Coop like he's her date and not Heath.

"I figured you were done with her since you said you had a date." Heath's blue eyes rake over my body, like he's imagining me naked.

I close the distance between Coop and me.

"You remember our new assistant, Madison?"

"Of course. She's a hard one to forget." Heath winks at me.

The guys continued to speak while Becca gives me a once-over before dismissing me and giving Coop a seductive smile. Who was this woman to him? I forgot to ask him after the phone call. She definitely wants to be on Coop's arm tonight. Or at least in his bed.

Not that I blame her. The things he can do to me always make me come back for more. So while I don't blame her, he's not hers to want.

This man is mine, so I arch my eyebrow at her to back off my man. She raises her eyebrows at my look. I'm sure many have tried to claim Coop before, but this time he's mine and I won't share him.

"It's not official yet," Coop's voice registers.

"Well, congratulations are in order." Heath's words are loud and boisterous. Heads turn on the dance floor. I catch sight of Noah and Sara dancing. It's dancing, so they have to stand that close together. There's no other reason.

My chest aches, and I lean into Coop, letting his solid frame hold me.

"When you know, you know." Coop rubs his hand down my back, bringing me back to the strange conversation.

Becca outright glares at me now. What's up her butt?

Ew, I remembered them commenting about her butt on the phone and really don't want to think about that now.

"I can't wait to console the weeping beauties at your wedding." Heath slaps Coop on the shoulder. "We're doing lunch this week, so you can tell me about your whirlwind affair. Maybe you should bring your little lady with you."

Heath winks at me.

Wedding? What the hell is he talking about?

Chapter 89

Train Wreck

Madison

Coop maneuvers us away from Heath, but that brings us closer to Noah and Sara. I refuse to look at them dancing. My stomach lurches at the sound of Sara's laugh. Coop leans in close to my ear.

"Just go with it. We'll discuss it more at home." Coop lifts his head and gazes down into my eyes. For a second, I get a little lost in his smiling eyes. That feeling of being connected with Coop surges inside me.

"I'm not sure what's going on," I admit.

When the song finishes, Coop takes my hand and places it in the crook of his elbow. Before we take a step, a gorgeous woman in black and a man stop in front of us.

"Is this your fiancée, Cooper?" The woman's words carry in the silence before the next song can start. She gives me a look like I'm beneath her.

My heart stalls on the word *fiancée*. What the hell is happening? Some of the conversation with Heath makes sense now. Mostly.

"Leighton Porter, this is Madison Harris, my fiancée."

I keep the smile glued to my face. Even though I'm shocked as hell to be called his fiancée. I want to give him a *what the fuck* look, but I can't take my eyes off the woman in front of me.

This is Leighton. The woman Coop once loved. The woman who tried to break apart the guys. She's taller than me, with sleek brown hair and startling blue eyes. She holds herself like royalty and looks down her nose at me like I'm a commoner.

"This is Drew Young, my date for the evening. Drew, Cooper Graham." Leighton smiles at Coop like she's caught him. Her gaze goes to my left hand on his elbow. "When you told me about your engagement, I couldn't resist finding the lucky girl. I was hoping to see what diamond your fiancée chose from your family's collection. I always loved the yellow diamond we talked about."

"We haven't had a chance to look over the collection yet." Coop reaches out and touches my earrings. Our eyes meet briefly, and he gives me a little encouraging smile. "I think the one that matches this set will be perfect for her, but I wanted to let her choose."

Leighton's gaze roams over the jewels draped around my neck and dangling from my ears. I take in a shaky breath. She's almost as terrifying as Elizabeth. Right now, my best bet is to remain quiet and let Coop weave whatever lies he needs to. I can't imagine why I got an upgrade from girlfriend to fiancée though.

Noah and Sara stop beside us. I can't meet Noah's eyes. He wanted to be my date for tonight. He wanted to claim me until circumstance dictated Coop be the one to claim me. So I keep my smile on.

"I'm sure that will be lovely. Where is your family from?" Leighton's blue eyes pin me in place. Her smile doesn't reach her eyes. Whatever I say, she'll pick apart just like she hopes to do to me.

"She doesn't have to answer your questions, Leighton." Coop draws me tighter against his side. His warmth helps with the coldness. "This isn't an interview."

"So mysterious, Coop." Leighton snuggles into her date's side. He hasn't spoken the whole time. Maybe he's just arm candy. "I can't wait for the engagement party."

Can we have an engagement party if he hasn't proposed to me? Dating Coop is already a stretch with what everyone, even Coop, said about his past. A thought pops into my head, right before Leighton speaks it into existence.

"I assume the tight timeline is because of special . . . circumstances?" Leighton's gaze drops to my flat abdomen with an almost evil smile. If I was pregnant, I'd cover my stomach from whatever evil this woman cast on it.

"No other reason besides Madison being the love of my life."

My eyes widen at the bold statement but I keep my smile soft. My heart trips over itself a little. Coop's just playing a part. He doesn't really love me. This arrangement isn't about love. I have to remind myself of that until it's lodged in my brain.

Leighton flinches slightly at that. Did she love Coop too? I've never learned the complete story besides her wanting Coop not to hang out with the others. I almost feel sorry for her for losing him.

Coop nods his head to Leighton and Drew. "If you'll excuse us, we need to return to our party."

As we walk away, Noah and Sara follow us.

"I didn't know you two were engaged," Sara exclaims as we reach the table. "Congratulations."

I lift my eyes to the others. Blake looks like he wants to break something, and that something might be Coop's face. Seth is quiet and still, but his eye twitches a little. Elizabeth seems taken aback.

"Kayla, why don't you and the other women go dance?" Blake stands. A fast song plays on the speakers.

"You two will make the most exquisite children." Kayla grabs my hand and tugs me away from Coop as the guys converge on him. I should go with the guys. This is about me.

Sara releases Noah, and that's when I meet Noah's eyes. For a second, we connect and nothing around us matters. I'm his and he's mine. My heart settles with that knowledge. Even if everything else is crazy around us, we still have each other.

He nods as Kayla pulls me away. I'll be in the loop later. For now, I guess I'll dance.

Seth

"Elizabeth, if you'll excuse us." I don't wait to hear what she has to say. I'm ready to be away from her. She keeps touching me, trying to build a new relationship on the toxic dust of the one we had in college.

It won't happen. Not now. Not ever.

It wouldn't matter if Madison didn't exist. I could never trust Elizabeth. Her mother's machinations will always rule her.

We move to the access door Coop took Madison out earlier. Blake leads the way to the Graham Wing and we fall in step. No one talks yet, but we need to know what the fuck Coop's done.

Engaged? This is a fucking train wreck.

When we move into the room, Noah and I settle on the low leather benches for visitors to sit and admire the paintings and furnishings. Blake paces like a caged tiger.

"Explain," I bite out.

Coop straightens, walks to one of the marble columns, and places his hand on it. "Leighton—"

"Of course this is because of that bitch." Blake leans against the wall opposite Coop, crossing his arms over his chest, which always makes him seem larger than life. "She always fucks with your brain. You let her dig her way inside every fucking time."

"What happened?" Noah seems like the least unsettled by this development. My mind spins around why. He wanted to claim Madison as his own. Now Coop has upped the stakes, claiming he and Madison are engaged.

"I told Leighton Madison is my fiancée." Coop turns, puts his hands in his pockets, and leans his shoulder against the column like he doesn't have a care in the world. "And then I told Heath."

"What the fuck, Coop?" The words pop out of my mouth before I can stop them. Noah and Blake both raise an eyebrow at my tone. I can't seem to stop myself though. "What the hell were you thinking?"

"That Leighton wants me back as much as Elizabeth wants you back." Coop shrugs. "So instead of asking the bitch out, I put her in her place."

The dig lodges in my stomach.

"Are you fucking kidding me right now?" I stand. My hands clench at my sides as I hold back from wrapping them around his neck. "You dating Madison was fucking damage control. Us bringing dates was damage control. This is just petty bullshit."

"Right, because if you could've rubbed Madison in Elizabeth's face, you wouldn't have taken the opportunity." Coop scoffs. "It's not like I ran off and married Madison. It's just a fancy girlfriend title."

"It also keeps her locked in a relationship with you." Noah leans back on his hands as he shakes his head at Coop. "It would be one thing if you 'dated' Madison for a while and then dropped her. One of us could have easily 'comforted' her and dated after a respectable amount of time."

Coop crosses his arms over his chest as he watches Noah.

"Your ex-girlfriend might have been testing the bro code, but for any of us to make a move on your ex-fiancée would make us a huge asshole." Noah laughs bitterly. "But tell us how this will work in our favor."

Looking down, Coop sighs. "Fuck."

I glance around the empty hall. This isn't the best place to have a conversation. "We may need to talk about this at home. This isn't a secure location."

Coop rubs the back of his neck. "Madison and I fucked in here earlier. We heard a door close when we finished. But we didn't see anyone."

"Because you were too busy fucking?" Blake steps forward. His fists are clenched, and he looks like he's on the verge of losing control. "Too busy getting off to make sure she's protected?"

Noah steps in front of Blake. "We can review the security feed."

"Not possible." Coop pushes off the column and points to the camera. "My buddy shut them off for me so I wouldn't have to have security erase them later."

Both Noah and Blake erupt at that. I don't pay attention to their words because I'm thinking the same damned thing. He brought Madison to an unsecured area of the event where anything could have happened to either of them.

Fuck. This is a mess.

"Are you saying she's not safe with me?" Coop's voice is louder than usual. I focus on him. Gone is the smooth-talking playboy. "Fuck you both. I can protect her. I can take care of her without your fucking help. She's as much mine as she is yours."

And that's the rub. We're all falling for her. We all want to protect her. Claim her.

"Enough." I hold up my hand. "All of us are worried about her and what might happen. We're doing everything we can."

"We need to do what's right for Madison. Not just what's good for our own petty revenge." Noah shakes his head as he and Blake step away from Coop.

"This engagement might make the stalker escalate. Did you even consider that?" Blake's mouth is a firm line. His words are clipped. "That news is going to spread like wildfire, most likely because of Leighton. She'll want to prove you're lying about the engagement."

"Fuck." Coop smacks his hand against the column. His eyes narrow on me. "I fucked up. But you brought that snake back into our group. Elizabeth shouldn't even be at our table. I don't give a fuck how much money her family's company could bring in."

"For one night." I sit. Elizabeth was a misstep, but not as big as Coop made. "You couldn't get over yourself for one night."

Coop takes a step toward me. "She came to my bedroom from yours, Seth. She wanted to see if I was as good as Leighton claimed. Elizabeth used you, my brother, to get to me. And you want to reward that bitch by parading her around the benefit."

"It's business."

"No, it fucking isn't." Coop steps closer. "She wants back in. You're wealthy and powerful now. She wants a taste. She doesn't care how she gets it. You can't be that fucking blind."

I shake my head. "This isn't about Elizabeth."

"Of course it is." Coop runs a hand through his hair. "These greedy bitches just want to use us for our money, our power, our status. And you let her. Fuck, you didn't see Madison's face when you walked in with Elizabeth. You crushed her."

My chest aches as fire engulfs my lungs. The pain on Madison's face every time she looks at Elizabeth is like a dagger deep in my gut. Madison won't even look at me.

"This whole evening was supposed to solve a problem that keeps creeping up, but maybe we shouldn't worry so fucking much about that problem." Coop straightens. "Who cares who we fuck and how? Seriously, fuck them."

Chapter 90

Hostile Takeover

Madison

"I love this song!" Sara yells to be heard over the music. We're on the dance floor in a small circle while Elizabeth sits at the table looking like she's eating something sour.

Trying to be nice, I smile at her, but my gaze goes to the door the guys disappeared behind. What are they talking about? This engagement between Coop and me? Because that's ridiculous. The whole concept is ridiculous. We've known each other a few weeks.

Even Leighton thought I might be pregnant and that's the only way someone like Coop would marry someone like me. Of course, that would be the only reason that made sense. Not that I'm the love of his life like he claimed. My heart skips a beat.

This is such a mess.

"If you want to go to them, I can walk you." Kayla leans in close to my ear.

"No, it's okay." I give her a smile that I'm sure looks fake, but it's enough for Kayla to back off.

This whole night is a mess. The guys and their dates. Me and

Coop. I just want to go home, crawl into bed, and wait until it's tomorrow.

"What the fuck are you doing here?" A gorgeous man cuts across the dance floor. He looks like a Viking in a tuxedo. Huge, with a wide chest and narrow waist. A tip of black ink on his neck peeks out over his collar. His long, wavy blond hair falls around his shoulders. His icy blue eyes hold me frozen in place as he comes toward me. My breath catches.

Fuck, I don't know this guy, and trust me, he's someone I wouldn't forget, but his focus is beyond me.

Sara backs up as the guy approaches. Her eyes dart to the sides like she's searching for an escape. Her mouth moves as she whispers, "Fuck."

"Oh, no you don't." He reaches out and grabs her arm, drawing her to him. What the hell is happening?

"Hey." Kayla steps between them, while all I can do is gawk. "Let her go."

"Let me go, Dante. You don't have the right to do this." Sara tugs on her arm. But Dante is stronger and reels her into his side. The crowd around us parts as he makes his way off the dance floor, dragging Sara with him. Kayla and I follow as Sara keeps glancing back at us.

"What's going on? Where are you taking her?" Kayla tries to step in his way again. The guy towers over all of us. Fuck, he might be taller than my guys.

Dante stops and glares down at Kayla, who straightens and glares right back at him. "This isn't any of your business."

"These are my friends." Sara tugs at her arm again now that he's stopped. "Release me."

His cold eyes scan both of us before he scoffs. "Sara and I have some unfinished business."

Her eyes widen as he drags her down an empty hallway. Kayla glances at me before she follows. I turn to look for the guys. Blake could stop this monster of a man, but they still aren't anywhere in sight. Maybe I should go back to the table. When I turn to follow Dante and Sara, I see Kayla slipping around a corner.

Shit.

Lifting my skirt, I hurry to catch up, not wanting to lose them. As I rush by a hallway, someone hooks my arm and drags me the other way.

"Hey," I call out.

As I turn to face whoever grabbed me, I'm pushed up against a wall. My breath escapes my lungs from the impact. I force myself to focus on the man detaining me.

My professor, Jimi Alan, holds my shoulders as he leans in, way too close. His dark eyes search mine as a grin forms. He's maybe ten years older than me.

"Madison Harris. I thought I'd never see you again." His breath smells like one-hundred-proof liquor. My heart thrashes, making my chest ache. I can't move.

This isn't good. Shoving my panic to the background, I push against his chest, and he stumbles back. For a moment, I'm free. I need to get away. We're the only ones in the hallway. Fuck, I need to get back to the benefit and people.

I rush toward the hallway I just came from. My heels slip on the marble floor, slowing me down.

"Nah." Jimi grabs my shoulder and shoves me against the wall again. This time his whole body presses against me, trapping my hands between us. I can't push him away without leverage.

"Get off me." Realizing I can still speak, I open my mouth to yell for help. He covers it with his hand. I still yell but it's muffled. His hand is damp over my mouth, and I resist the urge to gag at the salty taste of his skin. My legs shake as I try desperately to think of another way out.

"Shh. Come on, little girl." Jimi's brown eyes skim down to the diamond necklace before dropping to my cleavage. He licks his lips. "We both know you liked to taunt me with those sweet sundresses you wore to class. Such a fucking tease."

My blood runs cold. The dress. The pictures. The taunts.

His smile is evil as his eyes meet mine. "I saw you flirt with those guys. Right in front of me, testing me. You'd give it up to just about any guy, but not me. Not your professor. You were too good for me."

I lift my knee, but he angles his hips away so I miss his junk.

He grabs my neck with his other hand and adds just a little pressure. Enough to make me still. Not again. My heart races, and I look around to see if I can find anyone else, but just like in the apartment, I'm alone and helpless.

"I figured you were a slut, but it wasn't until I saw you sucking that guy's cock that I realized how much you want it." His fingers soften on my neck. "So eager for his cock and fucking yourself too. I nearly came in my pants, but don't worry, I saved it for you."

Icy, cold dread pours through me. The door. He'd seen Coop and me. He watched that private moment. Jimi drags his hand down toward my breast.

"Don't touch me," I protest against his hand, but it comes out muffled. Pushing with all my might to get him off me, I move off the wall a little, even with his hand pressing against my mouth. As I begin to twist, he slams my head back.

The blow to my head stuns me as bursts of light sparkle through my vision. My head aches, and he uses my distraction to slip his hand under my dress to cup my breast. I don't want to be a victim again. I lift my knee but he's ready for that.

At the same time, I try to bite his hand.

His chuckle is dark as he pinches my nipple painfully hard. "Fuck, I hoped you'd struggle. Little girls like you need someone to teach them exactly how to take a cock."

"What the fuck do you think you're doing?" A male voice rings out in the hallway.

Jimi turns. "Fuck off."

I struggle more and yell "Help" into Jimi's hand.

"Let the woman go." His voice is commanding and familiar, but right now, I'm just grateful someone has rescued me.

Please don't leave. Please help me.

"Why don't you mind your own—" A fist connects with Jimi's face, and he stumbles away from me.

I inhale fresh air and fix my dress while backing away from Jimi. I can't take my eyes off him. Not for a moment. I don't trust I'm safe yet.

My savior moves around me and grabs Jimi's neck. When he straightens, I recognize Patrick Beck. He holds Jimi by his neck against the wall and glances at me.

"Are you okay?"

I blink at him. I'm still stuck against that wall. Fingers tightening around my neck. I can't breathe. Hands touching me. My face is wet. My vision swims.

"Fuck." He decks Jimi who crumples to the ground. "Stay down."

Patrick moves slowly toward me with his hands outstretched like he's trying to calm a wild animal. "Madison, you remember me, right? I'm not going to hurt you."

My hands shake, and I can't seem to get any air into my lungs. I reach up to pry the hands away from my neck, but my fingers only find my own skin.

"Shit." Hands grab my shoulders. "Breathe. You need to breathe or you're going to pass out."

Kayla

"Seriously stop. You can't just take her. She's here with someone." I follow Sara and Dante doggedly. Honestly, it's not a hardship. No offense to Coop and Madison, but holy heck what a sandwich Sara and Dante would be.

"Sara, control your friend." Dante doesn't slow down but keeps dragging her down another hallway until we're a distance away from the party.

When I look back, Madison isn't behind me. She must have gone back to the table. A pang goes through me. I promised Blake I'd watch over her, but she's safe as long as she's with everyone. No one's made a move toward her all night.

"Let me go, Dante." Sara pulls free and stops.

He rounds on her. And woof, there he is. Tall, wavy blond hair falling to his shoulders, icy blue eyes. The tux had to be custom made for him because it clings to him the way I want to.

"And what, Sara? Let you go so you can try to rile him up?" Even his voice makes me want to follow him, but he's also pissing me off because this is my new friend.

"Rile who up?" I take Sara's arm and step a little in front of her, putting myself between them.

Sara's cheeks are bright red, and Dante's perfect lips are pressed into a thin line. Apparently neither of them is going to tell me anything.

"It's better if you leave now. Your brother hasn't seen you yet." Dante holds his hand out to Sara.

She looks at it for a moment as if weighing her options. "You know what, no. I'm here with a date. My mom set me up with Noah and I'm not leaving him because you're afraid of what? That Tom will see me here?"

Sara puts her hands on her hips and stands in front of me. I'm a little more in love with my new friend. She's standing up to all this hotness.

"You guys don't get to decide where I can and can't go. I'm a fucking grown-up."

I want to say *yeah* and back her up, but Dante steps forward, and when he looks down at Sara, even I get shivers. That's not a normal *I'm just getting you out of the way* look. His eyes are burning with heat and I'm feeling the secondary burns.

"Pipsqueak, you shouldn't be here."

"I have every right."

"You do." He puts his hand on her shoulder and she trembles

beneath his touch. "Let me take you home. I'm sure your friend will tell your date where you went. Come with me."

He slides his hand down to take hers. Chills. Fucking chills.

Ummm, I'm not even here to either of them right now, but I fucking volunteer as tribute. Yes, please. I don't know what he intends to do to her, but it's gotta be better than whatever is happening at this dance.

"You should go," I whisper and give her a little push toward the hot Viking. She could climb him like a tree.

Sara glances back over her shoulder at where the benefit is still going on and then returns her gaze to Dante's. Resignation swims in her eyes. "Fine."

He nods and waits for her as she turns to me. I thought tonight was going to be boring. Fuck, I've never been more happy to be wrong.

She swallows and meets my eyes. "Can you tell Noah I'll text him? And tell Madison I really enjoyed meeting her and everyone else."

"You text me." I glance up at the Viking and give him a smile. "If you find yourself needing a plus one or two, let me know."

He arches an eyebrow like he doesn't know. But he does. I give him a wink.

She chuckles and hugs me. "I really enjoyed meeting you. I'll text you later."

I hug her back. Tonight was a good night. Good drama and new friends. But that's definitely enough drama for the night.

She takes Dante's hand and they disappear down the hallway. I need to get back. I turn to find my way back to the party, except I really didn't pay attention to how we got here. Well, fuck.

Noah

Nothing got decided, but we head back into the benefit. Until we get back to the apartment and can include Madison in the discussion, Coop and Madison are currently engaged. Fuck.

I don't think Coop was truly thinking when he threw that out there. But it fucks everything up. Because Coop's not marrying anyone, especially when his mother hears about it. Victoria Graham is a storm to be reckoned with. Not even Coop has much luck against her.

But Coop has a point. Why do we have to hide our relationship? So what if a few customers leave? Why can't we live our lives the way we want to? Date who we want to and not have to put on a dog and pony show to protect the one we love?

When we reach the table, the only person there is Elizabeth. Her expectations for this evening clearly haven't been met. She has a fresh glass of wine in her hand. Her eyes are a little glassy as she glances over all of us before her calculating gaze settles on Seth.

Seth nods to her but looks out at the crowded dance floor. It's hard to see in the dim light.

Elizabeth sighs and lifts her wineglass. "If you're looking for your other dates, they disappeared down that hallway with a very determined man."

"What?" Blake's eyes widen, and he's already headed that direction with Coop on his heels.

The stalker? My chest tightens.

Seth and I exchange looks before taking off after them. The hallway continues on in multiple directions. The women could be anywhere.

Kayla rounds a corner, breathless. "Have you seen Madison? She was just behind me."

My heart clenches as I shove past the guys. "Where's Madison? Where's Sara?"

"Oh." Kayla blushes and looks down before a small smile plays on her lips. "Well, there's this guy. His name's Dante and he dragged Sara off that way. Madison and I tried to help her."

"Where's Madison?" Blake growls.

"I don't know. I'm sorry, Blake." Kayla glances around. Her eyes tear up. "She was right behind me, and then I turned around and she was gone."

"We need to split up." Seth nods to all of us. "She can't have gone far."

"She wouldn't have wandered off on her own." Coop's fists are tight against his sides.

"Someone would have stopped anyone from dragging her out of the museum." I try to remain rational. I try to keep my cool, but this is Madison. My heart is racing and my blood thunders in my ears.

"I'll check with security." Blake heads off the way we came.

"She was right behind me," Kayla murmurs to Coop. Tears roll down her cheeks. "This guy took Sara from the dance floor, and we were both following to help her. I didn't mean to go too fast. I thought Madison was right there."

Coop pats her on the back. "We just need to find Madison. Now."

Coop's eyes meet mine. We're on the same page. This is our girl.

"Show us where you last saw her." Seth takes Kayla's arm. She leads us to where she lost sight of her.

"Kayla, check the ladies' rooms, just in case." Seth sighs and runs a hand over his hair.

I'm sure we all have the same bad feeling coursing through us.

Seth directs each of us to branch out. I barely keep myself from yelling her name as I hurry down the darkened hallways. As I turn a corner, someone stumbles into me, almost knocking me down.

"Watch it." The guy staggers to the side and keeps going.

A faint moan comes from around the corner. Fuck. My heart feels like it's going to burst out of my chest as I rush forward.

"It's okay," a voice says.

A guy hovers over Madison on the ground. I don't think. My blood boils. My vision turns red around the edges. I lurch forward and shove the guy away from her.

"Whoa." The guy lands on his ass with his hands up to protect himself.

I kneel next to Madison and check her over, afraid to touch her for a second. Her face is pale, but as I watch, her chest rises and falls. Relief pours through me. I cup her cheek. "Madison?"

"Noah," the guy says. I finally look at him and see it's our attorney. Patrick.

Glaring, I lift Madison onto my lap and into my arms, needing her close. "What were you doing?"

"Punching the guy who was assaulting your assistant." He glances to a wall and sighs. "Who must have escaped when she fainted."

"What were you doing here?" This is an odd place to just walk by. I didn't miss the fact that the asshole who ran into me just then was probably the one who assaulted Madison. The urge to tear through the benefit to find him races through me. But she's in my arms and safe for the moment.

I still don't know how Patrick "stumbled" upon them. I'm a mixed bag of feelings right now. Worry, relief. Suspicion, gratitude.

"I was meeting someone." Patrick looks embarrassed, rubbing the back of his neck. "She was supposed to meet me in the medieval wing."

Madison sighs and turns into me. Fuck it. The guy was heading off to cheat on his wife but stopped my girl from being assaulted. Gratitude wins.

I glance at Madison and run my finger down the side of her face. "Hey, kitten."

She breathes out and smiles with her eyes still shut. "Noah."

"Yeah, love. You need to open your eyes."

Patrick stands and fixes his tuxedo. "The guy was a little shorter than me. Brown hair. Brown eyes. Smelled like a bar."

"He ran into me on the way here." I nod at him but focus on Madison.

Her eyes finally open, and she blinks at me for a second before she focuses.

"You okay, kitten?"

"You're here?" She seems confused.

"Did she hit her head?" My fingers run over her scalp, but I don't feel any swelling.

"I caught her before she hit the floor and just lowered her down." Patrick glances over his shoulder. "We should contact the police."

"Would you mind texting the others?" I don't take my eyes off Madison's as I ask Patrick that. He knows everything about us. He's the one who drew up our contracts for Madison.

"Noah!" Suddenly, Madison grabs my hand. Her eyes are wide and scared. "My professor."

"Your professor?" Shit, maybe she hit her head before she fainted. "You need to rest. Do you know who assaulted you?"

This time rings in my head. The overwhelming urge to wrap her in bubble wrap and keep her in the apartment isn't rational, but I can't stand the thought of her being hurt again. I should have been here. I should have been the one to punch the guy hurting her.

"My stalker," she says. "Jimi Alan. He mentioned my sundress." She grabs my hand and squeezes it.

I glance over at Patrick.

He nods. "I'll call the police."

Chapter 91

Synergy

Madison

Noah never released me. Not when the others came. Not when the police came. Not when the paramedics came. He touched me or held me the entire time.

Jimi left the benefit. But the police took my statement, and Patrick told them we'd come down to the station to answer questions tomorrow afternoon. Thankfully, the paramedics determined I didn't need to go to the hospital.

My panic attack caused the fainting. I just stopped breathing.

They kept the whole thing away from the benefit. Blake had security let them in through a back door. I'm sure the dancing and laughter continue down the hallway like none of this happened.

"I'm so sorry." Kayla grabs my hand and squeezes it for the twentieth time.

Noah holds my other hand and sits close to me on the bench. Coop paces back and forth in front of us, his brow furrowed. Seth and Blake lean against the wall, silently taking in everything.

The police just left, and Patrick assured us he would come with us to the station tomorrow before he headed out. I can't help but feel grateful to him. He stopped Jimi from doing anything more.

"He would have found me alone at some point. I just hesitated too long." I give Kayla a smile to let her know I don't blame her. We were trying to help Sara. Speaking of. "Where's Sara?"

"That guy Dante, she left with him. She told me it was okay." Kayla glances nervously at Noah. Probably worried about his feelings for Sara.

"She told me there was a guy she was trying to make jealous." Noah's brown eyes meet mine. "She and I both went on this date for appearances only."

I take a deep breath in as a pressure releases from my chest. I like Sara, but she and Noah were getting along so well. He squeezes my hand like he knows my thoughts. I want to rest my head on his shoulder, but I don't.

As much as I want to bask in his warmth, I have to stay aware of appearances. It's okay for my friend Noah to comfort me, but he can't look like my lover Noah.

Besides, I seriously need a shower after being groped by my professor. Unlike Jeff, he didn't leave any visible marks on me. The paramedic passed me a card for trauma counseling, which is tucked in Noah's jacket pocket. The jacket I'm wearing. Being wrapped in his outdoor scent and warmth comforts me almost as much as his hand in mine.

"We should head home." Seth pushes off the wall.

We all rise, preparing to leave. Noah doesn't release my hand and Coop takes my other one. I'm too exhausted to think or care about how it will look.

"We'll drop Kayla on the way." Blake joins us and looks at Seth.

"I'll see Elizabeth home and then meet you all at the apartment." Seth's blue eyes search mine. I want to fall into his arms and let him make me feel safe. Instead, I nod and lean my head against Noah's shoulder.

I don't want to be separated from any of them right now.

But it makes sense. I'm not up for dealing with Elizabeth or even acknowledging that I'm leaning on Noah and holding Coop's hand. She wouldn't understand, and the guys don't need to deal with all the consequences from this.

Kayla hasn't said much about Noah and me, but I can tell she feels bad for accidentally leaving me alone. I don't blame her for leaving me. Sara might have been in trouble.

Tim gives me a nod as he holds the limousine door open. After we all get in, Tim drives us to Kayla's hotel. As she gets up to leave, Kayla hugs me tight.

"Don't stay a stranger," she whispers in my ear. She pulls back and sighs. "Are you sure about dick? I mean, sure Coop is pretty. They all are. Not you, Blake. But I'm pretty too."

When she winks, a laugh bursts out of me and some of that tension inside me unwinds.

"Stop hitting on my woman, Kayla." Coop draws me into his side.

She laughs and turns to wink at him. "I wouldn't mind both of you."

"Come on." Blake holds his hand out to her. "I'll walk you in."

The door shuts, and it's just Coop, Noah, and me. Tim puts up the privacy screen, leaving us completely alone.

"Are you okay?" Coop's fingers brush my jaw.

I release a breath. As much as I'm hating those words, his heart is in the right place. "I'll feel better when the police have him in custody, but yes, I'm fine."

"Bath and bed?" Noah lifts my hand to his lips and presses a kiss to my knuckles.

"Definitely shower." A chill races over me, and Noah wraps me in his arms. I'm not sure how to say this. "I don't want this to affect us."

"You don't have to—" Noah starts, but I press my fingers against his lips.

"I want to fuck tonight. I need to feel you buried inside me, so deep, so thoroughly, that I can't imagine anyone but you there. All of you."

The door opens and Blake resumes his seat across from us. "Kayla is a wild card. I never know what I'm going to get with her. Are you okay, tiger?"

I swear I feel like screaming *I'm fine*. But I know they worry.

"I'd feel better with you between my legs." I raise my eyebrow at him in a challenge.

He smirks as he kneels between my legs and sweeps my dress up over my knees. "Like this, tiger?"

Noah and Coop take ahold of my legs next to them and hook them over their knees, spreading me open for Blake. Desire swells inside me as Blake's gaze devours my pussy like I know his mouth will.

"Yes, please," I whisper.

"We aim to please." Blake leans in and drags his tongue along my slit. A bolt of lust sweeps through me, and my skin tingles with the need to be touched. When his mouth closes over my clit and sucks, Coop tips my chin his way and claims my mouth.

A deep, thorough, toe-curling kiss. Coop takes everything I have to offer and captures all my gasps and moans from Blake's tongue driving me crazy.

Noah tentatively slips his fingers along the neckline of my dress. Maybe he's worried, after hearing me tell the police what happened, that I won't want him to touch me. Taking his hand, I slide it inside my dress over my breast. My insides clench. His touch is gentle and exploring and so different from the assault earlier.

Blake slides his finger inside me while he explores my pussy with his tongue and lips. Coop takes his time kissing me so thoroughly that I don't know if we'll ever come up for air. When cool air caresses my breast, I'm startled, until a second later Noah's mouth closes over my nipple. I moan into Coop's mouth as Noah's draw on my breast pulsates through me.

My fingers trail up Coop's and Noah's thighs to their hard cocks.

As I stroke them through their pants, heat engulfs me, taking me higher, knowing they're hard for me and only me. Blake's finger slides in and out of my pussy while he sucks on my clit, making the fire rage out of control.

Their mouths work together to bring me to the edge. My insides are an inferno. I don't hold back as my release rushes through me. My body arches into them, needing to feel all of them, knowing they won't let me down.

Blake straightens. The sound of his zipper fills the car. My pussy still throbs from my release as the head of his cock presses against my entrance.

"Do you want this, tiger?"

I pull my mouth from Coop's and meet Blake's darkened eyes. I can't think of anything else. "Yes, fuck me."

When he slides his cock deep inside me, we both groan at the feeling of being connected. Coop kisses down my neck before he sucks on it. His fingers brush aside the silk on my other breast and explore my tight nipple.

Noah doesn't release my other breast, suckling on it while I rub his cock over his pants. Both Coop and Noah brush my hands away. They lower their zippers. Noah lifts from my breast as Coop lowers to suck my nipple into his mouth.

I find their cocks with my hands and stroke them. Tipping my head his way, Noah takes my mouth. The fire burns hotter with every stroke of Noah's tongue against mine. Blake thrusts his cock deep inside me as the guys hold my legs open wide. When I arch into Blake, Coop tugs on my breast.

Desire, lust, and passion flood my body, and I shatter all around Blake and the others. Blake thrusts deep and fills me. His hands caress my thighs as we both come down.

"You're not done yet, sweetheart," Coop whispers against my ear.

Blake draws out of me. Noah lifts me to straddle his lap. Holding his cock, I lower onto it as we kiss. My hands go to his shoulders as I ride him. Coop's hand sweeps my hair to the side, and his lips find the nape of my neck as his front presses against my back.

His hands trail down my sides, setting off sparks in his wake. I love this. I gasp into Noah's mouth.

"You're divine, goddess," Coop whispers against my skin, sending shivers coursing through me. His hands wrap around my thighs as I rise and fall over Noah's cock. "I need some of your wetness. You're soaking for me, aren't you? Like a good little whore?"

His fingers press against my clit before sliding inside me with Noah's cock. I lift my mouth from Noah's, moaning at the stretch. My forehead rests against Noah's as I look down.

"That's it, goddess. Get my hand nice and wet and I'll fuck your ass while Noah fucks your pussy." As Coop's mouth torments my neck, I slide down on Noah's cock and Coop's fingers. "You want that, sweetheart. Both of us inside you, deep, filling you with our cum."

I want that and more.

"Coop." I whimper his name, not really knowing how to communicate anymore. All I can do is feel. Coop's thumb brushes my clit and I cry out as I come. Noah presses his forehead against mine as I convulse around him.

"You better hurry and do it, Coop. She's so fucking tight on me I won't last much longer." Noah presses his lips against mine as Coop's hand slips from inside me.

"I could probably join Noah in your cunt as wet as you are, goddess."

Coop's words make me moan as aftershocks rip through me. Noah grabs the back of my neck and kisses my mouth like he's never tasted anything better. Like we may never have a chance to kiss again.

Coop's hands are on my hips, pulling my ass cheeks apart. His fingers slide inside my ass for a second before he withdraws. Then the soft head of his cock presses against my asshole.

"Are you watching our girl, Blake?" Coop asks. "Do you see what she likes?"

"I know what she likes, you cocky bastard." Blake's words are breathy. "She likes it hard. She wants you to ride her ass like it's the last time you'll ever fuck."

"Fuck," I whisper into Noah's mouth.

"We know what you like, kitten." Noah's words work me up, and my pussy pulses in response. "You like us talking about fucking you, but you like it better when we just do it."

He punches up into me as Coop slams his cock into my ass. I cry out at the intrusion, and my muscles tighten around the cocks in my body. Fire bursts through my vision as I come. They both groan before they work their cocks in and out of me, riding the waves of my orgasm, keeping me under.

Their lips caress my neck. My eyes find Blake's. His bow tie is undone and the top buttons of his shirt are released. He lounges back against the seat as his fist works his cock. His hand pumps up and down in rhythm with Noah and Coop.

"You look exquisite when you're being fucked, tiger."

My release tears through me again. Biting down on my shoulders, Noah and Coop thrust deep, pushing me higher as their cocks pulse inside me, filling me with their cum. Their bodies smash me between them.

Blake's dark green eyes hold me as he strokes himself. "Do you want me to come, tiger?"

I shake my head. "I want it."

I want all of them, inside me. Coop thrusts his still-hard cock deep, and I groan at the ripple of aftershocks that work through me. His teeth graze my shoulder as he pulls out. Noah lifts his head and meets my eyes.

"We're good?" His dark eyes search mine.

Cupping his jaw, I nod and lower my mouth to his. "We're very good."

His mouth takes mine. Blake closes in behind me. Keeping me on his lap, Noah lifts me off his cock, holding my ass up, and Blake slides inside my pussy. I groan into Noah's mouth as Blake fucks me. The sounds of our bodies coming together fill the car.

Noah's hand slips between us and he rubs my clit. I cry out into his mouth as I come, drawing Blake into his release. He pulses deep inside me, filling me. My body is limp between them.

"Good girl," he whispers in my ear. He kisses the nape of my neck, making shivers course through me before he withdraws back to his seat.

Coop takes a wet towel to my pussy and ass before he helps me adjust my dress to cover me again. I curl into his side as the others fix their clothing. Drawing in a deep breath, I release it. This is what I need.

Noah snuggles into my other side. Their warmth fills me. Blake gives me a smirk from his seat as I yawn. All I need is Seth and everything will be just right.

My gut clenches, remembering the possessive hold Elizabeth kept on Seth all night. He's still mine, but I don't think that knot will release until he's back in my arms.

Chapter 92

The Viper In Waiting

Seth

The benefit is winding down as I walk back into the ballroom. Elizabeth sits with a glass of wine at the table. Earlier, I offered to have our driver take her home, but she insisted on waiting for me. This won't end well.

Coop's words replay in my head. Why are we hiding behind other people? So what if our relationship isn't conventional?

The real question is, could we really share a woman long-term? Why complicate everything and our business if this thing with Madison isn't going to last? Madison is great, but we didn't ask her to be our girlfriend. Well, not technically.

We asked her to fuck us because it's convenient. Is that a good way to start a relationship? Probably not. But it doesn't mean our feelings aren't involved at this point.

Elizabeth straightens as I approach.

"Are you ready to go?" I reach my hand down for hers.

She smiles and uses my hand to stand. She stumbles a little and falls against my chest.

"I'm so sorry." She smiles up at me. "I must have had too much to drink."

Her eyes spark with a hint of cunning. She's not *that* drunk. She'd never give up that much control. It's one of the reasons we didn't work well as a couple. She couldn't relinquish control to me.

Holding her shoulders, I help her straighten. It's time to make this clear. "I'm not into playing games, Elizabeth. This was a favor to your mother. Nothing more. I don't want you back in my life."

She purses her lips and narrows her eyes at me. "I don't know what you expect me to say to that. Obviously, I hoped to rekindle our romance. You seem lonely and worked to the bone, like me. You have so much on your plate with your assistant and the guys, I just thought you might like a distraction from the toils of your life. I know I could use a distraction."

"Not going to happen."

Aware we're still in public, I offer her my elbow and she puts her hand on my arm. As I'm leading her out, we get stopped by some clients and by some of her friends. It takes much longer to get to the car than I'd hoped.

Everything in me wants to get back to Madison and hold her in my arms. We could have lost her tonight. If Patrick hadn't stopped him, what fresh hell would Madison have gone through? How far can she bend before she breaks?

At least this guy, this Jimi Alan, can't go underground as easily as Val and her boyfriend did. He has a life and can't just disappear. Some pieces of this whole mess don't quite fit though. That's one piece. Why go after her in a public place when he's had her cornered and alone?

"Seth?" Elizabeth looks at me expectantly.

"Yes?" I gaze down at her, not really seeing her as my mind tries to piece together all that we know.

"The car is here." She sighs and her lips press into a flat line. "What's on your mind?"

I cock an eyebrow her way as I guide her down the steps.

"What?" she persists. "I'm a good sounding board. Even if you don't trust me, you obviously have something racing through your mind. You always figured things out best by talking to me. So talk to me."

I give her my hand to help lower her into the car before I go around to the other side to get in. As much as I don't want to talk to Elizabeth, my mind is spinning out.

"Fine." I close the door, and the driver heads to Elizabeth's place.

She crosses her legs and folds her hands on her lap as she turns to me.

"Our assistant has a stalker."

"You mean Coop's fiancée?"

"Yes." That burn in my chest goes out faster this time. "We think he revealed himself tonight, but something isn't adding up."

"Okay."

"It's someone she knew from school, which makes sense with the timeline. But something is bothering me."

"Maybe the fact that you want what you can't have." She arches her eyebrow. Her words are still a little slurred.

I press my lips together and wait. She's been chewing on something herself and it's time she let it out.

"You want that woman. I can tell. I think a blind person could probably tell." She chuckles. "You want what you can't have because she's Coop's. Don't think I didn't notice how tense you got when he announced their engagement. It's kind of funny if you think about it. I went after Coop while dating you, and now you want Coop's fiancée."

Leaning back in my seat, I watch her. This woman who at one point I thought I might love. She's just as cold today as she was back then. If not more so. She doesn't care that I want someone else. She just wants to use me any way she can get me.

"If you need someone to fuck, I haven't gotten any for a year and you were good at what you did." Drawing closer, she puts her hand on my thigh. "Of everything we did together, fucking was the only thing we could get right."

I pick up her hand from my thigh and put it back on her lap. "When are you going to get this through your head, Elizabeth?"

Her eyes widen.

"I don't want you. I don't want to fuck you. I don't want to see you. I don't want to use you. You fucked with Coop's and my lives without any consideration for what you were doing. The only reason you're here tonight is because I needed a date and your mother threw you at me. I figured why not, because it wouldn't matter. Because I don't want you."

She draws in a deep breath and turns her face to the window. Her features are flat.

"You hurt my relationship with my brothers back then, but you can't now. Tonight was a business transaction."

A sharp laugh comes from her as she turns back to glare at me. "You should know about business transactions. I tried to downplay the rumors, but then I saw you in action tonight."

My heart speeds up. The rumors. The whole purpose of bringing dates was to suppress them.

"Coop's not the only one fucking the charity case, is he?" Elizabeth spits it out harshly.

"You don't know what you're talking about," I say carefully.

"It's all anyone who's anyone talks about. The fucked-up little world of Morrigan Technology Group. That first assistant, Amber? No, Andrea, spread a rumor that you all wanted to fuck her. Most people didn't believe it, but I knew." Her eyes sparkle in the streetlights.

I sit back. Let her fucking talk. Who cares? It won't hurt us. We could spin it that she's a bitter ex.

"You guys were so close even back in college. And I know how you like to watch. Pretty sure Coop likes to be watched." She laughs bitterly. "I always wondered, if I'd just asked you, would you have wanted to watch me fuck Coop? Mother wanted me to get pregnant and blame it on him. She wanted his family's power merged with ours."

"This is all ancient history." It's over and done with.

"But is it?" She taps her fingernail against her lower lip. "Because it's weird how your assistant lives in the building. From what the rumors said, it's shared living space. Do you all fuck her together? Or do you just get off on watching?"

"You know nothing about me." I keep my face expressionless.

She's too close to the truth, but how much of that is the liquor talking? I'm sure she wouldn't be saying any of this to me if she were sober.

"Am I hitting a sore spot, Seth?" She fake pouts. "I played nice all night, but I should have been drawing blood. It's definitely more fun than pretending I want you back. You know that's Mother's idea, right?"

My lips tighten, and the car can't drop this bitch off fast enough.

"She even figured I could convince you to sleep with me." She lets out a sharp laugh. "That's how she ended up with me, after all. She didn't realize you're probably getting everything you need at home."

The car stops in front of her house.

"It's been enlightening as always," I say as the driver opens her door.

"It's been an awful evening." She slips out of the car and stumbles up the steps.

When the driver gets back in, I have him wait until she's in the house before we leave for home. After opening the door, she turns and watches me drive off.

I hate it when Coop is right.

The kitchen light is on when I walk into the apartment. I'm dead tired and I need a shower. Elizabeth's heavy perfume clings to me.

"Hey." Her voice is soft, and I almost didn't notice her sitting at the island. Madison.

"Where's everyone else?" I'm surprised the guys let her out of their sight. Noah kept her hand the entire time after the attack. It took me longer than I wanted to get here, but now with her before me, my chest loosens.

"Bed." Wearing a silky camisole and shorts pajama set, she stands and flicks off the light in the kitchen. The city lights pour in through the windows, casting us in shadows as she moves toward me. She takes my jacket out of my hands and folds it over her arm. "How was your night?"

We walk toward my room.

"Exhausting. Yours?" I open my door and she leans in the doorway.

"Confusing."

I gesture for her to come in. When she sits on the edge of my bed, I feel more settled and take off my cuff links. "How was it confusing?"

"Watching you guys with other women. It's not as easy as it sounds." She pulls her feet up on the bed and wraps her arms around her legs. I long to hold her, but I need to wash tonight off me first.

I strip off my shirt and pants and hang them on the chair. My undershirt, socks, and boxers go in the hamper. When I'm stripped bare, I hold out my hand for her.

She eyes it before slipping off the bed and taking it. Once we're in the bathroom, I turn on the shower. When I close in on her, she takes a deep breath. Her eyes devour me like she's starving.

I reach for her top and pull it off. "Did you enjoy the night before . . . ?"

"Before I was attacked?"

I drop to a knee before her and slide off her shorts. She's not wearing any panties. Unable to resist, I lean forward and press my lips against her stomach. She releases a breath as her fingers thread into my hair.

I lift my eyes to hers.

She cradles my jaw in her hand. "Before the incident was good. Sara and Kayla seem nice. But I didn't like seeing you with Elizabeth."

"Why?" I stand and take her hand, drawing her into the shower. When the warm water rains down on us and her soft skin brushes against mine, more tension unwinds from my gut. Fuck, it's good to be home.

She grabs my shower scrub and loads it with soap, her attention on her task. "You two fit."

Fuck that. "We don't."

She doesn't look up at me as she runs the soap over my body. Her touch makes me need to make sure she understands. Elizabeth doesn't hold a candle to her.

"Madison." I tip her chin up so her blue eyes meet mine. There's worry in them beside the desire that always burns between us. That worry won't do. "She and I don't fit. Who I fell in love with in college was a lie. What I had with her was all a game she was playing. She never wanted me. She wanted Coop, and only because her mother wanted her to want him."

"But she's someone you could love." Her voice is strong but I can hear the hurt in it.

I lift her up to stand on the seat in my shower so her face is higher than mine. My hands rest on her hips. "If I could love an illusion, yes, but she never showed me who she really was until later."

I run my hands over her hips and press my forehead against her stomach. I turn and rest my head against her, needing her to know that I'm hers. Her hands cradle my head. My chest expands as I breathe in her soft floral scent and feel her warm skin against my cheek.

"I was afraid to lose you," she whispers. "She's so much more than me."

I look up to find tears swimming in her eyes.

"She's not even half of you. I almost lost you." The words fall out of me, and I draw her down off the seat to wrap her in my arms. "He almost took you from me."

"He didn't." She sighs against my chest. "I was scared, but he didn't hurt me. I'm here."

I kiss the top of her head and breathe her in. This whole evening was horrible. But now, with her in my arms, everything feels right again.

Drawing her under the shower spray, I tip her face up and claim her lips. I could lose myself in the taste of her. The need for her overwhelms me. My hands grab her hips and pull her into me like I can't get close enough. She presses against me, wrapping her arms around my neck, clinging to me. But it's still not close enough.

Turning off the shower, I grab a towel to wrap around her. I lift her against me, still exploring her mouth with mine. Her hands cup my jaw as I lay her on the bed and follow her down, still dripping wet.

Unwilling to take the time to dry off before I feel her against me, I take her lips with mine. My hands roam her sides and she opens beneath me, parting her lips and her legs, giving herself to me. Lifting her knees and spreading her wide, I slide my cock deep into her. I groan as her tight, wet pussy engulfs me, taking all of me. I swallow her gasp as her fingers clutch at my short hair.

"Seth," she breathes out. She meets my every thrust with the same desperate energy. The need to be one. To connect with her, just the two of us. To feel her open for me, let me in.

I break away from her lips and press my forehead to hers. "You wouldn't look at me."

"I couldn't." She arches up against me.

"Why not?" Taking her hands, I hold them down against the bed next to her head, refusing to let her hide from me, waiting for her to look at me and answer me. Her eyes open and lock on mine.

"Because I couldn't see you look at her the way you look at me." Her eyes are dark pools of desire and want. "I couldn't see you want someone like her."

"Fuck, princess." I thrust deep inside her. Her legs wrap around my hips, clenching me tight. "I will never want anyone the way I want you."

The words are true. I can see her trying to deny them, struggling to accept them.

"Seth, I—" She closes her eyes.

"Don't close your eyes. Stay here. Stay with me. Don't shut me out."

She opens her eyes and I see it all. I see her. This magnificent woman we've lucked into. She's brilliant, loving, caring, and so damned sexy.

"Never shut me out." Our hands are locked together as she keeps her eyes open. I change the angle of my thrusts slightly, rubbing her clit with my pelvis. She sucks in a breath.

So close. She's on the edge. I want to fall over it with her.

"I won't." She arches into me. Her hips follow mine. "Seth."

"Madison." I quicken my pace and feel her pulse around me. "Come for me, princess."

She bites her lip as she moans through her release, drawing me deeper inside her. Her pussy convulses around me, squeezing and releasing until I can't hold back. I capture her lips with mine as my release shatters through me.

For a moment, it feels like we're suspended in time. Clinging together as our hearts race. Gathering her into my arms, I hold her against me as we both come down.

I won't let her go. She's mine.

Chapter 93

Integration

Madison

After we finish drying ourselves, he holds me against his side as we walk through the dark apartment to my room. Coop, Noah, and Blake are passed out on the bed where I left them. As exhausted as I felt, I couldn't fall asleep without Seth.

When he walked into the apartment, everything inside me settled, knowing I had them all again. I wanted to take care of him. Make sure we were all good.

His fingers smooth over my forehead. "Stop thinking so hard, princess. We'll work everything out."

I nod, and he pulls me down onto the enormous bed. Noah reaches out as I settle, and he tugs me back into his arms against his body. I cuddle into him and lift my gaze to Seth as he closes in on my front.

He brushes my hair out of my face and leans in to give me a kiss. Need throbs through me. I can't seem to get enough of them tonight. He slides his hand between my legs and rubs my clit. "I didn't give you everything you needed, did I?"

I cup his cheek. "You always give me what I need."

Noah's hands follow my curves up to my breasts, which grow heavy as he rubs on my tight nipples. Liquid fire flows through my veins. Wanting, needing more. Seth slides his fingers inside me, thrusting gently while teasing my clit with his thumb, pushing me closer to the edge. My breath quickens as I cling to Seth's shoulders. When Noah shifts behind me, his cock bumps against my entrance and Seth's fingers.

Seth curls his fingers against my G-spot, making me see stars, and Noah thrusts his cock deep inside me. Both of them inside me, stretching me. I cry out at the fullness. Noah kisses the back of my neck as Seth rubs my clit and watches my face. Taking in my every expression, watching the fire within me build until I combust.

"Tomorrow," Noah whispers in my ear, "Coop and I will fuck this greedy cunt together, while Seth fucks your ass and Blake fucks your mouth. You'll be stuffed full of cocks. How hard are you going to come for me, kitten?"

Seth rubs my G-spot as Noah continues to thrust into me until everything blurs. My body trapped between their warm bodies, skin rubbing against skin. Noah's hand teasing my breast. All the while, the fire within me explodes into flames. I convulse and gush around them both. I shatter into so many pieces it will take forever to put me back together.

"Fuck, princess." Seth kisses me.

"She likes the sound of that. Don't you, kitten?" Noah thrusts harder into me, driving me to the edge again until I explode. I cry out and moan as Seth rubs my clit.

My breath is difficult to catch as I start to come down, but Noah is still hard inside me. Seth looks beyond me at Noah and grins. Sliding his fingers out of me, he moves down and takes my breast into his mouth, sucking, licking, biting, keying me back up.

Noah hooks his arm under my knee and hikes my leg up high, thrusting deeper in and out of me. The tickle of hair against my inner thigh is the only warning I have before Coop's mouth closes around my clit. I writhe against them.

They move as one, and I stop being able to process what's happening. Lust dances through my veins and all I am is a mass of sensation as I reach the edge again. These men are out to ruin me. Make me need them. A scream builds inside me. As I come, the scream releases. Noah groans before he thrusts deep and comes.

Someone grabs my hips and tugs me into a kneeling position before a cock fills me.

"Blake," I say his name as he fills me with his thick cock.

A hand lifts my chin, and I meet Coop's dancing eyes before his hard cock bobs in front of me.

"Open up, sweetheart."

I lick my lips and open them wide as Coop's cock slides inside my mouth. They fuck me in time together. Someone toys with my nipples while someone teases my puckered hole with their wet fingers.

My skin sizzles with sparks and heat. Feeling everything but not able to process it all. I come faster this time, clenching around Blake's cock as Coop comes in my mouth. I swallow him down before Blake picks up his pace and groans as he releases his seed deep inside me.

"Color, kitten." Noah lifts me onto his lap.

I hold his jaw between my hands and stare into his dark eyes as I lower onto his cock. "Green."

We both moan as I rock against him. Our eyes hold and our souls connect. He's mine and I'm his. I'm all of theirs and they're mine. Seth moves behind me, and Noah falls back on the bed with me on top of him. Seth's cock presses against my puckered hole. My pussy spasms with anticipation as he slides into my ass.

So fucking full of them. Their cocks press against each other inside me.

I take Noah's mouth with mine as Seth fucks my ass. His hands guiding my hips onto his huge cock and pulling me down onto Noah's with each thrust.

I can't catch my breath. I can't move as he guides me. It's as if someone has lit a spark inside me and tossed it onto gasoline-soaked cloth. My climax tears through me, dragging Noah and Seth into theirs. I convulse around their pulsing cocks filling me full.

We collapse against each other as we catch our breath. Little aftershocks ripple around their still-hard cocks. I snuggle into Noah's chest, content to stay like this until morning.

Seth kisses my shoulder and pulls out before falling onto his back beside us. His hand trails down my side. "I missed you, princess."

I meet his captivating blue eyes. "I'm right here, boss."

Noah rubs a hand down my back, making me want to fall into sleep.

"Come on, sweetheart. We need to get you cleaned up." Coop lifts me from Noah. Turning, I curl into his arms, wrapping myself around him. He takes me into the bathroom where the shower's already running.

I love when they take care of me. He steps inside and Blake joins us.

Hands clean me, slipping over my curves, thrusting inside me. Mouths capture mine until we're doing a dizzying dance and I'm a mess of desire and lust. I need more. I want more. Whimpering, I cling to Blake's chest.

"Fuck, sweetheart." Coop's hands stroke over my hips. His fingers toy with my asshole as his mouth tastes my neck, nipping, sucking, licking. "You need to be fucked, don't you, my little whore?"

"Please," I sigh.

Blake lifts me against him and I wrap my legs around his waist. His cock slides inside me, and I feel whole again. When Coop thrusts his cock into my asshole, I shatter, pressed between them. So full, so completely and thoroughly fucked, that I never come down as they both work their cocks in me. It feels so intense, but so fucking good.

I cry out as the orgasm crescendos. Blake and Coop both groan. Their breathing heavy in my ears as their cocks pulse their release inside me. Coop kisses my shoulder tenderly as he withdraws.

When Blake claims my mouth, our tongues slide against each other as an aftershock pulses around his cock.

"Fuck, tiger." Blake rests his forehead against mine. "You're amazing."

He sets me down on my feet, and I rest my head against his chest. His heart beats steady and strong beneath my ear. They wash me while I cling to Blake. When we're done, Blake kisses my head, and Coop carries me out of the shower. Taking his time, he dries me before lowering me into bed between Noah and Seth.

I roll into Noah's heat, and he kisses the top of my head as he draws me into his warmth. Seth closes in behind me and I release a breath. I'm safe here in their arms.

I wake up to soft kisses down my stomach. My knees are spread wide and a tongue sweeps over my clit before burying itself in my pussy. I can't move my legs. The tongue keeps moving, stroking, tasting until I moan my release.

The tongue doesn't let up, taking me higher. My breath catches as I fall over the edge again into oblivion. Soft, wet kisses move up my body, taking a moment to tease my breasts before those lips meet mine.

"Noah," I breathe out on a smile.

"Good morning, kitten."

I open my eyes and meet his dark ones as his cock slides inside my still pulsing pussy. "Oh, fuck."

He leans over me with a smile on his face and his blond hair falling into his dark eyes. He reaches between us and rubs my clit. I don't know if we're alone on the bed or not, but I don't care as I wrap my arms around his neck and drag him down onto me. Skin to skin. The weight of him sinking me into the mattress.

Our mouths collide in a meeting of lips, tongues, and teeth as he fucks me, slowly and thoroughly. My insides explode with sensation. Everything tightening and releasing. Noah grabs hold of the headboard and fucks me harder.

"I wanted to fuck you last night at the benefit." Noah grabs my knee with his free hand and lifts it higher. "Take you into a dark corner and ravish you."

My neck arches as he hits a spot deep inside me. I wanted that too. "Noah."

"I wanted to fuck you until your legs trembled and couldn't hold you up anymore." His voice is dark as he watches my face beneath him. "Have my cum dripping down your thighs so you know who you belong to."

I catch his gaze with mine. "I belong to you."

"I belong to no one else, kitten. You have me body, heart, and soul." His words burn into my heart as his cock drives deep inside me, pushing me over the edge, shattering me.

I cry out and arch into him as he rides the waves with me before thrusting deep and groaning through his climax, holding me close as we sink back down into our bodies. His weight on me makes me sigh in contentment. I could lie here all day like this.

Someone brushes a finger over my foot. Jerking away, I squeak at the tickle.

"Time to get up, sweetheart." Coop chuckles.

Noah groans and rolls to lie beside me. "Fuck off, Coop."

I take a deep breath and rise on my elbows to look at Coop. He wears a t-shirt and jeans that show off his muscular build. He looks yummy this morning.

"Keep looking at me that way, and I'll be in that bed with you instead of upstairs working like I'm supposed to." He raises an eyebrow but grabs my ankle and drags me down to the edge of the bed.

"I'm getting up." I begin to rise, but Coop presses his hand to my stomach.

He looks behind me. "Hold her still, will you?"

Noah's hands lock around my wrists, holding them down on the bed.

Coop's gaze roams over my naked body as he opens his jeans and pulls his cock out. My mouth waters at his thick, hard cock. He shakes his head and smirks at me.

"This is going to be fast and hard, but you'll take it any way you can get it. Isn't that right, my little whore?"

I don't have time to come back at him as he grabs my legs and thrusts deep inside me. My protest comes out as a moan instead.

Coop rests my ankles against his shoulders and lowers his hands to my hips, lifting them off the bed. "I need you to get off quickly, like a good slut."

He nods to Noah before he pistons in and out of me. Each stroke makes the fire within me spread. Noah leans over my face and latches onto my breast. He licks and sucks my nipple as Coop pounds my pussy.

He lifts my hips. The change in angle makes me explode.

"Oh, fuck!" I come around his cock. Neither of them let up, keeping me shattering all around them until I squirm to move away.

Coop laughs and smacks my ass before burying his cock deep inside with a powerful thrust and climaxing. Noah trails kisses up my neck before kissing my jawline. He claims my mouth upside down.

Coop's finger strokes my clit until I go off like a rocket. Noah takes my cry into his mouth as Coop strokes his still-hard cock in me a few times before pulling out.

He lowers me to the mattress as Noah sits back and releases my wrists. I couldn't move if there was a fire. My body sinks into the bed. Coop pushes his cum back inside me with two fingers, and an aftershock ripples through me.

"Good little whore." Coop thrusts a few more times as my pussy convulses around his fingers before he draws them out. "Be a good slut and clean my fingers."

I sit up and grab his hand. Meeting his eyes, I bring his fingers to my mouth and take them deep, sucking Coop, Noah, and my cum off his fingers.

Coop draws his fingers out and leans down to kiss me, taking the taste of us into his mouth. He stands and shakes his head. "Get showered and dressed. You need to be upstairs in—" He glances at his watch. "Now you have ten minutes."

Smiling, I shake my head. How much time did I begin with? Standing, I head into my bathroom, determined to get ready for the day. Bare feet pad up behind me as warmth closes in on me. I turn to the mirror to see Noah. I lean back into him, and he takes me in his arms.

"Shower?" He kisses the top of my head. His hard cock presses against my ass.

I catch his dark eyes in the mirror. I'm pretty sure this shower will take longer than ten minutes.

Chapter 94

Hard Stop

Blake

It's a working Saturday, meaning this week got away from us and now we're paying for it. We also have to go down to the police station to give statements. Fuck. Something I wish we didn't have to do.

Madison sits quietly at her desk working. We let her and Noah sleep in but should have sent someone besides Coop to go get them if the smug smile on his face is any indication.

The door buzzes. The building is locked up tight. I disabled all key cards except ours, so if someone plans to come in and work, they'll need to ask to be let in. While it's the right thing to do, given Madison's stalker got in on a weekend, it's annoying as fuck.

I pull up the security feed and see Patrick Beck at the door. Clicking on the intercom, I say, "I'll come down and get you."

I won't be getting any more work done until we return, so I close out of my computer. This week has been a mess. When I walk out my door, Madison lifts her head to look at me.

Today, she wears jeans and a long-sleeved blouse. Her hair is pulled into a bun with golden tendrils falling around her face. She's not wearing makeup, but she doesn't need it. She's just as stunning as she was last night dripping in gold and diamonds.

"Good morning." When she smiles, it's like sunshine cutting through the clouds on a gloomy day. My heart kicks up a notch. I'm a fool for this woman.

"Patrick is here." I gesture to the elevator.

"Oh." She straightens and her hand goes to where a necklace would hang, but she's not wearing one. Her fingers linger for a second, then fall to her lap. "We're going to the police station soon?"

I nod. It's not what we wanted to accomplish today. I hope this whole stalker thing is over and we can get on with our lives. But something doesn't sit right about this whole thing.

Getting in the elevator, I think over all the facts we have so far and how those might point to a professor in college who wanted Madison and couldn't have her. Then attacks her at the benefit?

So far, her stalker has been meticulous, and that attack seems out of character.

I walk across the lobby toward the door and push it open for Patrick.

"Thank you for coming in." I lock the door behind him.

"Not a problem. Besides being your lawyer, I'm a witness and need to give a statement too." Patrick follows me to the elevator. "They think that guy is the stalker? The same one that sent the dress?"

I'd almost forgotten Patrick was in our office that day.

"Yeah." I push a hand through my hair as the elevator heads up. "He was her teacher and made passes at her."

"Do we know why he was at the benefit?"

"The college had a table." I lean back against the wall and watch the numbers creep by. "Why would a guy like that risk his job over an attempted assault?"

Every other move the stalker made was calculated. This just seems sloppy.

"The guy was drunk. Maybe he saw an opportunity and grabbed

it." Patrick shrugs and the elevator stops on the office floor. "We'll just have to wait and see if they catch the guy."

I lead Patrick toward the conference room. Madison stands and smiles as we pass her. When Seth comes out of his office, he shakes Patrick's hand before going over to Madison. He guides her into the conference room with his hand on the small of her back.

When everyone is in the conference room, Patrick leans back in his chair and watches us. "A few things to clear up first. If you don't mind?"

Seth nods his head.

"Are you two actually engaged?" Patrick asks as Coop sits down.

Coop rubs the back of his neck as he glances at Madison. She blushes and looks down in her lap. "No, it's not a formal announcement."

Patrick scoffs and opens his briefcase. He pulls out a file folder and opens it. "It's already out. Along with the news that you're expecting. Congratulations."

His tone is dry but the message is clear. He lays out some pictures of Coop and Madison. This isn't something that will easily fade into the background. That lump forms in my stomach as I gaze across the table at Madison. Everything happened so fast with us. Maybe too quickly.

"Also, there's another story buzzing around." He spreads out some pictures of Seth and Elizabeth. The last one is of her pressed up against Seth's chest, gazing up at him with a smile. His hands are on her upper arms like he's holding her there.

Madison goes pale when her eyes fix on the picture.

"That one isn't what it looks like." Seth leans his elbows on the table. His gaze holds Madison's. "When Elizabeth stood from the table, she stumbled into me. I made it clear to her that last night was purely business and I want nothing more to do with her personally."

"Her publicist reached out to ours this morning. Our publicist looped me in since she saw our appointment on my calendar." Patrick leans back in his chair as he looks over all of us. His focus stops on

Seth. "Elizabeth wants to roll with this fantasy of you two dating again, at least for a few months. Or she's willing to come forward and say you're having an affair with Coop's fiancée."

"What if we just say we're in a relationship?" Noah straightens. His brown eyes determined. "All of us."

Madison gasps softly.

Patrick blows out his breath. "You know what happened with Andrea and Rachel. It's a PR nightmare. What you do behind closed doors is your own business. But the image we project to the media and clients has to remain consistent."

"Then let's be consistent and say we're all dating Madison." Coop puts his feet up on the table. "I don't see why this should be as big an issue as everyone makes it out to be."

"Because it will lose us clients." Seth runs his hand over his hair. "We already have someone warning clients away from us. This would be another nail in the coffin. Our reputation is everything."

I let out a harsh breath. "As much as I want to claim Madison, Seth's right. So is Patrick. This company is ours and what we do matters. How we present ourselves to the world matters. What happens years down the road when Madison starts her own business? If this doesn't last, it will be brought up every time she makes a move. We already have our business, but she's just starting out."

My gaze meets Madison's blue eyes. "I can't fuck with your future like that. I won't."

Her eyes soften and she nods. Her future needs protection too.

"So that's two for blowing up the company and two for not blowing up the company." Coop shakes his head. "Honestly, I don't think it would hurt Madison that much."

"Let's just deal with one crisis at a time before we create a whole new thing to worry about. I'll think about the Elizabeth thing, but I'm not committing right now." Seth nods to Patrick. "When are we due at the police station?"

Patrick glances at his phone. "We should leave shortly."

We all stand as Patrick gathers the photos back into his file. I pick up one of Coop and Madison dancing. Something about it strikes me. I'm not sure if it's just that they look really good together or what it is exactly that catches my eye.

Madison passes me, but I put a hand out across her hip, stopping her. She looks up at me.

"It's not that I don't want to claim you as mine," I whisper.

She takes a breath and blows it out. "I know. It's complicated. I don't think you're wrong either."

I tip her chin up and lean down to kiss her softly. "You're amazing at what you do, tiger, and I never want to hold you back. Not now and not in the future."

Her hand cups my jaw. Her blue eyes search mine. "I don't know how this will all play out. But I appreciate you looking out for me."

———

"We apprehended Jimi Alan this morning." Bill Carr, my friend on the force, meets us at the front desk. Those are the first words he says to us.

Madison sags against Coop. He wraps his arms around her and kisses her forehead.

"Follow me. We have more to discuss."

We follow Bill to a conference room. He waits until we're all seated. "The timelines don't add up for him to be the stalker."

"What does that mean?" Seth asks.

"Mr. Alan has been out of the country for the past six months on sabbatical. He returned a few days ago. Which is why the drinks hit him so hard last night, alcohol combined with jet lag. It's no excuse for what he did to you though, ma'am."

Coop holds Madison's hand on the table.

Bill clears his throat. "The texts and videos came from within the country. That doesn't rule out an accomplice. We'll hold him on the sexual assault charges while we look into it. We don't think stalking charges would stick."

"Does that mean the stalker is still out there?" Madison's voice trembles.

"Honestly, we don't know, ma'am." Bill leans back in his chair and looks over all of us. "We'll do what we can to see if we can pin any of this on him."

"Let us know if you need anything from us." I glance over at Madison. She's pale and her lip trembles a little.

"Keep us informed if the stalker contacts you again."

"Of course."

Bill takes our statements. Mostly Madison's and Patrick's. Patrick leaves after his interview. His kids have stuff today.

When we head back to the office, everyone is quiet. We thought we caught him, but it's possible that whoever is after Madison is still out there. Not to mention Jeff and Val. They might never reemerge from the underground. If we're lucky, they'll run into other trouble that keeps them out of our lives permanently.

Once we're in the office, everyone returns to work. Something still feels off about the whole situation, but I'm not sure what it is.

A movement in my doorway draws my attention. Madison stands there with her hand holding her elbow, looking so uncertain.

"Do you need something?"

She walks in and glances at the door. "Do you mind?"

She gestures to the door. I nod and she closes it before stepping up to my desk.

"I can't focus." She drops her gaze to my desk. "My mind keeps spinning."

Her eyes lift to mine and my cock twitches.

"Do you need me to help you?" I ask carefully. She may just need someone to talk to, but . . .

"When you spanked me in the apartment, it helped me gain focus." She bites her lip as I stand.

Fuck. This is something that will help clear my mind too. "Come here."

She walks around my desk to me.

"Hands on the desk." I reach in my drawer and retrieve a leather paddle.

She leans over in front of me, pushing her hips out and spreading her legs. I trail my hand over her ass, and she shivers beneath my touch.

"Ten blows shouldn't be too much with your jeans on." I grip her ass and she presses her head on the desk. "No crying out. The only thing I want to hear from you is counting."

"Yes, sir."

I run my hand under her shirt, touching her warm skin. She sighs.

"Ready to count, tiger?" I fix my grip on the paddle.

"Yes, sir."

Aiming for the fleshy part of her ass, I land the first strike.

"One."

I don't let up, alternating cheeks and using the paddle as she moans out numbers. By the time we reach ten, both of us are panting. My cock strains against my zipper.

"Pull down your pants so I can see how red your ass is."

She does as she's told, bringing her pants down over her hips before leaning forward on the desk again. Her pale skin is red from the paddle. I run my hands over it to feel the warmth. Easing my hand lower, I press my fingers into her soaking cunt.

She moans and pushes back against my hand.

"Do you need release, love?" With one hand, I undo my belt and unfasten my pants to draw my cock out.

"Yes, Blake. Fuck me." She moans as I thrust deep with my fingers before pulling them out.

I press the head of my cock against her entrance. She whimpers in need. Her jeans keep her from spreading her legs wide. I tease her with a few shallow thrusts before she tries to press back against me to take me in deep.

"No moving," I order and smack her sore ass cheek.

She hisses in a breath but stops rocking her hips. "Sorry, sir."

Rubbing at her reddened skin, I slide my cock an inch into her pussy, wanting to thrust all the way in. She's so hot and wet, but I can't reward her bad behavior. "Are you going to be a good girl, tiger?"

"Yes, sir." She trembles beneath me, needing more than what I'm giving her. Her pussy is always tight around my cock, but with her legs pressed together, it makes her even snugger.

Rocking my hips, I ease deeper inside her with every forward thrust. It's slow, and it takes all the control I have not to bury myself deep inside her cunt. Her fingers curl on my wooden desk, looking for something to hold on to. She makes needy noises as her warmth engulfs me.

The door downstairs buzzes. I withdraw from her pussy and she whimpers.

"Work, tiger. Give me a second and then I'll fuck you." I sit on my office chair and pull up the feed from the door. Our employee Peter is at the door. Pretty sure he wasn't scheduled to come in today.

He glances over his shoulder while he waits.

"Madison, on your knees in front of me. Suck my cock to keep it hard while I deal with this."

She straightens and her darkened eyes meet mine as she lowers between my knees. Her mouth is hot and wet as she takes me in. I love her mouth almost as much as her pussy and ass.

"Quietly, love. Hands on my thighs."

When she's settled, bobbing up and down over my cock, I click on the intercom. "Peter, what are you doing here today?"

"Oh, uh." Looking away from the camera, he runs a hand through his unruly dirty blond hair. "I forgot something at my desk and wanted to get it."

Fuck, there goes playtime. "Okay, give me a few minutes and I'll be down to let you up."

Madison's tongue curls around my cock, making it throb. I cut off the intercom and lean back in my chair. Her blue eyes look up at me as she sucks on the head of my cock. I could probably fuck her mouth and come in a few minutes, but I don't want that to be the end of our playtime.

"Good girl. Now stand and go back to lying across my desk. Don't move an inch when I leave."

She stands and looks at me for a second like she's going to question me.

"Do you need more punishment, love?" I rise before her and tuck my cock back in my pants.

"No, sir." Her eyes sparkle with need, but she lowers herself to the desk, baring her pussy to me again. Fuck. I'll hurry back.

"Don't move," I remind her as I walk around the desk. Opening the door, I walk into the lobby and grab the knob to close it. My eyes meet Madison's again, and I smirk at her as I leave the door wide open.

Will the others walk by and see it as an open invitation? Maybe. But she better still be there when I return, or she'll definitely earn a punishment.

Chapter 95

Progress Check Meeting

Madison

My pussy throbs as I watch Blake walk away. I'm completely exposed here, waiting for him. The only thing I need now is an orgasm or two.

My jeans keep my legs together. I could reach down and get myself off easily, but that's not the point. The point is to wait until he's back to fuck me. If I got off and he came back, he'd probably punish me and just come in my mouth with no other stimulation.

That would suck, because his cock pressing into me, filling me, felt so fucking fantastic. I can't wait for him to be deep inside me. So I'll wait.

Someone walking beyond the door catches my attention. I glance up and see Seth. His gaze is on a tablet as he strides to my desk. When he finally looks up, his brow furrows as he glances around.

I'm allowed to speak, just not move. "In here."

Seth turns and his blue eyes light up. He closes in on me at the desk. He takes a moment to get a good look at my pulled-down pants and probably still red ass. "Punishment?"

"Yes. Blake had to go let someone in." I don't shift my position even though I want to. "Did you want something?"

Seth sets his tablet down on the desk and goes around behind me. His finger strokes over my ass cheek, and I suck in a breath at the tender flesh. "What are your rules, princess?"

"No moving." Every nerve ending tingles waiting to see if he'll touch me more. He could fuck me. As long as I don't move, I won't get punished. I get wetter thinking about it.

"Hmm." The chair creaks behind me, and he reaches forward for his tablet. "I need to go over some figures with you."

I tense. "If you need me to get up—"

"No need." The chair rolls and the arm of it taps my leg. "We can get into it when you finish in here with Blake."

Is he just looking at my pussy? Heat floods my abdomen.

"Fuck." Noah's voice makes me tip my head toward him, standing in the doorway. "I needed to talk to Blake."

"He's downstairs. He should be back in a few." I act like I'm not lying on his desk with my ass hanging out and Seth staring at my pussy. Just a normal day in the office.

"Do you mind if I wait in here?" Noah's eyebrow cocks up and he smirks.

"The more the merrier." I sigh, feeling the flames rage higher as Noah sits down. They could so easily take care of this burning inside of me. But I get the feeling neither of them are going to.

"Did you get the quarterly report I sent you?" Noah leans back and looks over me, I assume at Seth.

"Is there a reason for the fluctuation in office supplies?" Seth leans forward, and his warm breath caresses my pussy, making me inhale sharply.

"I need to go over that with the office manager. Sometimes they make a larger order in anticipation of a growing need." Noah's dark eyes lower to mine and he smiles.

"Good. We should stay on top of that. Wouldn't want anyone's needs to go unmet." Seth's voice sounds like he's holding back a chuckle.

Fuckers. Teasing me. I'll propose I tie them up tonight. I'll bring them right to the edge and then back off until they squirm for me to give them release.

"What's happening in here?" Coop asks.

"Waiting for Blake." Noah looks over his shoulder at Coop.

"Waiting for Blake to be finished with Madison." Seth leans away from me again, taking his warmth with him. "Did you need something?"

"Now that you mention it." He takes the seat next to Noah. His gaze roams over me.

Three cocks in the room and none in my pussy. Thoroughly dissatisfying experience.

"I wanted to discuss the new technology coming in next week with Seth. Though the CFO and our assistant would be helpful in the conversation." Smirking, Coop crosses his leg over his knee. "I assume you all have time since we're waiting."

"You have my undivided attention," I chime in.

Coop chuckles. "Our storage needs to be inventoried, and we might need to move some items around to make room for the new products."

"We can put together a team on Monday to do the inventory." Noah's fingers flex on his ankle.

How long will Blake be gone? Do I really have to stay like this the whole time? It's part of being Blake's. And if I really want to get fucked, I probably do. I sigh. But isn't the whole point of having multiple men at your disposal that you don't have to wait to have a cock buried in your pussy?

The guys discuss some of the technology coming in. I keep notes in my head, but Coop will also send me the relevant information. It's kind of difficult to focus lying on a hard wooden desk, with my ass exposed, waiting to be fucked.

The only thing keeping me aroused is the fact Seth is directly behind me and his breath keeps teasing my pussy. I have to admit, I thought when Blake left the door open someone would take it as an invitation to fuck me. Not sit around and wait like good boys.

The elevator dings and I release a happy sigh. Blake is back. He'll fuck me.

He pauses in his office doorway. "May I help you?"

His green eyes focus on me. I'd squirm for him, but I'm not allowed to move.

"Seth is here for me. Noah is here for you. Coop needed to discuss new technology arriving with all of us," I inform him, ready to carry on with where we left off.

Blake lifts his eyebrow but nods in acknowledgment. "You're welcome to stay, but I need to finish a project first."

"Go right ahead." Seth stands from the chair, but he doesn't come around to the front of the desk so I don't know where he is. But I know he'll be watching.

"Have you moved, tiger?" Blake strolls around the desk to stand behind me. His hands grab my hips and his thumbs trace over the paddle marks.

"No, sir." I'd been on a low simmer for the past few minutes. But with his touch, my insides turn molten again.

"Hmm." His thumb draws closer to my aching pussy. "Did anyone touch you while I was gone?"

"Seth touched my ass cheek briefly." Not enough to do anything more than stir up a need that no one felt inclined to satisfy.

"Sounds like you wanted them to touch you, tiger." Blake's tone is a little gruff.

I definitely wouldn't have minded it. But I don't think he'd like to hear I just wanted to be fucked. I love all the guys' cocks. But each of my bosses gives me something different.

Blake smacks my ass with his palm, and I cry out at the unexpected strike. "Answer me, tiger."

"I didn't know it was a question."

He spanks my other cheek. Heat floods through me, warming my face.

"Did you want them to fuck you?" Blake growls out.

"I wanted *you* to fuck me, but you left me here. So if they had wanted to fuck me, I certainly wouldn't have stopped them. You only said, *Don't move*. I haven't moved." And I don't feel like I should have been spanked because he didn't ask a question, but something tells me to keep that to myself.

"You came to me to help you focus, love." Blake's belt clanks as he opens his pants.

My pussy throbs in anticipation of his punishing thrusts. My jeans still bind my legs or I would have spread them wide to welcome him.

"For your punishment—"

"Wait, what?" I almost move but stop myself.

He smacks my ass twice. Fuck, that hurts. I was already a little sore from the paddle, and each smack lands where he spanked me before.

"As I was saying." He clears his throat and thrusts his cock deep inside me.

I moan as my pussy stretches to accommodate him. He's so fucking thick.

Grabbing my hips, he draws me upright against him. His voice is directly in my ear. "You're going to sit on my cock and the boss is going to fuck your face, followed by Noah, and then Coop. You aren't allowed to come or move until I tell you to. If you do, everything stops and you go back to work. Got it, tiger?"

Even if I come it won't be as intense as the one he's building up inside me. The one that will ravage me after taking all of them.

"Yes, sir."

He sits down in his chair, pulling me with him, keeping his cock buried deep inside me. Seth stands before me and undoes his pants. I lick my lips while I wait. This is the type of punishment I could take all day long.

Seth pulls out his cock, but I can't move to lean in to taste it. I meet his eyes, and the corner of his lips tips up. Taking my hands, Blake puts them on the arms of his chair. Then he slowly pulls the pins holding my hair up until it's tumbling around my face.

My pussy pulses around his thick cock, needing friction. The urge to move is overwhelming, but I don't want this to stop. Seth steps forward and threads his fingers through my hair, grabbing it. Pulling just a little to add a sting, shooting tingles through my veins.

"Open up, princess."

I part my lips. He thrusts and pulls my mouth over his cock until my nose touches his belly. I breathe as best as I can through my nose and swallow around his cock lodged in my throat. My eyes water. He holds me there until I desperately need more air.

He pulls me off, and I gasp in a breath before he plunges back in. I get even wetter around Blake's cock, and the need to move wrestles with my need to behave. My fingers clench the chair's arms as tears roll down my face. But I refuse to move.

"Such a good little slut." Coop's voice rings through my head.

Seth pulls out a little, letting me gasp in a breath before he fucks my mouth. He thrusts deep before drawing out over and over. My breathing follows his cock. My clit throbs restlessly as he fucks my face.

All the while, our eyes are locked on each other. His are a dark, endless lagoon where the surface is just the beginning. I want to sink into them and just float there for all eternity.

Blake's hands slip under my hips. I tense as he lifts me slightly before letting me slide down on his cock. Flames erupt within me. I moan around Seth's cock, tensing against the orgasm just waiting to explode.

Pressing into my throat deep again and groaning his release, Seth spills his cum in my throat as I swallow it greedily. He releases my hair and steps back, putting his cock away before rubbing my lower lip with his thumb.

"Good girl." Seth's eyes fill with a dark tenderness that tugs at something aching inside me. A ripple of happiness flows through me, but I'm fighting back the need to come. He steps away and Noah steps into place.

His cock is already out. I lick my lips, ready for more. He grabs my hair while aiming his cock at my mouth. When I part my lips, he fills me all the way back to my throat. He doesn't have the same need for control that Seth does. His dark eyes burn into mine as he fucks my mouth, hard and fast.

I want to move my hips in the same rhythm, follow this dark desire he stirs in me until we both succumb. I suck and his cock rubs against my tongue with every thrust. His fingers massage the back of my neck in sharp contrast to the way he takes my mouth.

My body hums with pleasure, spiraling down to where Blake fills my pussy. Noah groans and buries himself deep inside my throat as his release spurts out of his cock. I swallow around his head, loving the feel of him so deep inside me. Tugging my hair, he tips my head back before his lips crash down on mine.

I ache with need as his tongue caresses mine. Drawing away, he gives me a smile. "Thanks, kitten."

"Take a breather, tiger." Blake's voice reverberates through me. His cock twitches inside my pussy, and I feel like one graze of my clit will make me explode at this point.

I take a few deep breaths, trying to calm down as Coop steps up. Out of the corner of my eye, I catch Seth standing off to the side, watching. I have to be dripping down Blake's lap at this point. Absolutely soaking his pants.

Coop takes his cock out and strokes it in front of my face before rubbing his tip over my lips, spreading precum over them. "Fuck, sweetheart. When are you going to let me cover you in my cum?"

My heart ratchets up and I lick my lips. I remember the times Noah fucked my breasts, spilling his warm cum over my skin. "We can talk later."

His eyes light up. "Right now, I want you to be a good slut and suck me off."

I meet his eyes and open my mouth for him. Groaning, he grips my hair.

"I love your fucking mouth, my little whore." He pushes inside but keeps from thrusting into my throat, rocking back and forth so I can suck on him while he bobs my mouth over his cock.

The slow, steady rhythm is almost more devastating than Noah's fast and hard pace. It isn't long before I'm hanging on the edge again. Blake shifts below me and slides me up his cock again before dropping me down.

I moan around Coop's cock. His wicked blue eyes smile down at me.

"Blake, our girl is a greedy little whore. She wants to come so bad right now." Coop's words make me throb.

Blake rocks his hips against mine, and I almost lose it. "Is that what you want, tiger? You want to come all over my cock?"

Yes. Fuck yes, I want to come so fucking bad. Coop thrusts deep in my throat, preventing me from saying anything.

"I bet if I flicked your clit right now, you'd explode like a good slut." Coop leans down and I whimper.

I will, and that's a problem. I don't want this to end, so I can't come until Blake tells me to.

"Take her off your cock, Coop." Blake waits for Coop to withdraw before lifting me to stand on wobbly legs.

"Easy." Coop catches my hips, steadying me.

"Trade me places." Blake stands behind me. His wet cock nestles against my ass crack as he draws me back. Coop sits in Blake's chair.

Turning me to face Coop, Blake presses down on my back, bending me at the waist. Coop grabs my hair and lowers my open mouth down to his cock. As soon as Coop thrusts inside, so does Blake in my pussy.

Moaning, I know I won't be able to hold back as the fires rage through me.

"I'm going to fuck you, tiger. Don't come until I tell you to."

Coop slowly bobs my head over his cock, feeding me more of him as I suck and lick to distract myself. My pussy is tighter with my legs pressed together. Blake's hands part my ass cheeks as he pushes all the way into my pussy.

He's watching his cock disappear inside me. I want to watch it all. See them fucking me. Maybe tonight we can record it. As much as I worry about it falling into the wrong hands, I want to see it even more.

Blake withdraws slowly before thrusting in deep. I take Coop deeper and almost slip over the edge. I'm holding on by a thread as Blake fucks me. Coop controls the depth of his cock in my mouth as Blake slams into me from behind.

It's too much, but I'm not about to give in until Blake lets me. I can feel it right there, just waiting.

"Come for us, love." Blake's words wash over me, and my body follows his command.

I keen around Coop's cock as the orgasm rushes through my body. My pussy convulses around Blake's cock while I remember to suck on Coop's.

They follow me into oblivion as they both come, filling me at the same time, triggering a second climax. If Blake weren't holding my hips, I would collapse. I swallow down Coop's cum as Blake's cock pulses warm cum deep inside me. Each pulse triggers an aftershock until I'm spent.

Coop lifts my mouth to his, taking his time to taste me. Blake pulls out and pushes my pants down to my ankles before lifting me to straddle Coop's lap. Coop reaches between us and presses his still hard cock against my entrance. Our mouths claiming each other as I slide down his cock, filling my pussy with him.

We rock together. Exploring each other's mouth as the wave rises again. Coop reaches between us and rubs on my clit while Blake's fingers slide into my puckered hole. I couldn't hold back my orgasm if I wanted to. It races over me like a freight train, shaking me down to my core.

I arch into Coop as I clench around them.

Coop thrusts deep inside me as he groans his release. I breathe in his breath as we come down.

"Think you can focus now, princess?" Seth's voice makes me turn to face him, resting my head against Coop's. Seth gives me a smirk. "Come on. Get cleaned up. We have work to do."

Chapter 96

Game Time

Madison

> **HOPE:**
>
> How did the benefit go?

> **ME:**
>
> Amazing until the end. My professor tried to assault me.

My phone rings, and I glance toward the guys' office doors before answering Hope.

"I'm fine. Someone stopped him." I stand and stretch. The past few hours, I've focused on work. And sitting on my ass hurts a little. But the pain is good, it reminds me I'm here. I'm safe.

"Oh, shit! What happened?"

I walk to the break room as I tell Hope the whole sordid story. Leaving out how jealous I was of the women Seth and Noah brought. I also tell her the police don't think he's the stalker but haven't ruled him out entirely.

"You'd like Sara and Kayla, Blake's sister." I dump out the

remnants of the coffee and load the dishwasher. "They were both really nice."

"That's good. Especially if Noah dates Sara since she'll probably end up hanging out with you and Coop." Hope sighs. I ignore the twist in my heart about Noah and Sara. It doesn't sting quite as bad, especially since Sara definitely has something else going on. "The way Coop looked at you. Jeez Louise, I almost got scorched from the smolder."

My cheeks grow warm. There's another piece I have to tell her. "Okay, so it's not official so don't say anything, but there's a rumor that Coop and I are engaged."

"What? That's fantastic! You'll make the cutest babies. You aren't pregnant, are you? Because if you are, it doesn't matter. He's lucky to have trapped you." Hope squeals. "A wedding."

I sink into the chair in the break room and pick at a napkin on the table. "It's a rumor, but I don't know if it will blow up or not. It's really confusing, actually."

Her tone is gentle when she says, "Do you want to talk about it?"

"No. Yes. I don't know." I don't know what I can tell her and what I should keep to myself. This whole situation makes my brain hurt. The NDA binds me from talking about my relationship with the guys, but this thing with Coop isn't part of it. Can I tell her the truth? We aren't engaged, but then she might ask why fake it. I rub my forehead. "Do you want to come over tomorrow and watch *The Witcher* and drink wine?"

That I know I can do. It's safe.

"Oh, yes. That sounds great. Afternoon?"

"I'll text you when I clear it with the bosses."

A movement next to the door makes me lift my gaze. Coop leans in the doorway with a smirk on his lips and his hands in his pockets. Everything about him is stylish, from his shirt to his designer jeans to his leather shoes. His dark hair is gathered in a bun. His light blue eyes hide a hint of mischief in them.

"Sounds great! I'll see you tomorrow."

Ending the call, I set my phone down on the table in front of me.

"I was just talking to Hope." I gesture to my phone. My cheeks warm and my insides melt remembering him deep inside my mouth and pussy just a few hours ago. Coop in the break room seems to be our thing, so I buzz with anticipation for his next move.

He gives me a nod and glances over his shoulder before approaching the table and taking the chair next to me.

"You don't have to clear anything with us." He takes my hand in his. His clear blue eyes capture my attention, like a beautiful sky I can't help but stop to admire. "You can see your friend when you want to."

"It's just all a little odd. I don't know what I can tell her and what I have to keep secret." I shrug and lower my gaze to our hands.

"I got you something when I dropped off the diamonds in the vault this afternoon." Coop lifts a box from his pocket and hands it to me. "Normally I'd let you choose, but this one reminded me of you."

My heartbeat quickens and I'm afraid to blink. It's one thing to pretend to get back at his ex, but this is a whole other level that makes my heart pound. My fingers twitch toward the box, but I hesitate and sigh. "It's just a rumor, Coop. We could just let it die. Ignore it or say you were just messing with your ex."

He catches my chin and tips my gaze up to meet his. "Don't do that. I know I'm not the perfect guy, but I'm not about to go back on my word."

He opens the box and takes out the ring. I keep my gaze on his, afraid to look. Afraid to hope for something more than right now. I'm good with what I have with the guys. I don't need more. But this could make me long for something we can't have. A future.

"I'm not good at the emotional stuff, but this is something I'm good at. Offering expensive things to gorgeous women." He slides the ring on my finger and the weight of it startles me. I glance down at this beautiful setting of diamonds similar to the earrings and necklace from last night.

"It's exquisite, Coop," I whisper. A waterfall of diamonds clustered on a platinum band. It's definitely too much, possibly priceless, and probably an heirloom of his family. "But I can't wear this. What if I lose it? I'd never forgive myself."

Before I can take it off, he closes my hand and brings my knuckles to his lips, placing a gentle kiss on each one.

"You won't lose it, sweetheart. I trust you with this."

My eyes meet his again, and there's that tenderness I saw last night. It makes my throat thick and my heart feel too big for my chest. I lurch forward, throwing my arms around him and holding him close. He pulls me onto his lap and holds me against him, stroking his hand down my back.

It's sweet and so unlike Coop. I sigh against him and look at the ring again. This is a complication I'm not sure any of us are prepared for.

Dinner is a quiet affair. Well, conversation is quiet at least. We're all in the living room with the game on when the pizzas arrive. Seth brings them up and sets them on the coffee table while Blake carries plates over for us.

When I reach for my pizza, Coop grabs my left hand.

"Where's your ring?"

I sigh and glance around at all their faces before returning to Coop's. "I left it in a dish in the bathroom."

He lifts an eyebrow. I hoped this wouldn't be an issue.

"It's gorgeous, but huge." I tug my hand back and reach for the pizza again. Not looking him in the eye. "I'm afraid someone might end up with an eye gouged."

Besides, it didn't seem right to wear an engagement ring while being fucked by four men. Sure, one is technically my fiancé, even though he still hasn't actually asked. And the eye gouging could take place during sex or sleeping.

"I'm sure it would be fine." Coop grabs a slice and takes a bite. "You'll get used to it if you wear it more."

"I'll wear it all day tomorrow," I promise and give him a smile before biting into the best pizza ever. I moan around the bite of cheesy, saucy perfection. When I look up, everyone is looking at me with curiosity and that edge of heat that always stirs when we're together. "What? It's good."

Noah chuckles and pulls me into his side. I settle in beside him as I eat until I can't eat any more. The game occupies the others. Noah takes my plate and his and heads to the kitchen. Feeling the need to move, I follow him.

"How long does the game last?" I lean against the counter opposite the dishwasher as he loads the dishes. I haven't changed for bed, and I might take a shower.

"An hour more, probably." Noah glances my way and gives me a look. "Did you want to do something?"

I smile at him. "Eventually. But I might change first."

He closes the dishwasher and washes his hands before coming over to me and trapping me against the counter. Tingles scatter through me with him so close. I breathe in his outdoor scent and want to fall into him. I'm barefoot and he towers over me. His unruly blond hair tumbles over his dark eyes.

Unable to resist, I push my hand through his hair, holding it up to see his eyes. "Are we going to play tonight?"

"Yes, kitten. We're going to play. Do you want me to help you get ready?" His eyes darken as he lowers his mouth to hover over mine.

My skin tingles in anticipation of his touch. His lips brush over mine, and I let out a small sigh.

I keep my eyes locked with his, and my hand tightens in his hair. I want his kiss more than I want my next breath. He hovers just out of reach, teasing me.

"We're going to ruin you, kitten," he whispers against my lips. "We're going to take everything you have to give. You'll be so fucking full of cock you won't want it any other way."

My breath catches, and I slide my other hand around the back of his neck. "Maybe I'm the one who will ruin you."

"I certainly hope so."

His lips capture mine, and I'm swept up in the closeness of his body. Every nerve ending stands at attention waiting for his next move. Our tongues slide together, sending shivers of pleasure through me. His heart pounds against mine.

I'm briefly aware of the guys cheering on the game in the background as Noah's hands run down my sides. His fingers trail along the waist of my jeans until he reaches my snap and zipper.

Opening them both, his hand slips down the front of my pants. I pull my mouth free to inhale a breath. His dark eyes hold me motionless as he slides his hand beneath my panties and between my legs. His fingers brush my skin, but he doesn't really touch me.

Our lips brush with every breath, but I'm locked on his eyes, wanting to watch that moment when he first touches me. He smirks. Fuck, I love the glint in his eyes.

"You think they'll notice?"

We turn our heads to the guys engrossed in their game. Warmth fills my chest seeing all of them here. I couldn't imagine not having them all. Noah makes me feel loved. Blake is my constant protector. Coop takes care of me in so many ways.

And Seth, he makes us all a family. Like I belong. I haven't felt that before. I don't want to lose this feeling.

My gaze returns to Noah's smiling eyes as he thrusts his fingers inside me. My lips part on a gasp at the satisfaction reflected in his eyes before he claims my mouth again. He swirls his thumb around my clit while his tongue devastates me.

Tingles spread through me. He lifts his mouth from mine, and our foreheads press together. Our chests rise and fall as our breathing quickens.

"So fucking wet already, kitten." His dark eyes roam over my face as he pumps his fingers in and out of me. "I need you so fucking wet and needy that taking all of us will be the only thing you need to feel complete."

I tug his hair, drawing his gaze back to mine. "Make me need you more, Noah? I don't think it's possible, but I want you to try."

His smile turns wicked. "Watch what you ask for, kitten."

He thrusts another finger into me, stretching me around them as he fucks them in and out of my pussy, confined by my jeans once again. I reach my hand down to tug them off, but his other hand captures mine.

"No. You don't undress until I let you. You don't touch until I allow. I want you to come all over my hand, Madison. Drench me in your pleasure." His lips tease mine with every word. He tightens his hand around my wrist. "I'm going to fuck you so hard you're going to want to scream."

I flick the tip of my tongue against his lips. Wanting to torment him the way he's tormenting me. "You want me to scream for you?"

"No, kitten." He twists me in his arms, making me lose the grip on his hair, pressing me against the island with his hard cock against my ass. "I want you to be as quiet as a mouse."

He presses my hand flat on the island. The game is loud even in the kitchen. Seth and Blake are tense on the edge of their seats while Coop has his hands on top of his head. On TV, a guy runs down the field avoiding everyone.

"Both hands on the counter. I'd tie you up, but I'm a little occupied." He thrusts his fingers in and out of me in a slow, steady pace designed to drive me insane. His breath ruffles the hair next to my ear, sending shivers down my spine. His thumb rubs my clit, spiraling desire with every touch. I do as he asks and put my other hand on the island in front of me. "Good kitten."

A rush of euphoria races through me. I'm so close. Knowing Noah is getting me off and the others aren't even aware makes it a little more exciting. My orgasm crashes over me, and I bite my lip to stop from crying out as I arch back into Noah.

My pussy pulses around his fingers as he works me through my climax before he pulls them out. He takes ahold of my jeans and panties on both sides and strips them down my legs. I kick them off my feet. Thankfully, I prefer to go barefoot around the apartment.

He nudges my feet apart, spreading me open. The tense moment on the screen seems to have rolled into the next play.

"Go. Come on!" Coop yells, almost masking the zipper of Noah's jeans.

I suck in a breath as Noah's cock prods against my entrance before he sinks inside me. I lean down to rest my head on the cool marble as he eases in and out of me so fucking slowly while holding my hips in place.

"Come on!" Blake yells at the screen as the others join in to encourage whoever is making the play, but it feels like they are cheering me on.

My orgasm builds again. I want it faster and harder, but Noah keeps up the same insanely slow rhythm until I can't take it anymore.

I straighten, lifting my hands from the island.

"Bad kitty," Noah says in my ear before pulling his cock out of me entirely.

I groan at the empty feeling, but he shoves me back down. His hand in the center of my back holds me down, and I feel the soft head of his cock against my puckered hole before he shoves himself deep inside my ass.

I release a breath as he fills me, giving me a moment to adjust before finally taking me hard and fast. His cock works me over until I shatter around him. He pushes in one final time before his release fills me.

The guys all cheer as the stadium goes wild. Chuckling, I agree that was a pretty excellent fuck. I melt into the island as the intensity of my climax fades. Noah slips his cock out, and his fingers thrust back into my pussy.

I gasp and the spell is broken. Seth turns and meets my eyes. He lifts his eyebrow before taking a drink from his bottle of beer. Noah's fingers torment me hard and fast again. Seth's gaze drops down to Noah's hand, and he licks the opening of his beer bottle.

It's all too much, pushing me over the edge until I can't help crying out, alerting the others to what was happening right behind them.

Hungry gazes meet mine, and anticipation sizzles along my skin.

Let the real games begin.

Chapter 97

Move the Needle

Madison

The TV screen goes dark, and Coop tosses the remote on the couch. Blake, Seth, and Coop stalk toward the kitchen. I straighten off the counter with my back against Noah. My pants are gone but my shirt is still on. Noah is still completely dressed with his cock out.

Seeing their hunger has anticipation welling within me, making my skin tingle. The intent in their eyes has my blood boiling.

Noah lifts off my shirt and tosses my bra to the side, leaving me naked. His hands rest on my hips. His cock nestles in between my ass cheeks. My pulse flutters, and even though I've already come twice, my pussy grows wetter as they take in every inch of me.

They gather around the island like we've called a meeting. They all tower over me, and with them fully dressed, I feel vulnerable, standing naked, waiting.

"What about your game?" My words are light as I meet each of their eyes. Coop smiles and licks his lips. Blake smirks. When Noah cups my breast, I catch my breath. He pinches my nipple before rubbing it better. A groan escapes me as heat spreads through me like a wildfire.

"There are some games I prefer to watch live." Seth slides onto the stool opposite me. His darkened eyes lower to Noah's fingers toying with my nipple. I love when he watches me with the others. That look in his eyes, knowing he's resisting the urge to touch me himself. An ache throbs in my pussy.

I want them all.

"Should we move to the play room?" Coop closes in on my side and his hand ghosts down it. The warmth of his fingers skims the surface, sending ripples coursing through me. I want to lean into his touch, feel his smooth fingers on my skin.

Noah's hand in the center of my back presses my front down on the island. The cool stone is a sharp contrast to my heated skin. I hiss as my nipples meet the cold. "Blake, would you mind? I need to clean up."

"Of course." Blake's hand rests on my back next to Noah's. A zipper sounds in the silence as Blake steps behind me. My stomach flutters. The brief kiss of his cockhead against my entrance is the only warning I have before he slides in deep.

My eyes close and my lips part, but no sound comes out. Oh, fuck. He's so thick and different than Noah. He holds his cock deep inside me as my body adjusts to his size.

"She needs to work up to taking us all," Noah says conversationally as the sink runs. "We'll need to prep. Should we edge her?"

"Not sure edging is a good idea." Coop runs his hand up my side and catches my arm, dragging my hand up over my head on the island. Seth links his fingers with mine, and Coop reaches over me to drag my other hand up to Seth. "If she's that needy, she'll come as soon as we get our cocks into her. Making us come too quickly. I want to enjoy the tight squeeze of her cunt around my cock for as long as possible."

His words cause my pussy to clench around Blake. My skin burns from every touch, and the cool stone beneath me makes it sizzle. Blake rocks his hips against mine, grinding against me. My toes curl in need.

"If we aren't withholding orgasms, maybe blissed out on orgasms is the way to go." Noah returns to my side and runs his hand up the inside of my thigh, leaving a trail of tingles in his wake. He leans in close to my ear as he whispers loudly, "You want to dip into subspace, kitten?"

Remembering the euphoria that filled me when I reached subspace excites me. The need to touch and be touched. I turn my head to look at him and lick my lips. His gaze drops to my mouth like he's considering taking it, claiming it as his own. I tremble with the ache inside burning to break free.

I achieved subspace one time. They stopped playing with me in the play room, though, because I couldn't tell them to stop if I needed to. But I couldn't get enough of touching or fucking. There was no pain, only pleasure.

I definitely wouldn't mind going back to that.

"Not subspace. She needs to be aware. We could unintentionally hurt her if she can't feel her pain." Blake pulls his cock almost all the way out before slowly easing back in, like lazily swimming the backstroke in a pool. It's smooth and easy but touches every nerve, lighting them up. "Just a lot of orgasms leading up to the big event."

Noah's fingers lift from my inner thigh to flick my clit. I draw in a deep breath as my pulse ratchets up higher. I can't move at all to seek more stimulation. The smooth surface of the island is cool, and my skin glides over it.

Seth holds my hands. Blake's cock and hips keep my legs in place. I'm a slave to their desires. Theirs to command. Accepting their control over my body and my pleasure, I relax into the counter.

"We need to get her soaking wet." Coop's fingers work their way beneath me to tease my nipple, rubbing his warm fingers over my cool flesh. "We could just fill her with our cum until she's so lubed anything would slide into her."

I moan at the thought of them fucking me until their cum coats my thighs.

It hasn't escaped my attention they're talking about me and not to me. They touch me almost absent-mindedly. A rub here, a flick there. Making me feel like an object of pleasure for them to use, to torment, to worship.

The thought burns through me, making my pussy even wetter.

Noah rubs my clit in slow, steady circles. "It shouldn't be difficult to get her ready. She's a little slut for being fucked. She likes to be toyed with like a good kitty."

I moan as he winds me tighter and tighter. Coop's fingers zing bursts of pleasure from my nipples to my pussy. Then Blake does that slow ease out of me until he's almost all the way out, just the tip barely clinging to my entrance, before he presses back in mind-blowingly slow.

The only one who hasn't chimed in during the discussion is our boss. I tip my head up to meet Seth's eyes. His gaze is on what the others are doing to my body while he holds my hands captive.

When he realizes he has my attention, he meets my gaze with his heated eyes. Need flows between the two of us. He wants to watch, and I want him to. I love the way I look in his eyes.

"I want to record it," I say directly to Seth because he'll understand. The flare of heat in his eyes tells me he knows what I want.

"We can do that." His hand squeezes mine. "You want to watch yourself get fucked by us, princess?"

The slow and steady torment of Coop, Blake, and Noah makes me moan and suck in a breath as I draw closer to the edge. It's such a slow build.

"Yes, please." Meeting Seth's eyes, I hold them. "I want to see what you do when you watch us. I want to see everyone's cock penetrating my body and making me come. I want to watch you fuck my ass while Coop and Noah fuck my pussy and Blake fucks my mouth. I want to see it all."

Saying the words out loud is enough to push me over the edge. It's not like most climaxes that build and build until the dam breaks. This release flows over me, making me moan and spasm around

Blake's cock as he leisurely moves inside me. I'm not overwhelmed by it. Just a gentle wave of bliss.

Seth pulls my hands toward him, stretching me out before he orders, "Harder."

Fuck. The pace picks up as Coop chuckles darkly. His fingers pinch my nipple before his other hand runs down the curve of my back to my ass. He slides his fingers between my cheeks before slipping into my asshole.

I gasp and clench a little.

"Shh, kitten." Noah's fingers rub my clit before he works them back toward my entrance.

Fuck, he's about to put his fingers inside me with Blake's cock. I stiffen. It's one thing with the others, but Blake is already stretching me out.

"Relax, princess."

My gaze lifts at Seth's voice. He raises an eyebrow.

"You know how to pause or stop things if you need to." Seth's tone is calming. Remembering the colors can make things stop relaxes me more. "*Green* is all good. *Yellow* is pause or slow down."

"And *red* is stop," I say.

The guys stop but don't pull away from me. They all hover, ready to withdraw or continue on my word. It's heady and intoxicating. The control I have to stop everything. To withhold their pleasure.

"What do you want, princess?"

But I don't want to stop. I want to be their object. "Green."

Blake's cock slides out of me right before Noah's fingers rub along my entrance, pressing at the muscles the same way they prepped my ass to take them. Coop's fingers remain in my ass unmoving.

"Good kitty," Noah murmurs. His fingers slide deeper and curve to rub against my G-spot. I hiss at the sensation before Blake's cock presses in with Noah's fingers. It's tight and I whimper slightly.

"Good girl, tiger." Blake presses deep, making me feel so full with Noah's fingers stretching my pussy and Coop's long fingers filling my ass. "I can't wait for you to watch me fucking you."

I bite my lip as they all slide out and thrust back in. It's amazing and overwhelming and so fucking powerful. All these men hell-bent on making me come.

"We're going to stretch your cunt out like a good whore." Coop leans down to whisper in my ear. "We'll stuff you full of cock until you beg for more. Until all you can think about is our cocks inside you, fucking you, filling you with our cum until it leaks out. Making you come so hard you scream your release until you're hoarse from it."

His fingers pinch and pluck at my nipple as he fucks my ass with his other hand. "You want that, don't you, my little whore? You want our cocks and our cum so fucking bad it hurts to not have them."

I moan as I come, gushing around Noah's hand and Blake's cock, squeezing Seth's hands while Coop makes me come again around his fingers, taking me even higher.

"Fuck, tiger." Blake thrusts deep and floods my pussy with his cum.

Noah withdraws his hand and Blake pulls out. I whimper slightly at the loss.

"Don't worry, kitten. I've got you." Noah thrusts his cock into my pussy, making me explode again as he thrusts hard and fast. Dragging out my orgasm with his every thrust. He finds his release, filling me up before squeezing my ass cheeks and pulling out.

Coop removes his hands from me and steps behind me. His cock surges into me, and I moan as he thrusts wildly, like a man possessed. Grabbing my hips roughly to center himself. I wouldn't be surprised to find bruises on my hip bones from the hard marble island. Need claws at my insides as he hits a spot that makes me rocket to the moon. I cry out and he thrusts deep before releasing his cum to mix with the others.

I lie on the island panting. My hands clutch Seth's like he can ground me to the here and now. I release a breath as Coop pulls out. He kisses my ass cheek as his fingers gather the cum running down my leg and push it back inside my pussy.

"Good girl." Seth squeezes my hands and releases them.

A little thrill goes through me at the compliment. I don't think I can move as Coop thrusts his fingers into me, making little ripples of aftershocks work their way through my body.

Seth stands and walks around behind me. Coop steps out of the way, but Seth doesn't move in or touch me at all. He just looks at my ravished pussy and asshole.

As the time lengthens, I squirm under his gaze. I'm tempted to ask him to take a picture so I can see what he sees.

"Coop, set up the camera in the play room. Noah and Blake, move the furniture around and set up the lighting. Something soft and moody. Find some music." His arm wraps around my waist and pulls me upright against his hard body. "I'll get the star ready."

Chapter 98

Taking the Boss's Lead

Seth

Madison rests against me like all her bones have turned to mush. Lifting her into my arms, I carry her through her room into her bathroom. Her head rests against my chest the entire time.

"You aren't sleepy, are you, princess?" I set her down on the counter beside the sink.

She leans back against the mirror and watches me with her huge blue eyes and licks her lips. "Not sleepy."

Grabbing a washcloth, I run the water to get it nice and warm before wetting it.

"Spread your legs for me." I meet her darkened eyes and she opens her legs. I wipe down her pussy thoroughly. She makes little needy noises and squirms as my fingers part her and skim along her clit. "You want more, princess?"

"I want you, Seth." Her gaze drops to my erection straining against my zipper. My hard cock twitches. "I need you deep inside me."

Her fingers trail over the counter like she wants to touch me. I step over to the sink and rinse the cloth.

"Stand and lean over the counter." I squeeze the excess out of the washcloth before looking at her. She's bent over like she was in the kitchen, spread out before me like a beautiful flower waiting to be plucked.

I run the washcloth over her ass. Her lips part in the mirror as her gaze meets mine in it. Control is my thing. It's what keeps me from giving into my baser desires. It's what makes me a strong leader and businessman.

But Madison tests my control like no other. I crave her. I ache to take her. And her eyes tell me she feels the same. I toss the washcloth in the sink and wash my hands before turning off the water.

"Put your hands on the mirror." I undo my belt and draw it from my jeans.

She lifts to put her hands on the mirror, never taking her reflected gaze from me. Her legs are spread, opening her up to me. Her pussy glistens with her wetness. The temptation to have her touch herself fills me. To watch her fall apart under my instruction.

But I need to ruin her myself, feel her hot cunt spasming around my cock.

"Are you ready for tonight?" I take my shirt off and toss it to the side with my belt.

The heat in her eyes almost makes me groan. "Yes, sir."

My cock jerks as I reach for the button of my jeans. I strip off my jeans and boxers until I stand naked behind her.

"I have an outfit in mind for tonight." I trail my finger down her spine with the lightest touch. She arches into it like a cat seeking more.

"What I'm wearing won't do?" She gives me a smile.

"I always like this particular look." I palm her ass cheek, massaging the muscle. "But if you're going to watch it later, we should add a little something to make it special."

I drag my fingers down the back of her thigh. She trembles beneath me. So sensitive to touch.

"Seth?" Her voice is breathless.

"Yes, princess?" I trail my fingers up the inside of her thigh, toward the spot that needs me the most.

"Are you going to fuck me, sir?"

I lift my gaze to hers in the mirror. "Do you want me?"

"Yes, sir." She doesn't blink as she holds my gaze.

"Do you ache for me?" My finger brushes over her pussy, so light that it will do nothing but tease.

"Yes, sir." Her lips part as she waits in anticipation of my next move.

I close in on her hips and brush the tip of my cock over her throbbing clit. She exhales sharply.

"Please."

"Please, what?" I brush it again, loving the wetness gathering on my tip. Her need for me glistens on my flesh.

"Please, sir. Fuck my pussy with your cock." Her hands press against the mirror as she holds my gaze. "Seth, I need you."

I slide my cock to her entrance and she sucks in a breath. Her legs spread more. She rocks back, dipping the tip of my cock into her warm, tight cunt. Fuck, I want to pound into her, take everything she has to offer me, but I need to maintain control.

Meeting her eyes in the mirror, I bite out, "If you want it, take it."

"Yes, sir." She shoves herself back on me, impaling herself on my cock. I bite back a groan at how good she feels surrounding me. Her moan fills the room. Her ass presses against my abs as she takes me as deep as she can before she slides forward.

Her wet cunt clings to my cock like it doesn't want to let go. She whimpers as she almost slides all the way off me. Our eyes lock, and she thrusts herself back on me.

Fuck. I close my eyes briefly at the perfection of her pussy. My hands trail up her inner thighs before parting her lips and toying with her clit.

"That feels so fucking good," she whispers. She rocks back and forth, letting me slide out a few inches before greedily taking it back into her.

I rub her clit. It pulses beneath my touch as I let her do all the work to fuck us.

She jerks forward all the way off my cock and turns. "I want to watch myself take you."

She presses her fingers against my chest and pushes me back to the bench in front of the full-length mirror. "Sit, please."

I don't usually take commands, but right now I'm more intent on getting her off. This is what she wants, and I'm willing to bend to give it to her. I drop onto the bench and sit facing the mirror.

She straddles my legs, her back to my front, and lowers herself down slowly. I help guide her hips before positioning my cock at her entrance. She takes me in slowly this time, and we both groan as she fully seats herself on me.

"Touch my breasts," she whispers as she leans back against my chest. Her gaze focused on where I'm buried inside her.

I stroke my hands up her sides before palming her breasts, massaging them before teasing her nipples with my fingertips. She lifts off my cock a little before sliding back down. The bench is low enough she has leverage to lift with her legs spread around mine.

She rises and falls, building a steady rhythm while I tease her breasts with my hands. When her hand strokes down her stomach, I follow it with one of mine. She parts her pussy lips even wider so she can watch her cunt take me.

Sliding my finger down over her clit, I rub in slow circles. Both of us watch our bodies moving together. Erotic and stimulating.

"Seth," she breathes out. "I'm so fucking close."

"Come for me, princess." My lips press against her ear before I suck on the spot behind it.

Her movement becomes chaotic as she races toward her climax. I slide my fingertip back and thrust it inside her cunt with my cock, pressing deep to sweep it over her G-spot.

"Fuck!" She comes hard, tightening around my cock and finger.

I drag my finger out and grab her hips, thrusting into her, needing to watch her take all of me.

Her breasts bounce with every thrust. She doesn't come down from her release. Her pussy flutters all around me as I buck up into her. Her hips try to move with mine, but her gaze is latched on to where we're connected, watching me piston into her.

I groan as she convulses around my cock again, dragging me into my release. My cock jerks as I unload my cum into her cunt, claiming her as mine in the most barbaric way possible.

She sags against my chest. Our skin glistens with sweat. The air is filled with our heavy breaths and the smell of sex. Her breasts heave. Reaching up, I cup them, tracing her nipples with my fingers. I bite down on her shoulder, and a little aftershock flutters through her cunt around my still-hard cock.

Her hand reaches back and threads through my hair. "We need to get cleaned up again."

I smirk at her in the mirror before I lift her with me. My cock still buried in her cunt as I walk to the shower and step in. Turning on the water, I take the brunt of the cold water as I set her on her feet and press her hands against the tile wall.

My cock is already hard again. I thrust in and out of her a couple of times before I pull out and ease into her ass.

"Oh, fuck." Her hand clenches against the wall as I bury my cock into her ass, barely allowing her time to adjust before thrusting hard in and out.

"This belongs to me when we all take you. Your ass is mine, princess. I won't care that you have other cocks to attend to. I want you to feel mine all the way through you as I bury myself in your ass over and over again until you come so hard."

"Yes, sir. Oh, fuck, yes." She pushes against me, meeting every thrust with her own until she clenches around me, coming hard again. I drag out of her before she can make me come.

As she catches her breath, I grab soap and wash my hard, aching cock thoroughly.

"On your knees, princess."

She turns and lowers to her knees, eyeing my cock.

"Open wide." I close the distance between us as she does as I ask. "Who's in control?"

"You are." She doesn't hesitate as she licks her lips and opens for me again.

"Suck my cock."

Leaning in, she licks the tip before taking me into her mouth, running her tongue over me and sucking. Her blue eyes meet mine and I grab her hair. She stops sucking and relaxes, giving me all the control.

"Slide your fingers into your cunt and fuck yourself slowly." Waiting for her to follow orders, I bob her mouth over me, making her take me deep before pulling back. Her fingers slide between her thighs, and she moans around my cock.

While I fuck her mouth slowly, she watches me and sucks and licks when she can. Water pours over her face from the shower. "Don't come on those fingers, princess."

She whimpers. I press even farther into her mouth until her nose brushes my abs. Her throat swallows around me, but she doesn't panic. She trusts me to let her breathe. She trusts me to know when it's enough.

When I pull her back, she sucks until her cheeks hollow out and I'm a goner. My cum sprays in her mouth as she swallows greedily. I thrust deep again, and she swallows around my head, draining me.

I jerk her off of me completely and drop to my knees with her, taking her mouth with mine. I thrust my fingers with hers into her warm, dripping pussy and brush my thumb over her clit while we kiss, tasting each other.

Our hands stretch her tight pussy, but she follows my lead until she cries out her release as she comes on our hands. Her head drops to my shoulder as I gather her into my arms and just hold her, kneeling under the warm water.

"You're going to wear me out," she whispers, pressing a kiss to my shoulder.

"Not possible." I inhale and the tension from the week releases. There's plenty to worry about come Monday morning again. But this weekend I can just focus on Madison.

Standing, I reach down a hand to help her up. "They'll come looking for us if we take much longer. Let's get you ready."

Chapter 99

Executive Decision

Madison

The almost sheer negligee Seth picked out for me is barely fabric, but the silk feels divine against my skin. It just covers my ass, and he didn't give me panties to wear with it.

He helps me braid my hair to get it out of the way. I never thought much about a man helping with my hair. But as he draws the brush through it, there's something relaxing and sensual about it. His fingers light sparks beneath my skin.

It keeps that flame of desire lit within me even though he's barely touching me.

Seth remains naked, which makes me want to touch the contoured planes of his body. Tease a reaction from his hard cock. Wind him up the way I always feel when I'm near him.

"Let's go." He holds his hand out to me, and we walk through my living room into the main living space. The play room door is open, and I grow wet just thinking of what will happen when we enter that room. "Remember your words, Madison."

"Green, yellow, red." I still don't have a safe word specific to me, but these words will work.

"If you can't speak?" He pauses outside the door and takes me by my shoulders to face him.

"I tap on someone's thigh three times. Or whatever I can reach."

He tips my chin up. "Soft limits. Cum on your body? Yes or no?"

Noah and I discussed this before he came on my neck and breasts. I wanted to try it then, and while it's messy, it's not a solid no. My pulse races as I search his eyes. "Yes."

He nods. "Hands on your throat, not choking?"

I shake my head. Not in this scenario. Maybe never. My panic attack last night runs through my mind. My hand reaches up to touch my throat. His fingers trail over my neck as he looks at where the bruises were. They may have faded but the fear lingers.

"No. I don't think I'd like to see someone with their hands on you like that." Seth traces his thumb down my pulse point. "Anything new you want to exclude?"

While Jimi was aggressive last night, it wasn't the same as Jeff's and Val's attack. Jimi pushed me against a wall and touched my breast. Neither are things I want to exclude from our play. It's different when the guys do it. But no one has choked me except Jeff.

"If something changes, I'll say *red*."

He nods. "You need to trust us to stop. No matter what. If it gets to be too much, promise me you'll use your outs."

I cup his jaw. "I promise."

He lowers his lips to brush softly over mine. "You ready, princess?"

I draw in a breath and blow it out. "Yes."

Taking my hand, he leads me into the play room. The lighting is dimmed but still bright enough for the camera, which is set up in the corner on a tripod. Its focus is the leather bench with a low center and two sides that curve up sharply.

Coop, Noah, and Blake are already naked, waiting for us. My insides buzz, knowing what's about to happen. I expect a little pain, but the pleasure always comes too. I can't wait to see what they have in store for me.

"You look delicious." Coop prowls over to me. His fingers skate beneath the strap of my negligee and glide over my bare shoulder. His other hand slips under my negligee to grip my hip. A shiver ripples through me. His blue eyes blaze with heat as they meet mine. "I assume you'll be directing."

He lifts his gaze to Seth. I glance over my shoulder at him as well.

"I enjoy being in control." Seth runs his hand over my ass, making me inhale sharply at the tingles racing through me. "We also need to build up to the main event."

Coop lifts me against him.

"Oh." I wasn't expecting it, but my hands brace on his shoulders.

He chuckles as he meets my eyes. "Expect to be manhandled tonight."

"I just wasn't ready." I tug the holder out of his hair and the strands fall around his shoulders. Sinking my fingers into his silky hair, I tug his head back and kiss his throat, sucking slightly.

He sits on the bench and tugs me down to straddle his lap. His hard cock sits between us. "Am I correct in assuming this stays on?"

He lifts the skirt of the negligee, which starts under my breasts and falls slightly past my hips. My pussy is bare and the sheer fabric hides nothing.

Seth sits behind us on the edge of the bed. "For a while."

Noah steps up behind Coop and tugs my hair back, tipping my head to look up at him. "We need to play with her. Tease her. Make her scream and buck. Make her need us so much she doesn't question how many cocks she's taking as long as she takes them all."

Coop's hand slides between my legs. "She's already soaking wet."

I moan at the light touch. His fingers thrust into me as Noah lowers his mouth to mine. While Coop explores my neck with his lips, Noah dominates my mouth. His tongue finds mine and coaxes me to spar with him.

Coop raises me up on my knees, urging me forward. The head of his cock presses against my entrance. I want him inside me so badly.

He lowers me down. I gasp into Noah's mouth as I take Coop inside me.

"Are we coming or holding off?" Coop asks against my neck. His words are hot against my skin as I grind down on his cock.

"Holding off." Blake's fingers trail over my breasts, teasing my nipples through the fabric. "She needs hard cocks to fill her full."

My pussy clenches on Coop. He leans in and takes my other nipple into his mouth through the fabric. They're working me into a frenzy of need with their words and touches.

I grind on Coop's cock, little rises and falls to stimulate my clit. Noah lifts from our kiss. His dark eyes hold mine while I move my hips until I shatter.

"Fuck." Coop releases my breast and reaches between us to hold his cock. "I won't be the first one to blow, but your pussy is so fucking tight and perfect, sweetheart."

I squeeze my pelvic floor as I meet his eyes, and he grins evilly. A thrill goes through me.

"You want to play, my little whore?"

"Yes." I grab onto his shoulders and dig my knees into the bench, riding him while holding his gaze. Lifting and falling onto his cock with fast hard strokes. "I want to play with all of you."

Coop's laugh is delightfully wicked. He stands and I wrap myself around him. My mission is clear. Make Coop come before I come again.

Holding me like I weigh nothing, he swings his leg over the bench and lowers me back down on it while I grind my pussy against him. He withdraws as far as my legs will let him before punching back into me. I moan at the sensation. His blue eyes dance in delight as he fucks me hard.

"You want to be filled with cum like a good slut?" He presses down on me. Our bodies strain together. "You're going to beg me for my cum by the end of this. You'll be my little whore needing it, wanting it. But I won't give it to you until you beg."

I press up against him and grab his hair to bring his ear down to my lips. These words are only for him. "We'll see who ends up begging."

I lick the side of his face. Thrusting deep inside me, he sucks the spot where my shoulder and neck meet before biting down on it. My body arches into him, needing more.

"Princess." Seth's voice is stern and makes my heart skip.

Coop lifts his head, and his dark hair falls around us, enclosing us. He has this glint in his eyes that makes me pulse around his cock. Neither of us turns to look at Seth, too wrapped up in this battle of wills.

The second I look at Seth, I'll give in. I'll submit because that's what he wants. I want it when I'm under his control, but Coop likes to give me control, or at least fight me for it. Right now, I want to make him come.

"You want to submit, baby," Coop says softly. He punctuates each word with a punch of his hips into me. Each stroke takes me higher, closer to the peak. "You'll do anything to get all these men to fuck you like a good little slut."

"Maybe." I arch into him and squeeze around his cock again. "At least I'll get to come like a good slut."

Coop takes my mouth. Our fight for dominance continues in this kiss. But then he reaches between us and circles my clit with his finger as he fucks me hard. It's too much. I cry out into his mouth as I come.

He jerks out of me before I can draw him into his release. He smirks at me. The fucker. I'm not finished with him yet. But I don't have time to focus on him as Noah thrusts into me, covering me with his body and capturing my attention.

"Noah." I dig my hands into his blond hair, pushing it away from his dark eyes as he takes in all of me. His cock stays deep inside me as he leans over me. Aftershocks from my orgasm ripple all around him. His hands flow down my sides, making sparks light up beneath his touch.

"Kitten." He claims my mouth and slowly fucks me. It's the exact opposite of the battle between Coop and me. It's tender and breaks me down into pieces that I know Noah will help me put back together.

Noah presses his forehead against mine. He thrusts in deep. Someone's fingers rub where we're connected, teasing my opening. My eyes find Noah's. He cups my cheek and traces his thumb over my lower lip. He pulls down on my lip as the fingers press inside with Noah's cock, stretching me.

My tongue touches the tip of his thumb before he presses it into my mouth. I close my lips around it and suck. Noah's cock twitches inside me. The fingers work around his cock, spreading lube and opening me up. They press against my walls.

"I love how you suck, kitten." Noah pumps his hips. "I can't wait until my night with you. I want to tie you up and keep edging you until you finally burst. But I'm not withholding tonight. Tonight, I want you to shatter until you feel like you can't come any more. And then we'll ruin you."

I whimper as he winds me up. Flicking my tongue over his thumb, I bite down lightly. His dark eyes flare with heat and he thrusts into me harder. Arching against him, I shatter, releasing his thumb as I cry out.

He pulls out without coming and moves away. Sliding into his place, Blake kisses me, taking my lips with his. Hands flow over my body, making me tremble. It's almost too much. I'm lifted against Blake's body, our mouths still locked in a hungry kiss. His hard cock presses against my stomach and I ache with need for him.

He lays me on a straight bench and kisses down my body. Sliding my negligee out of the way, he latches onto my breast. A moan rises within me.

Coop claims my lips, teasing and tasting. No longer at war with me, but tempting me. Blake's mouth keeps traveling down my stomach before he spreads my thighs wide.

As his tongue flicks my clit, Coop kisses a trail down my neck to my other breast before closing over the nipple and drawing on it. It's getting hard to focus on what they do as everything just pushes me back toward the edge again. Blake closes his mouth over my clit and sucks as Noah takes over kissing my lips.

I'm drowning in a sea of sensation. Hands join lips in tormenting my writhing body. My breathing is ragged. My heart races. I can't distinguish one from the other as they all work me up until I explode. They don't let me come down as they taste and tease my overwrought body.

My mind slips a little, becoming a slave to the desire, to the need to come. I fall apart beneath their tongues, fingers, and caresses. I cry out and slowly they move away, leaving me.

I'm left a harshly breathing mess on the bench. My pussy flutters. My heart feels like I've run a race.

Then he's there. Those blue eyes so intricate with flecks of gold and silver stirring in their depths. He draws me onto his lap. Our skin sizzles as it touches, and I rub my body against his, craving more. More touch. More pleasure.

"Seth," I breathe out and my fingertips trace over his soft lips.

"Madison, check in, princess." His hands touch me, but not where I want them. I lean in and press my lips against his. When I open my mouth, but he doesn't. My lips trail to his jaw, kissing, sucking, licking.

His neck, fuck, his neck is perfection. Firm muscles and his pulse beneath my lips.

I crave his touch, need it to survive. "Why aren't you touching me?"

"Princess, I know you feel good, but focus. If you want us, we're yours. But if you want to continue the night like we planned, you need to feel us." Seth's words penetrate to some small part of me that knows I'm tipping into subspace, or something like it.

Part of me doesn't care, but the main part of me doesn't want to leave the play room. I want to stay. I want them all inside me. Together.

I'm ready.

Chapter 100

Benchmarking

Seth

"I'm here." Madison settles on my lap. Her hands cup my face as she focuses those beautiful blue eyes on mine.

I'd still fuck her if she wanted to let go, but tonight is about exploring our limits, and we can't do that if she's not one hundred percent present. She glances down at my hard cock.

"I want all of you inside me," she whispers and presses a kiss to my jaw before kissing down my neck. Her eyes lift to meet mine every few kisses. She lowers to kneel on the floor as she works her lips over my chest. Her hands leaving trails of sparks in their wake.

Her hand slips around my cock, her mouth hovering over the tip. She looks up at me, wetting her lips. Precum leaks out of my cock. "I want to make you all come for me."

Fuck, I want that too, but I need to hold off, show control.

Her mouth covers me as she licks around the head of my cock, gathering the precum along the slit before she sucks. My fingers dig into her hair as I keep her eyes on me.

"Blake, work her pussy."

She moans at my command before taking me deeper inside her

mouth. Blake kneels behind her and lifts her hips. Coop captures my attention as he lubes up a butt plug. I nod to Blake, and he slowly eases his cock into her wet cunt. She moans around my cock, sending vibrations through me.

I wrap my hand around her braid, knowing if I let her, she'll get me off, and that's not what we want. She sucks but relaxes into my hold.

"How does she feel?" I meet Blake's eyes. He's buried in her but hasn't actually fucked her yet.

"Tight, hot, wet." He draws his cock out slowly before thrusting back into her. "So fucking good."

She moans again, and I raise her head before lowering it until my cock is in her throat. Her throat clutches my tip, but she's still breathing through her nose.

"Good girl."

She gives a little noise in acknowledgment.

Coop kneels next to Madison and rubs lube over her ass, dipping his fingers into her puckered hole. When she whimpers at the feel, my cock twitches.

Needing a moment to gain control, I lift her so I can meet her eyes and watch her take both Blake and the toy. "Color?"

"Green." She licks her lips. Her eyes widen as Coop presses the tip of the plug to her ass and steadily eases it inside. Her fingers dig into my thighs as her lips part on a moan.

"You like that, my little whore?" Coop draws it out before pressing it deep again. "You like being opened up for all these cocks?"

"Yes," she breathes out. Her pupils are blown, making her normally light eyes dark. "More please."

Noah kneels on her other side. His fingers glide over her clit, and she lets out a harsh breath. "Good, kitten?"

"Mm-hmm." Her eyes close as she focuses on the sensation.

When Noah slides a finger in with Blake's cock, her lips part and her hips roll, trying to fuck herself on everything currently in her body. But no one moves—I haven't told them to yet.

I want to make sure she's present. "What are you thinking, princess?"

"Fuck," she whispers but opens her eyes. She searches mine for a moment. "That I want you all to fuck me. I want Noah to press on my G-spot while Blake fucks my pussy. I want Coop to thrust that plug in time with Blake's strokes. And I want to suck your cock until we all explode."

Need rages through me, but it won't control me. I capture her chin with my hand and stroke my thumb over her lips. She opens and licks my thumb as I press it into her mouth. She sucks and moans around it.

"I can't give you everything you want, princess."

She whimpers and her needy eyes meet mine.

"We'll make you explode, but we're not going to until we're all so deep inside you, you forget everything except the feel of our cocks stretching you, filling you. You'll feel empty when we aren't in you." I nod to Noah and he slides another finger inside her. When her lips part and a moan fills the room, I know he's hooked his fingers to press against her G-spot.

"You ready?" I search her eyes.

"Green, so fucking green." She gives me this look. "I'm not going anywhere. I want you to ruin me."

My cock throbs, aching for release. To do what she asks. To ruin her with our cocks. She's present and willing, not strung out on desire. I tighten my hand in her hair and bring her lips back to my cock. Coop and Blake draw out as one. We hover there for a few seconds before we all thrust inside her.

She trembles and moans as we slowly fuck in and out of her, wringing every ounce of pleasure from her body. It doesn't take long before she shatters around us, but we keep up our slow torment. My balls ache with the need to come, as I'm sure Blake's do, but we're not coming yet.

When she screams her next orgasm around my cock, I draw her off, and Blake withdraws. After giving her another climax that has her panting and resting her cheek against my thigh, Noah pulls his fingers out.

Coop removes the toy. She trembles and whimpers against my skin. Smoothing my hand over her hair, I feel something so tight in my chest. I want to hold her and fuck her. I want to show her what she means to me, over and over again.

Blake gathers her against him and sits on the floor with her in his lap. She leans her head against his chest, and his hand slowly teases her clit, keeping her wound tight. "Color, tiger?"

***

Madison

"Green." Meeting each of their gazes to assure them I'm here and present, I lick my lips. Their cocks all weep for me, want me, and fuck, do I want them. I love what they do to me. "I'm ready."

My body still pulses with aftershocks. I want to take them all. Need to take them all.

Coop and Noah lie back on the curves of the bench across from each other, face to face. They position their cocks against each other's, and a shiver races through me.

I've felt them rubbing against each other inside me, but it's another thing to see their cocks pressed together. For me. A wave of lust hits me hard, making my pussy pulse against Blake's fingers.

"You like that, tiger?" Blake says quietly in my ear. "You like watching them get ready for you?"

"Yes."

Chuckling, Blake grabs a bottle of lube and puts some in his hand. Noah and Coop recline on the bench with their two cocks together. Unable to resist, I crawl out of Blake's lap and kneel to the side of the bench.

"What do you think, kitten?" Noah's dark eyes hold mine as my breath catches in my throat. I want them inside me, filling me, stretching me. Making me ache with how thick they are together.

"I think you're all mine." I take hold of their cocks and bring them together before lowering my mouth to kiss both tips. It looks like too much, but I open my mouth, wrap it around both of their cocks, and suck.

"Fuck, sweetheart. You're going to make me blow." Coop lets out a harsh breath, and it makes me suck a little harder. I love challenging Coop, making him lose control.

"That's fucking hot." Blake's lubed fingers thrust into my pussy.

I moan as he gets me even wetter and prepares me to take them. He scissors his fingers inside me until I throb with need. He adds more fingers until the stretch aches. My mouth hurts a little from how wide their cocks make it, but I don't want to stop.

The feel of them in my mouth and Blake's fingers push me over the edge. Moaning on Coop's and Noah's cocks, I come.

"It's time."

I lift off their cocks to meet Seth's gaze. His cock glistens with lube as he strokes his hand over it. My pussy clenches thinking of what we're about to do. A little tingle of fear works its way through me. What if I'm not able to take them all? What if it hurts too much and I have to call a stop to it? I don't want this to stop.

"If it doesn't work this time, we can always try again." Noah's dark eyes reassure me. I love how he can almost read my mind. My heart pounds a little harder. But fuck, I want this to work.

Seth holds out his hand. I take it and stand, biting my lip.

"How do I . . . ?"

"Face me." Coop summons me forward with his finger. "You'll take us both at the same time."

My legs tremble and nerves race through me. What if I can't take them both? I've done it before, but they felt so much bigger in my mouth. My wetness runs down my thigh at the memory of both their cocks inside my pussy. And this time I'll be taking Seth and Blake too.

I swallow down my fear.

Holding Coop's hand, I swing my leg over them to straddle the bench. Noah grabs my hips, guiding me as I lower myself. Coop holds both their cocks steady. It blows my mind how comfortable these two guys are with each other.

Their cocks touch my entrance. Blake's fingers are there as he stands next to me, helping to open me up.

"Look at me, my little whore." Coop's voice draws my gaze. His light blue eyes smile, a hint of a challenge in them. "You wanted to get me off first. Now's your chance. Because I promise when your tight little cunt wraps around mine and Noah's cocks, I'm going to lose my fucking mind."

I bite my lip and lower, taking them both into me slowly. Every inch stretches me and fills me like I've never been filled before. Blake's fingers move to my clit, circling it slowly, teasing me.

"You're such a good slut, taking all that cock." Coop's fingers trail up my stomach before cupping my breasts and rubbing my nipples.

I moan and lower down as they work to key me up. Noah's finger slips into my asshole, and I can't stop myself from coming. I take them the rest of the way inside me as I keen my release.

"That's it. Good girl." Blake massages my clit through the orgasm.

My breath tears in and out of my lungs. My legs tremble, but I'm not coming down from the high of the orgasm. I'm still so full, so needy.

"More," I whimper. "Please, Seth."

Fuck I need them all.

Noah's fingers leave my ass. Seth's heat covers my back, and he presses me slightly toward Coop. I rest my hands on Coop's chest.

"You feel amazing, sweetheart." Coop clenches his jaw. "I hope you don't think less of me when I don't last much longer."

I would laugh, but Seth's cock pushes against my asshole. I gasp as he slips through the outer ring and presses steadily inside. My mouth opens, but no sound comes out as he fills me so fucking full.

"Fuck. Fuck. Fuck." Coop squeezes his eyes shut and his hands fist against his thighs.

"She's so tight," Noah says. "Better hurry, Blake, or this is going to be over before it begins."

Blake's hand wraps around my braid and he gently tips my face toward him. "Are you good to go, tiger?"

"Green. Yes," I groan as Seth is fully inside me with the other two. I meet Blake's darkened green eyes. His gaze goes to where I'm stuffed full. "Fuck my mouth."

He grins. "I can't wait to watch this video while my cock is buried in your cunt."

My pussy pulses around the guys and they all groan. Blake grips my hair, and I part my lips to take his cock into my mouth.

Holding my hips, Seth lifts me gently before I sink down onto Noah's and Coop's cocks. The friction is amazing. I moan around Blake's cock. My fingers tighten against Coop's chest.

Blake thrusts deeper into my throat and tears flow out of my eyes as I choke on his thick cock while Seth pumps a little in my ass. It's a slow, deliberate fuck as we all work to move while pressed so close together. Coop's and Noah's cocks in my pussy make me shudder as they both thrust as much as they're able, taking turns, rubbing against each other and my walls.

I love that they're willing to do this for me. For our pleasure. I love them all.

I open my eyes, losing myself in Blake's heavy gaze.

Coop groans. "Fuck!"

His cum fills my pussy. Every pulse of his cock ripples through my walls, setting off my climax. It rips through me, making my whole body shudder. The need to scream fills me as the orgasm clings to me, lifting me higher and darkening my vision, but I want to get Blake off.

Focusing, I suck hard on his cock, hollowing out my cheeks. Noah curses, and his cock twitches deep inside of me as he fills me while my pussy convulses around them both.

Seth continues to fuck my tight ass. He groans and his warm cum shoots deep inside.

I can feel every twitch, every jerk of their cocks. It's pushing me so much higher, keeping me on that edge.

Blake thrusts deep and comes down my throat. I swallow around him. He withdraws and cradles my jaw, holding my gaze. I'm lost in how much tenderness is in his eyes.

Coop's fingers rub on my swollen clit. I can't get away from the overstimulation. I shatter, clenching and convulsing around the cocks still buried inside me. For a moment, blackness fills my vision as the sensations overwhelm me. My head hangs over Coop's chest.

My men surround me. All working for my pleasure. All taking care of me. All enjoying me. And my heart swells, too big for my chest. I love them so much it's bursting.

Words thicken in my throat, refusing to be swallowed back. As an aftershock rips through me, I blurt out, "I love you."

Chapter 101

Key Takeaways

Coop

Madison's panicked blue eyes lift to meet mine. I cup her cheek and let the words no woman has ever said to me sink in. My chest fills like a balloon. Her fingers dig into my muscles. Everyone heard her, but no one makes a comment.

Does she mean all of us? Just this sex act? Only one of us? She *is* looking at me.

"We must have fucked her brain loose." I try to defuse the situation before it becomes a thing. "I love your tight pussy, too, sweetheart."

Relief fills her eyes. That warm, full feeling in my chest shrivels a little. She didn't mean it. Just caught up in the moment. Fuck.

Seth tips her head to the side and kisses her cheek. "You did beautifully, princess."

He's standing over Noah's waist with his cock buried in her ass while we remain inside her. Things are softening as Seth pulls out. She gasps and bites her lip.

How sore will she be after this?

Blake helps her stand, leaving me and Noah with a sticky mess.

"I think I prefer the other way to be inside her together." I catch the towel Seth throws my way and clean up as best I can.

"Sorry," Madison says with a blush on her cheeks.

"Never apologize for a good session, princess." Seth closes in on her and tips her chin up before taking her mouth.

She sways into him. Maybe she meant the L-word, but I refuse to believe it's me she loves. Noah. Seth. Even Blake. They all make sense, but me? I'm a selfish bastard who no one truly loves.

I walk away, unable to watch her make any declarations to the others. Stepping into the bathroom, I turn on the shower and meet my eyes in the mirror. I take a deep breath. She's an opportunity. Useful, beautiful, fragile. Just because I'm getting wrapped up in her doesn't mean she feels the same.

Fingers run up my back, sending sparks through my system and making me shiver. My eyes close slightly, allowing the feel of her to surround me. She wraps her arms around my waist and presses her breasts to my back before resting her cheek on my skin.

"You okay?" Her voice is soft.

I'm tempted to turn and wrap her in my arms. Hold her and let her warmth sink into me until I feel loved by someone. I release the breath I'm holding.

"Shouldn't I be asking you that?" I put my hands over her arms and smile because this woman lets me do whatever I want with her body. She challenges me and makes me want to please her.

She presses her lips to my spine, and my heart climbs into my throat. No other woman before her made me feel like this. I don't know what to do with it. Because they all leave. When they don't get what they want, usually diamonds or power, women leave me.

If I didn't have money, they wouldn't want me for anything more than sex. But Madison is soft and caring, and even though my brain keeps flashing warning signals, my heart is stupid when it comes to her.

She squeezes me against her and walks around me, taking my hand and lifting her blue eyes to mine. "Ready to shower?"

Her smile leads me into the water until it covers both of us.

"Are you sore?" The words are rough coming out of my mouth.

"A little, but . . ." She looks up at me through her lashes. Innocence and sin wrapped together.

Fuck, this woman gets to me on every level. She soaps her hands and rubs them all over my body. Her curves press into me as she reaches for certain spots, even when it's unnecessary, brushing her skin against mine. My hard cock throbs with need.

Stroking her soapy hand over my cock, she leans in and kisses my chest. When she reaches my nipple, she sucks on it, making me ache for her even more.

I step into the water and she follows me, refusing to release my cock or break contact with my chest. When all traces of soap are gone, I lift her and press her against the wall of the shower.

Lifting her legs, splaying her out before me, I thrust deep inside her. Her face is flushed. Her lips red and parted. She wraps her legs around my waist and her arms around my neck. This is all I am to her: a needy cock.

"You first this time," I say and lean into her and claim her mouth, plundering it with an intensity she matches. I fuck her hard and fast. My hips pumping my cock in and out of her probably sore cunt, but she doesn't seem to care as her nails score my shoulders and her moans echo in the bathroom.

I want to claim every inch of her, make her know that what I feel has become more than casual. That what I feel for her has never been casual. I'm obsessed with her body, her mind, her heart, her soul. I want it all.

Even though she would be stupid to give it to me, I want it.

And I'm the type of greedy bastard who would take her heart without deserving it.

She shakes against me as she shatters. Her ravenous cunt clutching at my cock. I slow my pace and gentle my kiss, showing her that there's more to me than a fantastic cock. She sighs and clings to me as I fuck her, getting as close to making love as I can.

When I release her mouth, I press my forehead to hers. "Look at me, baby. Let me see those eyes when you come."

Her eyes open, and it's like seeing sunlight after living in the dark for so long. Blinding, disorienting. Never before have I seen the emotion filling her eyes when she looks at me, but I don't shy away from it.

"Coop." Her fingers tangle in my hair.

"Give it to me, baby. One more time. Come for me. Come with me." The desperation in my voice almost makes me wince, but I can't hide from this woman.

"Coop," she cries out as she comes again, drawing me into my release.

I collapse against her on the wall as I fill her. Our bodies pressed tight like they were built to fit together. She kisses my cheek and along my jaw until she pushes her way to my mouth.

She claims my mouth like she's claiming my heart. Aftershocks ripple through her pussy around my cock, making me groan. I meet her with the same intense intimacy, like we're the only two people in the world.

It won't last.

Her heart will never belong to just me. But if I have to share it with someone, sharing it with the men who are like brothers to me wouldn't be a hardship. Even if they deserve it more than me, I'd take whatever part she chose to give me.

If she gives her heart to us at all.

Noah

I don't follow Madison into the bathroom. I want to. I want to tell her how I feel, but I don't know what her words really meant. All of us seem confused, but I know Coop, and he's never been loved before. So when she went after him, I let her go, knowing right now he needs her the most.

The others must have felt it too because we all go to our own showers to clean up. What we just did with Madison we've never done with anyone else. Never wanted to do with another woman. It was intimate with her, with my friends. More so than anything else we've done together. The warm water of the shower runs over my face, and I swipe it off.

Fuck. This isn't the way it's supposed to go. It's an arrangement, a contract, for fuck's sake. Not a relationship with feelings complicating it.

My hair falls over my eyes as I press my hands to the shower wall and let the water pour over me. I've known I love her and want to keep her for a while now. I don't know how the others feel, but I'm ready.

Ready to admit to the world that what I want is the same as my friends. I want to share her with them and keep her for myself at the same time. She's not just a fuck and never has been to me. But that may be all she is to the others.

We haven't discussed it. It's never been an issue before. We haven't talked about how this might work if we decide to take it to the next level. If we don't let her go when she moves on to the next big thing in her life. How we could continue to be by her side. How that would work as a relationship.

"Fuck." I smack my hand against the tile.

I get where Seth and Blake are coming from. The Andrea stuff hit all of us hard. I never trusted the bitch, and she didn't like me, but the rumors she spread still haunt us. And Rachel? Personally, I would have fucked her for relief and that's about it. Neither of them stirred anything in me.

But Madison . . .

She's like air. Something essential I need in my life but didn't realize I couldn't live without. I want quiet time on the couch with her. I want her sleeping in my arms.

Playing fucked-up games with Coop. Taking Seth's direction.

Fucking her into oblivion with Blake. We're all a part of the puzzle, and without any one piece, we'd fall apart.

Even when our arrangement ends, when we're done with her or she's done with us, I couldn't just date her and keep my friendship with the guys. I'd have to choose. And right now, I'm not sure I could.

The door to my shower opens and closes. I know it's her. My eyes are closed, but I can feel her slide up behind me. Her arms wrap around my center, and she presses her cheek to my back.

"What do you need?" she asks softly.

I'm not like the others. I can't bottle up my emotions for the sake of propriety.

"Did you mean it?" I open my eyes and see her painted toenails peeking between my feet.

"Noah—" Her tone tells me she's going to back away from it.

I turn, take her hands, and press her against the tile wall. Her blue eyes widen, but she doesn't drop her gaze from mine. "No, Madison. Don't give me a bullshit answer. You and I were never that. We're real and raw. Don't make us into some cardboard cutout of a relationship."

She presses her lips together, and then opens them and closes them like she can't figure out what to say.

"I know you didn't mean to say it then." The urge to close in on her, press my body against hers, is strong. "But those words mean something. Maybe you meant you loved our cocks, but you said *I love you*."

She bites her lip as she looks up at me. Her eyes beg me not to press.

"Fuck." I rub my thumb over her wrist and meet her frightened blue eyes. She's not scared of me though. She's afraid of what she feels.

Fuck, I'm scared too.

I drop my forehead against hers. "I love you, kitten. You don't have to say it back to me or even tell me you feel the same—"

Her lips cut me off, kissing me.

"I love you, Noah." The words are a breath against my lips, but I'll take them.

Pressing against her, I nudge her legs open with my knee. "I love you, Madison."

I claim her mouth, falling into a kiss that fills my heart with such happiness. I lower myself down so our chests are aligned. Heart to heart.

Maybe I should have let her hide like Coop would. Maybe I shouldn't have been the first to confess my feelings and wait like Blake would. Or maybe I'd be like Seth and ignore her outburst as part of her orgasmic bliss.

But not me. I know Madison. She wouldn't say it if she didn't feel it. And she didn't say it to any one of us. She said it to all of us.

She makes soft, needy noises into our kiss. I release her hands, and they dive into my hair as I lift her legs and thrust deep inside her, needing to be one with her. To feel her pulse around me.

I abandon her mouth as I fuck her, kissing down her jaw and onto her neck. I kiss and suck and bite her beautiful bare neck, marking her as mine while my cock takes what's mine.

"I love you. I love you." She keeps saying it over and over like it's a prayer.

I slow my thrusts and lean into her, taking her slowly as I lift my head to press our foreheads together. "I love you, and nothing that happens will change that, kitten. No matter what, I will always love you."

Her blue eyes widen as she shatters all around me. "Noah!"

I capture her mouth and feel her come all over my cock before I finish inside her, filling her with my essence, marking her as mine forever.

She can hide from the others, but she can't hide from me. She's mine.

Chapter 102

Giving 110%

Blake

Joining us in her bedroom, Noah carries Madison in with her legs wrapped around his waist. Seth, Coop, and I have been silently waiting for them. Her hands are in his wet hair, and their heads are locked together. He has on a pair of boxers and she wears his shirt. I glimpse lace panties under the shirt's hem.

"Good shower, tiger?"

Unlike the other two, who pace like actual tigers, I sit on the edge of the bed. All of us have on boxers, figuring the night's playtime is over.

Noah stops and Madison dives at me. I catch her as she knocks me onto my back on the bed. She's warm and soft. Noah helps keep her steady as she straddles my hips. My cock, which was semihard when she arrived, leaps to attention between her legs.

Her eyes widen and she smiles this smug little smile, knowing she's the reason I'm hard. Fuck, she's always the reason I'm hard these days. I spank her bouncy little ass and she pouts.

"What was that for?"

"Just felt like you deserved one." I raise an eyebrow, almost baiting her to pop off so I have an excuse to spank her and play with her little pussy some more.

"It's time for bed," Seth says.

"Our night doesn't have to be over." Madison rubs her pussy against the ridge of my cock. Her eyes find the boss standing in the corner and she smiles at him, giving him a look even a fool wouldn't turn down.

Seth leans against the wall and crosses his arms. "You should rest, especially since you had two showers already."

By "two showers," he's saying what we all know. She fucked both Coop and Noah again.

"Fine." She turns her hungry eyes back to me. "You don't have to play, Seth." She rubs her pussy over my cock through our underwear. "But I'm not tired. Neither is Blake. Are you?"

"Not particularly." My fingers trail up her thigh and pull her panties to the side. Her gaze follows my fingers. I press them into her pussy to gather some of her wetness before rubbing her clit. She bites her lip as she watches. Her hands ease my boxers down until she can pull out my cock to stroke me.

Noah lies beside me on the bed, watching her. He's so far gone for Madison. I'd call him a fool for falling in love with her, but I can't say I don't feel the same. Those words on her lips made something inside me lift. It was the heat of the moment though, so I don't trust those words as the truth. But it may mean there's more to us than we considered before.

She lifts her hips and positions my cock at her entrance. Our eyes meet as she sinks down onto me, moaning as she fills herself with my cock. Her hips roll on me. No hurry. No rush to get to the end. Just slow and steady.

Coop walks up behind her and lifts her shirt off over her head. "That's better."

He lies on my other side as she chases her pleasure on my cock.

Her breasts bounce with every roll of her hips. Her blond hair flows down her back. She presses her hands against my chest to ride me. She's beautiful to watch.

They both already had her in their showers. It makes sense why she went to them and not me or Seth.

Of our quartet, those two are the dreamers. Yes, they're the most logical and their jobs follow, but they need this to be more. Coop's whole life has been dictated by his wealth and family. Noah always found it hard to fit in.

Even I want this to be more. Each day with Madison makes that more obvious, but I'm not sure how we work this so it's more for all of us.

And then there's Seth. Women have burned him and he's not as trusting, not as open to a relationship. Neither of us are, but Madison . . .

She turns to look at Seth. His cock is in his hand, stroking slowly. She bites her lip and moans a little as I thrust up into her.

"Please, boss." She holds her hand out to him and clutches her fingers, beckoning him forward.

Unable to resist her, he sheds his boxers and grabs the lube on the nightstand. He coats his cock as he walks to us and tosses the lube on the bed next to Noah. His eyes meet mine.

We've been best friends for a long time, and I know he's about to do something different. I just don't know what that *different* is going to be.

He stands between my knees and grabs a handful of Madison's panties, then tugs hard enough to rip them off. She gasps almost in indignation, but her cunt drenches me. She likes it when we play rough. He pushes her down on my chest.

I startle when his fingers stroke my cock with lube inside her. Ah, fuck. Yup, this is new and different.

Madison's eyes widen as she feels what he's doing. Then his tip presses against my cock and he pushes into her tight cunt with me. I groan at the combined stimulation of his cock brushing mine and her tightening around me. She moans as she takes both of us. The press of his hot flesh against mine inside her tight little cunt almost makes me blow.

When he's all the way in, we all take in a breath.

Madison buries her face in my shoulder and bites down. "So fucking full."

Both Coop and Noah sit up to watch her take both of us. I continue to rub her clit, but she's already exploding, pulsing hard on our cocks. Moaning like a porn star.

"Fuck." Seth pulls out a little and presses back in, slowly building up a rhythm. I stroke my other hand down her back as she shudders between us. On his next thrust, I pull out a little with him and thrust back in.

Then we're fucking her together. In and out. Over and over, as she cries out and bites me with every thrust. I don't give a fuck if I'm covered in bite marks. This feels completely foreign and so fucking good.

"Oh fuck, oh fuck, oh fuck," Madison chants as we pick up our pace. She screams as she comes all over our cocks, drenching me in her cum.

That's game over. My balls tighten and my cock jerks as it fills her with my cum. Seth's cock jerks against mine as he groans his release.

They both collapse in a heap on top of me. The weight is almost too much, but I can't even move yet.

"Fuck, that is hot to watch." Coop lies back next to me. "Feels weird having another cock in there with you, doesn't it?"

He bats his eyelashes at me. I put my hand on his face and push him away.

Seth stands and pulls out. He rubs a hand on Madison's back. "Good girl."

Her pussy twitches on my cock as she stays immobile. "I don't think I can move anymore."

We all chuckle. I roll to Noah's side with her, and her gaze falls on my chest.

"It looks like I tried to eat you." She kisses each bite mark. "I'm sorry."

"I'm not." I pull out and stand, dropping my boxers on the floor before heading into the bathroom. The mirror shows all the little dents her teeth left as I clean up with a washcloth. I've never felt prouder to bear her marks.

"You were okay with that. Yeah?" Seth asks as he wets his own washcloth to clean his dick.

"I would have told you if I wasn't." I shrug and drop the washcloth on the rack before grabbing another and wetting it down to take care of our girl.

"It was weird, right?"

I laugh at the look on Seth's face. Glancing over my shoulder through the door into the bedroom, I see the other three still lying there. Their words are too low to hear.

"It's different than feeling each other through her body, yes. But it was good." I shrug and glance back into the room where Madison is. "It's tighter, and I couldn't move as much, but yeah, a little weird feeling your cock with mine."

Seth nods. "She's something special."

"We knew that in the interview." Fuck, I knew that on the phone with her. She's bright and intelligent, but there's a softness that tugs at me deep inside.

Seth grunts and we head back to the bedroom. Madison is almost asleep in Noah's arms. Coop notices me and parts her legs so I can clean her.

She blinks up at me. "Thank you."

She curls back into Noah and releases a sigh before falling asleep.

We aren't talking about the elephant in the room. I'm not sure we ever will. She said *I love you*. This is more than we bargained for. More than we prepared for.

Sure, she took it back, but at some point we'll need to discuss this.

Either the four of us or us with Madison, but it will need to happen. Seth gives me a look, and I know he's thinking the same thing.

But the problem is, I don't know what the answer is. Or if there even is an answer to this situation. Is there a way for us to be together and not destroy our business and her future?

Seth

I can't sleep. I'm on the edge of the bed, so I get up. Not sure what to do now. Madison's confession of love plays on repeat in my brain, keeping me awake. It was just a momentary lapse of judgment as she came so fucking hard around us.

Even things spilled in the heat of passion can have some truth to them. It's possible she's falling in love with us. The way it seems all of us are falling for her.

The question of where we go from here plagues me though. It pricks at my consciousness every time I close my eyes. What can we have after this?

She's our employee. Yes, having sex with her could create complications, but being in love is a whole other story. We could have sex and not get emotionally invested. We've done it before. It's never been an issue since we started fucking women together.

But Madison deserves more. Fuck, I knew it when we proposed this idea to her. It's complicated and every minute with her makes it harder to untangle. Could we go public with a relationship like this?

Maybe.

I walk to the bathroom and close the door before turning on one of the dim lights. As I get a glass of water from the sink, my eyes stray to the bench where Madison fucked me earlier. Fuck, I feel something deep for her.

I'm not sure I can admit it's love, even to myself.

The door opens and Madison stumbles in. There's blood running down the inside of her thigh. My heart lurches as I rush over to her. Groaning, she doubles over holding her stomach.

"Fuck." I hold her arm as I get her to the toilet. "Did we hurt you?"

"Cramps." Her pain-filled eyes lift to mine, but she gives me a weary smile. "It's my period. I thought I might have another day."

She groans and clutches her stomach. Okay, menstrual cycle. So much better than the alternative, that we hurt her. That I hurt her. My heart pounds as I straighten. Taking a deep breath, I get myself under control.

"What do you need?" I run a hand over my hair.

"Panties, and there's a box of pads and tampons under the sink."

"What else, princess? Pain relievers, heating pad?"

Her blue eyes lift to mine again, and she smiles appreciatively. "Yes, to both."

With my mission in mind, I go around collecting what she needs. When I return, she's cleaned up her thigh. I hand her the cotton panties and an overnight pad.

She takes them a little self-consciously. Stepping out of the water closet, I leave the door open a crack.

"Do we need to change the sheets? Or we could all move to another bed?" My brain gets to work on the logistics and where we could all fit. My hands clench the t-shirt I'm still holding for her.

"No. The cramping woke me up." The door muffles her voice slightly. She opens it and glances up at me. "The bed should be fine."

I hand her the t-shirt and then help her put it on. It's Noah's from earlier. It hangs halfway down her thighs.

"Do you always have bad cramps?" I follow her to the sink and stand behind her as she washes her hands. If what we did injured her somehow . . . Fuck, I didn't think. I just wanted to be inside her cunt, to feel her tight around me, to make her scream as she came.

Her eyes meet mine warily. "Sometimes."

I hand her a towel. When she finishes drying her hands, I hold out two pain relievers and a glass of water. She takes them and sets the water to the side.

"I hooked up the heating pad. It's on the bed waiting for you."

She steps forward and wraps her arms around my waist as her head rests on my chest. "Thank you for taking care of me."

Hugging her tight, I press my nose into her soft hair, drawing in her scent. "Whatever you need."

And I mean that. Whatever she needs. I'm willing to do anything, even if it blows up in my face.

Chapter 103

Personal Day

Madison

I wake with a hard cock grinding against my ass. For a moment, desire flows through me and the memories of last night make me want to roll over and take that cock into me any way I can.

My abdominal muscles tighten painfully. Groaning, I curl around the heating pad pressed there. It must have shut off. Sliding my fingers along the cord, I find the switch and turn it back on.

"Are you okay, sweetheart?" Coop's voice is soft as his hand strokes down my back. "Did we hurt you last night?"

The concern in his voice fills me with love. These guys. "No, just normal, kill-me-now menstrual cramps."

"Fuck. I'm sorry, sweetheart. What do you need?" he whispers against my ear.

My cramps wrap around my back like a vise. "Could you rub my lower back, please?"

His large hands land on the tops of my hips. His thumbs dig into the tight muscles, and I moan as they release a little. I open my eyes. No one else is awake yet.

"You need anything else, sweetheart?" His low whispers curl

through me, and I wish I could turn and do all the dirty things my mind can come up with to him, with him, for him.

But holy crap balls, my insides feel like they're in a trash compactor filled with glass.

"Some ibuprofen?" A new uterus to replace the one currently being destroyed?

Coop shifts slightly and I hear a dark grunt.

"Watch your elbow." Blake's gruff voice disturbs the silence around us.

"Girl's got cramps. Be a hero and grab her some meds." Coop continues to work his magic on my lower back. The bed shifts a little.

Blake sits up and runs a hand over his dark hair. His sleepy gaze meets mine and softens. "Yeah. I've got you, tiger."

He slips off the bed and out of the room. Coop kisses the nape of my neck.

"You know what relieves cramps, sweetheart." His voice is dark and dangerous. If he says sex, I might hurt him. "A nice hot shower followed by a soak in the bath."

Not where I thought he was going. But it sounds heavenly. Blake returns and sits on the edge of the bed, holding pills and a glass of water. Coop helps me up.

"Watch our girl. I'm going to get the tub ready." Coop walks to the bathroom before I can protest. I really just want to wallow in misery, but the cramps are definitely worse this time. Not to mention, I'm sore from last night.

I loved every minute, but damn, I definitely need a minibreak. My gaze falls on Seth. If he wants to play therapist again, I'm game. A shiver rushes through me, remembering the heat and the cold.

I move to sit beside Blake. Our shoulders and thighs brush. He hands me the pills and glass.

"Thank you." I glance over my shoulder at Noah and Seth. They're still sleeping. I swallow the pills and sigh. No more playtime for a few days, probably. Definitely not until these cramps go away.

"What else do you need, love?" Blake rubs my back a little.

I arch into his touch when he rubs my low back. "Oh, right there."

He chuckles and focuses his attention in the absolutely perfect spot.

"I've never been with someone when I've had my period." My voice is soft so as not to wake Noah or Seth. The bath filling is the only other sound. "I've always just taken care of myself."

"You've got us now." Blake's voice is low as he nods toward the bathroom. "That one loves to dote on you especially."

The L-word makes me tense up, but Blake continues to work my muscles until they're loose again. He said it like that word isn't a big deal. It slipped out last night. I couldn't seem to help myself. It's way too soon. They must think I'm crazy. I'm not supposed to fall in love with them.

But how could I not? The way they take care of me. The way they pleasure me. The way they support me.

I'm afraid it will slip out more. Like once it left my body, it's just lingering out there. Noah knows, but Noah and I have always had a connection. He wanted my confession. Last night, he needed my confession. And I was helpless against my own need to give it to him.

I'm sure the others suspect it wasn't just a pleasure-induced admission. Will they bring it up? Will they confront me?

Will me loving them mean we need to end things? Stop fucking before it goes too far?

My heart aches. And I feel a little weepy, but that's probably the PMS talking.

Coop walks out of the bathroom, and whatever he sees on my face makes him hesitate for just a second before stalking toward me and dragging me into his arms. Our eyes lock. His light blue eyes fill with something that makes my insides sing. He lifts me off my feet, making me squeal softly, and carries me into the bathroom.

Blake closes the door behind us. "Let us take care of you, love."

Fuck, that word. He's called me that before, but now it feels like more. Blake closes in behind me. I want their hands on me, but I need to take care of something first.

"Just a minute." I shuffle out from between them.

Closing myself in the water closet, I take a deep breath. Their kindness will make me admit I love them even more. I'm not used to this level of caring. I switch to a tampon and clean up. Taking a deep breath, I rein in my heart and head back out to the guys.

Naked and aroused, Coop gets in my space, making my breath catch. It would be easier if I wanted them less. But even in pain, I want him. He lifts my t-shirt off and leads me into the shower. Blake follows us in.

"Um, there might still be—"

Coop presses a finger to my lips. "You're good, sweetheart. We're just here to help you clean. Every inch. Before your bath."

Through the fogged glass of the shower, I see the steaming bathtub, layers of bubbles floating on the surface. An herbal scent lingers in the air. Excitement races up my spine. I haven't taken a bath in years. My apartment didn't really have a tub that was usable, even if I could've found the time.

The bathtub itself is beautiful, but I haven't indulged. Yet.

Coop grabs my sponge and soap, while Blake takes my shampoo. Before long, I'm covered in bubbles. My insides are warm, and the shower isn't the only thing wet. When Coop kneels before me to wash my legs, I bite my lip and hold my breath.

He lifts his blue eyes to mine and smirks. "My good little whore, always ready for more than you can take."

I put my finger under his chin and stare down into his eyes. "Make sure to clean every inch."

He leans in and kisses my abdomen. His grin grows as he bends to clean my legs before drawing the sponge up my inner thigh. Blake pulls me back against him as Coop lifts my leg over his shoulder. My breath quickens.

Tossing my sponge to the side, Coop soaps his hands and strokes over my pussy. I bite my lip and tip my head back against Blake's shoulder. Desire flows hot and heavy through me. Every touch winds me tighter. While Coop thoroughly cleans me, Blake rubs my abdomen and lower back.

It's impossible to miss their erections, but neither of them moves to take this to another level. I'm boiling with desire, but everything still hurts. Coop stands and draws me into the shower stream with him.

His mouth finds mine, and we kiss with our slick bodies pressed close together. His hands massage my lower back. Neither of us moves to make it more, and I'm grateful. As much as I want both of them, as much as my body wants them, it's definitely a rest day.

That doesn't mean I can't help them along though.

When I wrap my hand around Coop's cock, he threads his fingers through mine and holds my hand away. "Not today, baby."

Cupping my face, he kisses me softly before turning off the shower. Blake must have left while we were kissing. For a second, I worry, but then Coop rubs a towel over me.

"I'm getting in the tub," I say with an indulgent grin. I love the attention even if it's pointless. "I don't think I need to be dry."

"I always like to do a thorough job." He wraps the towel around me and draws me in for another kiss before groaning and resting his forehead against mine. "You tempt me beyond anything I've ever felt before," he confesses. Inhaling deeply with his eyes closed, he just stays there for a moment.

I breathe him in too. I didn't know if I could love Coop, but it seems my heart is just too damned soft. He turns me in the tub's direction and smacks my bottom.

I drop the towel and step into the warm bathwater. When I sink below the surface, I moan as my muscles loosen. My gaze lifts to Coop's. "You going to join me?"

Smirking, he pulls on a fresh pair of boxers. He strokes his hand over the front of his boxers and his obvious erection. "Not this time. I'd do more harm than good."

Before I can say I don't mind, Blake comes in with an armful of stuff. He sets it down on the counter, and I shift in the water to see better.

"I swear Seth only wants you in skimpy stuff, but I found a drawer way in the back on the bottom with some fuzzy socks and comfy pajamas. Kayla loves comfy stuff when she's not feeling great." Blake's green eyes meet mine. My heart beats hard as it tries to fill my chest and burst out.

I smile at his thoughtfulness. "Thank you."

He shrugs. "Kayla really likes you, by the way. She texted me about you and asked how you're doing. When she's in town in a few weeks, she's going to steal you and Sara and take you both out."

Blake's love for his sister is written all over his face. "I'd like that. I haven't really had friends before."

"Didn't you have friends in college?" Blake sits on the bench.

"Mmm, not really." I drag my fingers through the bubbles on the water's surface. "A few study buddies, but I always had to decline going out. I had too much to do for school, and work to make sure I could pay the bills."

"Hope's coming over today?" Coop draws my attention.

I grin. I can't help it. I have friends. Real friends.

"Yeah. I really like her. It's nice to have someone to talk to besides you guys. As much as I enjoy talking and spending time with all of you, it's different with women."

"I get that." Blake releases a breath. "You definitely have a fan in Kayla. She mentioned how she wants to get secondhand info on how good Coop is in bed."

I laugh. "You have a strange relationship with your sister."

"Do you have any siblings?" Coop leans against the counter with his arms crossed over his chest.

"No. Only child. It would've been nice though." I pop some bubbles with my fingertip. At least then I wouldn't have had to be the perfect one. Something I could never live up to no matter how hard I tried. "My parents really weren't that into having a child. They planned me, of course, but I wasn't their priority. So having a brother or sister would have been nice for the company, but really, we would have been ignored together."

The words pour out of me as I hunt bubble after bubble until the realization of what I just revealed hits me. I cringe. I just said my parents ignored me. That wasn't fair to them. After all, they were busy with work and each other. I was fine.

I glance up and Coop's watching me carefully.

"I'm an only child too." He doesn't grin or smirk. "It can be lonely."

That spark between us lights up. I can tell he gets it. I want to ask if he was ignored too. If he was an afterthought to who his parents were. If they even think to call him when he's away, or if it's like he never existed at all.

"You're going to become a prune." Blake clears his throat and grabs a dry towel, heading my way.

I stand automatically, and he wraps the towel around me. He helps me step out of the tub. When I'm on solid ground, he tips my chin up. His green eyes search mine.

What does he see in them? Can I even hide any part of myself away from him? From any of them? Or am I an open book? Does he realize I love them all from just a glance?

His thumb traces my jaw before he leans down and claims my lips softly. When he lifts his head, that softness remains in his gaze. "Get dressed. I'll make pancakes for breakfast."

Chapter 104

New Business

Madison

SARA:

> OMG! Kayla just texted me what happened
> Friday. Are you okay?

After eating way too much breakfast, Noah and I settled on the couch to snuggle and put on something to watch. I still haven't decided on anything. We've been watching trailers for the past thirty minutes.

It takes me a second to realize what she's talking about. Ah, the assault.

ME:

> I'm fine. The police have him in custody.

The end of Friday night was a shit show, but I never heard the story about the big guy who dragged her off.

ME:

> What happened with the guy you left with?

SARA:

...

The TV draws my attention as a new trailer plays. It seems like an interesting show. Hmm, maybe. But not today.

SARA:

Dante is a friend of my brother and a huge prick.

SARA:

What do you think about a double date this week? You and Coop, me and Noah. We can catch up and Noah won't feel so awkward with you two there.

Yeah, that wouldn't be awkward at all. Noah lifts his head at my attention on him.

"What?" He reaches out and brushes some hair behind my ear.

I bite my lip and glance at my phone. "Sara wants to ask you out on a date."

Noah straightens and his dark eyes hold mine. "It's just to keep her mother off her back. We had an enjoyable time talking, but that's it. You're the only one I want."

"I know," I say softly to reassure him that I know he loves me and only me. Wishing I could say the same to him. But I don't love *just* him. I love all of them. If I had to choose . . .

My throat thickens and my stomach drops at the thought of having to pick. I couldn't do it.

"Hey." He traces my lip with his fingertip. "What's happening in there?"

Inhaling, I let that worry go. Not something I need to think about now. Besides, I can't really keep any of them. Not long-term. "Sorry."

"We're good, kitten." He kisses me softly and not nearly long enough.

"She wants to make it a double date with me and Coop." I hold my breath. Not knowing what his reaction will be.

His laughter, rich and full, fills the room. He laughs like it's the most hysterical thing he's heard. The sound makes my chest feel full.

"What's wrong with him?" Coop walks over and sits on my other side. Seth and Blake glance over at us from the kitchen where they've been cleaning up.

"Sara wants to go on a double date with Noah, you, and me." My gaze keeps bouncing back to Noah.

Coop's dark eyebrow rises. "I'm not averse to adding another—"

When my eyes widen and I pull away from him, he stops and grins. He tugs me back against him.

"I know. You only go for cock. Right? No little fantasies hiding in there?" Coop tips my chin up and studies my face. "Shame. I might like watching you make out with another girl."

My mouth drops open and my brain stalls. What the actual fuck?

Noah collects himself and shakes his head. "Fuck off, Coop. You can go to your room and watch some porn if you want to see that. I'm not sharing Madison with any more people."

Coop shrugs. "You're the one dating another woman."

"I'm not dating her. We're going out to appease our parents and to keep the press from thinking we're all doing exactly what we're actually doing with Madison." Noah's gaze flicks to mine with an apologetic look.

I take his hand and squeeze. I know the deal. We need to get the press to believe what they see is true. I'm engaged to Coop, and the others are all single or dating someone else. Though I'd be proud to have all of these men as mine in real life outside of our apartment.

"We should do it then." Coop draws my back against him and wraps his arm around me possessively. "I should take my fiancée out on dates more often."

I rest my head against his chest. My eyes snag on the ring on my finger. He insisted I wear it today. After all, no one will be getting laid. Not with my cramps. So no eye gouging to worry about.

I release a breath. "Yes, it would definitely make a statement if we all went out together."

And I'd be able to make sure Sara isn't trying to move in on Noah. I trust Noah, but I also know what a catch he is. Sara would be crazy not to fall for him and try to lure him away.

With a sigh, I text her back.

ME:

That sounds great.

SARA:

Can't wait! I'll text Noah now.

Noah's phone buzzes on the coffee table. Coop and I look at him expectantly. Noah sighs and picks up his phone. He types briefly. What did she send him? Did she tell him she had a great time at the benefit? Did she apologize for leaving with another man?

My insides twist a little. He loves me, but he can't have all of me. Will that be a deal-breaker?

When he finishes typing, his phone buzzes and he nods. When he lifts his gaze to mine, his eyes soften. He holds out his phone to me. "Here."

I hesitate for a moment, knowing I should trust him. And I do.

He grabs my hand and puts the phone in it. "You don't need to worry, kitten. I'm yours."

I glance down at the text conversation.

SARA:

Thank you for Friday night. I hoped we could go out again.

SARA:

Thursday dinner? With Madison and Coop.

SARA:

Madison said it was okay.

NOAH:

Thursday sounds good. You got home okay Friday night?

SARA:

Yeah, thanks for understanding. Dante can be very demanding.

NOAH:

Did our ploy work?

SARA:

Dante wasn't the guy I was trying to make jealous, so no. But THE guy will be at the restaurant on Thursday.

NOAH:

Okay, send me the details. We'll be there.

"There's a guy?" I hand the phone back to Noah.

Noah nods. "Otherwise, I wouldn't go out with her again. But being seen with the same woman will help dispel the rumors surrounding us."

Looking over the back of the couch, I meet Seth's gaze. Not all rumors. What if Elizabeth says something? She threatened to say Seth and I are cheating on Coop. Seth is the one who doesn't want the rumors flying around. Which probably means Blake should actually go out on a date with someone other than his sister.

"Have you thought about the deal with Elizabeth, Seth?" I need to know what's going on in his head. She wants to have a relationship with him and will force the issue.

Seth rounds the island and comes over to sit in front of me on the ottoman. My insides flood with warmth, remembering that day when they all took me in front of him before he finally fucked me. The corner of his lip tips up when his eyes meet mine.

"We should discuss this as a group." Seth waits a second for Blake to sit on the couch opposite us. Then he takes a breath. "Elizabeth wants to use me to make her mother happy. It isn't about sex or anything else. She sees me as a way to appear more powerful."

Seth swallows and my insides twist.

"Her mother wanted her to use one of us to get pregnant. She's looking for an heir. A continuation of her line, and she doesn't care who she uses to get it as long as they have the right qualifications."

"Qualifications?" I raise an eyebrow.

"Attractive, intelligent, driven." Seth runs a hand across the back of his neck. "If we let Elizabeth into our lives again, she'll wreak havoc wherever she can. She'll want me to go out with her, to be seen. She'll insist I come in for cocktails and spend time in her house to make anyone watching believe we're more than just acquaintances meeting for dinner."

He searches my eyes, probably to see if I'm strong enough to deal with this. To see if I'll break from the pressure. I don't flinch. He's mine. They all are.

"She wants to push rumors I'm sleeping with you." Seth closes his eyes for a moment before he opens them for me again. "That you're cheating on Coop with me. How can I reward that?"

"What choice do we have?" Coop runs his hand down my arm. "If you aren't willing to come out and say we're all in a relationship, then we have to do damage control where we can."

"If people think Seth is fucking around behind Coop's back"—Blake draws our attention—"Elizabeth will cause just as much or more damage. We'll appear weak, breakable."

"Fuck." Seth drops his gaze to his hands.

Needing to be close to him, I climb off the couch and straddle his lap, cupping his face and raising it to be level with mine. His hands rest on my hips.

"You and I are fine. We're good. You don't want her." The words get tangled in my throat, but I force them out. "You should date her."

He presses his forehead to mine and breathes me in. "She's a snake I don't want to let into our lives."

"She's already here," I whisper. Even after all this time, the dark blue of his eyes fascinates me, captivates me.

"It will hold off the inevitable." Noah strokes a hand down my back and shivers race through me. "And it will also give us time to come up with our next move. We still need to figure out who the mole is in our organization. And if Madison's stalker isn't the professor, someone's still out there."

My hands thread through Seth's soft hair as our gazes remain locked.

"Don't forget the police haven't found Valerie and Jeff," Blake growls. "I hope they've gotten what they deserve in whatever hole they're hiding in."

"Were we going to work on the mole again this afternoon?" Coop leans back on the couch. "Madison's got her play date."

I turn to glare at him, but he gives me a playful smile. I sigh.

"When is it going to be okay for me to leave here?" I return my attention to Seth. "It was nice to get out on Friday, even with Tim watching over me. I can't live in this building all the time. I need to get out and be with my friends. Maybe go to Hope's brother's bar. Or have lunch with people other than you guys."

So many things I want to do. I love these men. Blake has on a fierce expression like he's never going to let me go out again. Coop smirks at me like he knows the others will say no so he doesn't have to. Noah's brows pinch together and his fingers clench and unclench like he wants to hold on to me forever.

Finally, I meet Seth's eyes and see resignation in his. My heart hurts a little at the ache in his eyes.

"I'm not saying all the time, boss." I press my lips against his briefly. Sparks float along my veins, and his hard cock twitches beneath me. "Just every now and then. With friends. Not alone."

I spent the past four years alone on campus. Studying in the library. Working jobs but keeping my head down and focusing on what was important. Graduating before I ended up with a pile of debt. Scholarships helped, but I still have debt which this job will help pay off.

I don't want to hang out by myself anymore. I want to find friends who can know me. The real me with all my flaws and problems. I want to have the ability to discuss with them my feelings about these wonderful men.

"How about we take it on a case-by-case basis?" Seth concedes.

I grin and kiss him again. This time he takes control of the kiss, making it last longer than a second and stoking the fire sizzling inside me into a bonfire. Seth's kisses are as controlled as he is, but just as dangerous.

When he breaks off the kiss, I sigh and trace my thumb over his smooth jaw.

"But maybe not today, princess. You should stay here."

My eyes lock with his. "Of course."

Chapter 105

Don't Go There

Madison

"Hey." I greet Hope at the lobby door. The guys all went up to the office to work after lunch and left me alone in the apartment until Hope arrived. It's a small win for me.

"Hey." Her messy bun has tendrils falling around her face. She clutches her phone like it's her lifeline. She smiles at me, but it doesn't reach the worried look in her eyes.

"I . . ." Hope sighs and looks over her shoulder. She nibbles on her lip. "Do you think . . . ? No, you probably shouldn't . . ."

She bites her lip and looks over her shoulder again. I step aside to let her into the lobby. Worry tugs at her brow as the door closes.

"What's going on?" I don't move from beside the door. Something is weighing on her.

"It's Jason." She releases a heavy breath. "He isn't answering his texts. I tried calling on the way over here and got nothing. I was going to stop by the bar, but I didn't want to be late to meet you and . . ."

"Do you want me to go to the bar with you?"

Things fall into place. I'm not supposed to leave the building, but Hope desperately wants to check on her brother. I'm not sure why she's worried, but everything about her screams she's on the verge of panic.

"I can't ask you to do that." Hope shakes her head and lifts her phone. She smiles as she lowers it. "I'll try him again in a half hour. I'm sure he's fine."

She heads toward the elevator, glancing at the blank screen of her phone again.

"We could just pop over there," I blurt out. "It's not far."

She spins to face me with a relieved smile. "You think? The guys won't mind? I'd go by myself, but I'm afraid of what I might find."

The bank of elevators is close. I could go up and get one of them to come with, or even call one of them. But it's daylight and the bar is only a block away. They need to concentrate to figure out who the mole is.

Besides, what could possibly happen on a sunny Sunday afternoon?

Fuck, why did I have to think that? That seems like something the stupid chick would say in a horror movie.

"We'll be fast. Ten minutes, maybe fifteen. I'll text them to let them know we've gone." I open the door and her shoulders relax. Blake will need to let me back in.

"Thank you." She hurries outside and I follow, making sure the door shuts behind us.

I pull out my phone.

ME:

Running with Hope to check on her brother. BRB

After sending it to Blake, I slip my phone into my pocket and catch up with Hope.

"He was a boxer." Hope wrings her hands as we hurry down the sidewalk. Unlike on a business day, only a few people wander these streets, leaving them fairly deserted. "He sustained quite a few head injuries and sometimes has balance issues and migraines. If he isn't

ME:

No issues. I'm fine.

Hope comes back toward me but veers to the left. "His apartment is up here. You can come with or stay here. I should only be a minute."

The bar that seemed so full of light and life a few weeks ago now feels empty and gutted. Even with the lights on, shivers ripple through me. Yeah, I'm not staying here alone. I follow her through the door leading upstairs.

She opens the door at the top with her key. "Jason? Jason, are you here?"

I step into the doorway and wait as she wanders into the apartment.

She slips through another doorway and keeps calling for her brother. A muffled groan reaches my ears.

"Jason!" Her voice is high pitched. I give up my sentry post and hurry to where she disappeared. When I get to the bedroom, she's kneeling next to her brother on the floor, one hand on his pulse, the other holding the phone to her ear.

I'm not sure what to do, so I just freeze in the doorway.

"Yes, McAvoy's on Grand." She rubs her hand over his sternum. "He was conscious a second ago, but he's not responding now."

I hold my hand over my mouth as my pounding heart beats against my ribs. What if we'd stayed and watched TV while he was lying helpless on the floor?

"Okay. Yes." She glances up at me. "We'll let you in when you get here."

She puts the phone on the wooden floor and rocks back on her heels. Her focus is on Jason's face as she holds his hand.

"What can I do?" I step into the room.

She startles like she forgot I was here for a second. "Can you go down and let the paramedics in when they get here?"

answering, that could be why. But it could be worse. I just di
want to be by myself. You know?"

"Is there anything we can do?" We turn the corner and his b
directly in front of us.

"If it's really bad, he'll need to go to the hospital again." H
glances at me with concern. "He hates the hospital. They alv
want to do tests. He's a big guy and claustrophobic. They usu
have to sedate him to get scans. He despises being under sedation.

We get to the front doors of the bar and it's closed. It's schedu
to open later this afternoon. Hope opens her purse and
through it.

"I have a key . . . Here it is." She pulls it out and opens the d
There's a small vestibule and another door that leads inside.
lights are all off. She locks the door behind us. "Wait here. I'll get
lights."

She walks away, and I pull out my phone to see the texts
have been buzzing in my pocket.

> BLAKE:
>
> No
>
> BLAKE:
>
> Where are you?
>
> BLAKE:
>
> Answer me.

The lights come on, filling the room with a soft glow against
wooden walls and beams.

> ME:
>
> Hope's brother owns McAvoy's Bar
>
> ME:
>
> We just got here. Going to check on her
> brother and then walk back.

Hope comes back toward me but veers to the left. "His apartment is up here. You can come with or stay here. I should only be a minute."

The bar that seemed so full of light and life a few weeks ago now feels empty and gutted. Even with the lights on, shivers ripple through me. Yeah, I'm not staying here alone. I follow her through the door leading upstairs.

She opens the door at the top with her key. "Jason? Jason, are you here?"

I step into the doorway and wait as she wanders into the apartment.

She slips through another doorway and keeps calling for her brother. A muffled groan reaches my ears.

"Jason!" Her voice is high pitched. I give up my sentry post and hurry to where she disappeared. When I get to the bedroom, she's kneeling next to her brother on the floor, one hand on his pulse, the other holding the phone to her ear.

I'm not sure what to do, so I just freeze in the doorway.

"Yes, McAvoy's on Grand." She rubs her hand over his sternum. "He was conscious a second ago, but he's not responding now."

I hold my hand over my mouth as my pounding heart beats against my ribs. What if we'd stayed and watched TV while he was lying helpless on the floor?

"Okay. Yes." She glances up at me. "We'll let you in when you get here."

She puts the phone on the wooden floor and rocks back on her heels. Her focus is on Jason's face as she holds his hand.

"What can I do?" I step into the room.

She startles like she forgot I was here for a second. "Can you go down and let the paramedics in when they get here?"

answering, that could be why. But it could be worse. I just didn't want to be by myself. You know?"

"Is there anything we can do?" We turn the corner and his bar is directly in front of us.

"If it's really bad, he'll need to go to the hospital again." Hope glances at me with concern. "He hates the hospital. They always want to do tests. He's a big guy and claustrophobic. They usually have to sedate him to get scans. He despises being under sedation."

We get to the front doors of the bar and it's closed. It's scheduled to open later this afternoon. Hope opens her purse and digs through it.

"I have a key . . . Here it is." She pulls it out and opens the door. There's a small vestibule and another door that leads inside. The lights are all off. She locks the door behind us. "Wait here. I'll get the lights."

She walks away, and I pull out my phone to see the texts that have been buzzing in my pocket.

> BLAKE:
>
> No
>
> BLAKE:
>
> Where are you?
>
> BLAKE:
>
> Answer me.

The lights come on, filling the room with a soft glow against the wooden walls and beams.

> ME:
>
> Hope's brother owns McAvoy's Bar
>
> ME:
>
> We just got here. Going to check on her brother and then walk back.

"Of course." I bite my lip and glance at her brother. "Is he going to be okay?"

Her eyes are dry, but her lower lip trembles. She's holding back tears. Staying strong. Her eyes soften as they meet mine. "I hope so. Thank you for coming with me."

"Of course."

She shifts back to sit next to Jason, her fingers against his pulse. I head downstairs. Someone is already knocking on the door. I hurry over, thinking it's too early for the paramedics.

Glancing through the glass on the door, I see Blake. His mouth presses in a thin line. Relief pours through me. I could handle this alone, but with him here, I don't have to. I unlock the door and he stalks in. After engaging the lock, I take a breath and turn to him.

"We're waiting for the paramedics. He's passed out upstairs. The bar is closed, so it's safe." The words fly out of me. I don't regret coming here. I straighten my shoulders. "Hope needed me, and as her friend, I was there for her. You didn't need to come."

Blake's jaw clenches as his fierce gaze holds me in place. But I don't wilt. I'm not a child. I don't need protection twenty-four seven. The stalker has already proven that it doesn't matter if I'm kept locked away in a tower, they can still get to me. Maybe not physically. But we're feeding into their game by limiting my movements.

"Someone has you in their sights. Waiting for any slipup. What happens when Hope needs to go to the hospital with her brother? You get left here alone? You walk back? Alone?" Blake runs a hand through his hair. It's less than a block away. He grabs my shoulders. "Do you even care about your own safety? Fuck, Madison."

Not wanting him to worry, I rest my hand over his. His gaze drops to my neck. Does he still see the bruises even though they're gone? Does he still feel guilty for not arriving earlier with Jeff? When our eyes meet, I can see it still eats at him.

My heart pitches in my chest.

"I'm here." Closing the distance between us, I place my hand on his jaw, rubbing at the twitching muscle there. "I'm safe. I can't let one person dictate the rest of my life."

He draws me into his arms. His spicy scent fills my nose as I press my face into his shirt.

"I know, but I can't . . . I can't." He buries his face in my hair.

My heart swells, knowing what he can't seem to say. We don't want to lose each other. It doesn't matter if Blake loves me or not. He wants me and needs me. I have enough love for both of us.

A knock brings me back to the present. I pull away from Blake to look out the door. This time it's the paramedics. After letting them in, I show them where Hope and her brother are. Blake holds my hand as they load Jason into the back of the ambulance.

Hope stops before me and hugs me tight. A tear slips down her cheek. "Thank you for coming with me. I'm glad I wasn't alone. I'll call you later."

Her gaze flicks to Blake briefly before she hands me the key to the bar. "Could you lock up? The bartender will be here in a few hours and he can open everything."

"Of course. I hope he gets better."

"Me too." A shadow plays in her eyes. What put it there? How often has this happened?

"Text me when you know something," I say after her.

She nods as she vanishes out the door.

Blake

Madison is quiet on the walk back to our building. I don't know what to say to her. I want to tell her she can't just do that. She can't just leave and act like everything is okay.

But I'm not her prison guard either. She's a young woman. We can't keep her locked in the building. Not long-term. Hell, even in the short-term, it's probably not healthy.

The elevator stops on the office floor. She glances at me, waiting for me to step off.

"Come on, tiger. You can hang out with us while we search files. Maybe you'll see something we don't." It's a lame excuse, but I wasn't the only one concerned.

Her lips press together. For a moment, I feel like she's going to refuse. When I got her text, all I could see was Jeff holding her, his hand tight around her throat. The panicked look in her eyes and then the relief when she saw me. And then she dropped to the ground like a rag doll.

I wasn't supposed to be there. If I hadn't gone . . .

I can't relive that. Back then, I didn't love her. Now . . .

Fuck, I can't lose her.

"Please, Madison." I hold my hand out to her.

Whatever she sees in my eyes makes her gaze soften. She takes my hand. Hers is so small and delicate compared to mine, but she isn't afraid of me. I don't think she ever was. Wary maybe, but never truly scared.

Something slips into place inside me. I don't know that I'll be able to let her go. That's the deal though. We let her go when the time comes. But maybe that time won't ever come.

"Everything okay?" Noah stops as he's carrying files to the conference room.

"Hope's brother was unconscious. She had to take him to the hospital." I clear my throat. "It's a good thing Madison was there for her."

Madison's gaze darts up to me, but I keep my focus on Noah. Her fingers tighten around mine.

"Good." Noah nods and jerks his head toward the conference room. "Let's get to work then."

"Come on," I say roughly and walk with Madison into the conference room.

Seth looks up when we enter. The tension eases from his shoulders when he sees her.

"Madison, you can work on those files." He straightens and gestures to a chair with a stack already in front of it. "We're looking for commonality among projects. So we're going through old files, trying to pick up on who we can eliminate from the staff as a suspect."

"Okay." She draws away from me with a glance over her shoulder. Our eyes meet, and that edge of stubbornness is gone now.

We all settle in to work, trying to unravel this puzzle. After a few hours, Madison stretches and covers a yawn. Seth nods to me. The amount of work we have in front of us is monumental. We're searching for a piece of hay in a pile of hay.

"All right, tiger." I stand and gesture to Madison.

"What?" She straightens and almost pulls off looking alert.

"You and me are headed downstairs." I move to the door.

She bites her lip and looks at the piles of paperwork remaining.

"Go take a nap, princess. You didn't sleep well last night." Seth takes her hand and presses a kiss to her knuckles. "We'll survive an hour without you."

She nods slightly and joins me at the door. "Only an hour."

"Sure, love." I wrap my arm around her shoulders and draw her into my side as we make our way to the elevator.

"Are you still mad at me?" She tips her face up to look at me.

The elevator doors open and I lead her in, pressing the button for our floor. "I wasn't mad at you. No one would be there if something happened to you. Again. Val, Jeff, your professor. I can't protect you if I don't know where you are."

She rests her head against my chest. "It's not your job to protect me. I need to protect myself."

The doors open on the apartment floor. Instead of leading her to the main door, I take her to my bedroom. She walks in and sits on the edge of the bed. Another yawn takes over for a second.

"We need to get you a self-defense instructor then." I brush her hair out of her face. "A woman self-defense instructor."

She smiles at my qualifying statement. "Are you going to be my attacker?"

I chuckle and press her shoulder so she lies back on the bed with me hovering over her. "Only if you submit to me afterward and take your punishment like a good girl."

"That seems reasonable." She smiles and wraps her arms around my neck, drawing me down until our lips meet.

We move farther up on the bed. Taking my time, I explore her mouth, knowing we're building a hunger that neither of us will quench. But I enjoy tasting her and exploring her without the rush to fulfill the ache.

I roll to lie beside her. She curls up on her side facing me.

"Thank you," she says.

I turn my face to meet her blue eyes. "For what?"

"For understanding. For knowing this time I didn't need to be dominated. That I need my space sometimes." She draws her fingers through my hair, sending little sparks through my veins.

"I'm here for you, love." Always.

Chapter 106

Immaterial Misstatement

Madison

Sunday night is low-key. We have a light dinner and watch a movie. When we all head to bed, Seth draws me into the closet.

"Sit." He gestures to the bench.

I sit while he opens drawers. It's still pretty unbelievable that this is my closet. That all these things are mine. They don't feel like they're mine. It feels like they'll all get taken away from me when I least expect it. Kind of like these guys.

This whole thing isn't permanent and I need to remember that. This is a stepping stone to my future. What we do here in this apartment is the experimenting I didn't have time for in college. And when I go, I'll leave all this behind me. No magical closet. No wonderful men. Just me and what I learned from them.

Taking a breath, I return my focus to Seth. He rummages through a few drawers.

"I figure you'd want something comfortable for tonight." He returns with a set of pink shorts and a sleep shirt that says *But First, Coffee.*

Smiling, I lift my gaze to his, trying to imagine Seth picking these out for me. After all, I didn't buy them. Imagining the man I thought he was buying these makes me smile. He sets them beside me.

"Stand."

My insides rejoice, knowing he's going to command me, control me, and I want it so bad. I love my independence, but giving in to Seth gives me something I didn't know I needed. Willingly, I stand.

"Arms up." He stops in front of me.

I lift my arms and he draws my shirt off over my head. When I start to drop my arms, he gives me a warning look. Straightening them, I give him a small smile.

"How are your cramps?" His fingers draw lines across my abdomen above the jeans I put on earlier. Tremors quake through me at his light touch.

"The pain meds and heat worked." My breath catches as his fingers tickle up my sides before his warm hands settle on my ribs. His thumbs brush just below my bra.

"Arms down."

I bring my arms down. He traces the band of my bra to the hook and releases it. He draws it off me, and my nipples tighten in anticipation of his touch. The guys haven't really played with me today.

"Are your breasts more sensitive?" He drops my bra into the hamper and reaches for the button and zipper of my jeans.

"A little tender, but usually only the first day." My breath catches as his hands skim over my hips beneath the denim, sliding it down my thighs. His lips graze my stomach as he lowers to the ground to push my jeans all the way off.

Fuck. If I weren't on my period, I'd be all over him. I'm not particularly shy, but I don't know how the guys feel about period sex. I've never actually had sex while on my period, and no one's really offered. It feels like we're all feeling each other out to see what we should do. Which means no one is doing anything.

After last night, maybe that's for the best. Between the multiple rounds of sex, and taking both Noah and Coop together *and* Seth and

Blake together, I should be worn out. Not craving the slightest touch from Seth now.

After I step out of my jeans, he rises before me and drops them in the hamper. The closet is warm, but I'm wearing only my panties at this point. Seth returns to me, and his hungry eyes devour my body, almost like a physical caress. A shiver runs down my spine.

When our eyes meet, I release the breath I didn't even know I was holding. Seth reaches for the pajama top and helps put it on me. His fingers graze my breasts, making me burn with the need for more. Our eyes catch again.

His eyes have darkened, and the fire burns in him too, but his control is firmly in place. I'm not sure there's anything I could do to shake that control. He reaches for the shorts and holds them out for me to step into. Taking ahold of his arms, I use them to steady myself.

Once I'm dressed, he kisses me. Before he can pull away, I wrap my arms around his neck and press up into him, opening my mouth beneath his. Willing him to let his control shatter and take me.

Groaning his surrender, he wraps his arms around me and lifts me against him so he can claim my mouth more thoroughly. My insides burst with joy. When his tongue brushes mine, I sigh and lift my legs around his waist. His hands grip my ass to help support me.

His cock is hard between my thighs and my pussy aches with need.

He lifts his mouth from mine. "Princess, we can wait. You took all of us last night. We don't want to hurt you. Even if you weren't on your period, you'd need to rest."

I groan as my pussy clenches. "You're right."

I don't unwrap from him though. As I tighten my legs around him, he quirks an almost-smile. Fuck, I love that smile.

"Let's go to bed." He strides out of the closet and into the bedroom.

"We almost sent someone in after you two." Coop comes up behind me and wraps his hands around my waist. His bare skin is hot where it touches mine. I'm tempted to sink into his heat.

"Let the boss get ready for bed, sweetheart."

I kiss Seth before letting go, knowing Coop has me. Coop doesn't drop me on the bed like I expect him to but carries me into the bathroom. He sets me down in front of the vanity.

"Do what you need to do to get ready for bed." He waves his hand at the water closet.

My eyes meet his in the mirror. His hands settle on my waist and slip beneath my waistband to touch my hip bones.

"Unless you want to do something else." He glances over his shoulder briefly before closing in on me. "Whatever you want, sweetheart. I'm always happy to oblige."

I give him a smile but Seth is right. Things are sore and achy down there, and messy. We can take a night off. "Maybe on our night."

"Hmm." His fingers tease my hips, playing with the edge of my panties, tugging them slightly to press against me. His eyes lock with mine, and he drops his head down so his lips are against my ear as he speaks. "Whatever you want. You want to be my naughty slut? Or maybe you want me to be your bad boy?"

A shiver races down my spine. I lean into him, craving his warmth and his touch. "We can figure that out in the moment."

He turns his head and his lips brush my pulse, sending sparks sizzling through my veins. Stepping back, he gives me a cocky smile in the mirror. "We'll all be waiting for you, sweetheart."

When he walks out, he closes the door behind him. I exhale and shake the desire off me. When I finish getting ready, I find all my guys on the bed, just like Coop said, waiting. I lean against the doorway to take them in. They all wear their boxers, showing off their cut abs and chests. Corded arms and thick legs.

When did this become my life? Except for the stalker and my ex-roommate, this is a fantasy come true. Four beautiful men who desire me. Who appreciate my intelligence and believe I bring something to the table at work.

Who I love with my whole heart.

I guess that's where the fantasy ends. Noah loves me. His dark eyes meet mine, and I know in my heart he'll always be mine, even long after this is over.

The others? I just don't know. They care about me, but love? I'm not perfect like the women Coop and Seth have fallen for before. Not that those women were the best people, but they're definitely perfect in the public eye.

Even dressed in the beautiful clothes Seth picks out for me, I'm just an impostor. A child playing dress-up and pretend. Could they even love me?

"Come on, love." Blake smiles and pats the bed. "Let's get some sleep."

I push off the doorframe and take his hand, climbing into bed beside him. Seth is on my other side. Coop and Noah lie down on the outside.

Blake wraps his arm around me, drawing my back to his front, and I release a happy sigh. Before I can get settled, Blake's phone buzzes on the nightstand. He sits up as an alarm blares. Fire? The guys all get out of bed in a hurry.

Seth takes my hand and pulls me with him.

"What's happening?" The alarm is persistent but not overly loud.

"We need to get out of the building." Seth drags me into the closet and grabs a huge sweatshirt to put on me before pulling on his jeans. He tosses a pair of sneakers on the floor before me, and I slip my feet into them.

We hurry into the main part of the apartment. The others have on jeans and are tugging shirts over their heads.

"The elevator is shut down." Blake nods his head back toward my bedroom. "We need to take the fire exit."

Seth's fingers squeeze mine as we all turn back to my bedroom. I have a million questions, but right now we have a goal: get out quickly. Once things calm down and we're safe from whatever, then we can talk.

Blake leads us to a door in my living room that I just don't think about. Coop told me about the fire escape in my room when he showed me the apartment, but my brain was focused on other things that day. How much I wanted him even though I didn't think I could have him.

Seth pulls me through the door into a huge staircase that winds down all the floors. "Hope you're ready for exercise, princess."

"If you get tired, let us know." Coop stops beside me and brushes my hair out of my face. "I can carry you if you need me to."

I nod and Blake strides by us.

"Let's get a move on."

We descend the stairway, our hurried steps and labored breathing echoing off the concrete walls. Mostly *my* labored breathing. I'm not as fit as they are.

"What do we know?" Seth asks two flights down.

"Fire alarm in the kitchen and on the third floor." Blake lets out a huff as he rounds the next landing. "They didn't go off at the same time. It's odd. The fire station has been notified, and they're on their way. So are the ambulance and police."

"Does this happen a lot?" I pause on the landing for a quick breath.

Noah grabs my hand and keeps me moving. "Not typically, but we keep up with the system, so in case of an emergency we're ready."

"Our goal is to make it outside and across the street." Blake pauses to look back at me. "We make sure everyone got out and then we evaluate the situation. Fortunately, tonight it's just us and the night guards on the main floor. Evacuating the entire building is almost a nightmare."

"Do we think it's a false alarm?" I don't smell any smoke. We were just in the kitchen. Everything was off.

"We won't know until we get out and make sure everyone's safe." Blake takes off down the stairs again. "I'll check the system when we know we're in the clear."

By the time we reach the bottom of the stairs, I'm winded and need a moment as Blake pushes open the door that leads out the back of the building.

"Come on."

I inhale the fresh, cool air as I step out and glance around. It's almost midnight. The lights back here overlap slightly, but they fight against the oppressive darkness trying to close in on us.

Coop draws me into his side, and Noah's hand slides from mine. Noah's dark eyes give me reassurance, but he steps away from me.

A shiver ripples through me as Coop leans close to my ear. "There might be cameras out there, sweetheart. We need to keep up appearances."

Coop takes my hand and slides the ring I left on the tray in the bathroom back onto my finger. "You need to keep this on."

I don't protest as he wraps his arm around my shoulder and we follow the others. It still feels wrong to wear this ring that someone in the past used to make the ultimate promise of love forever to someone else. Especially when the reason Coop gave it to me was to continue this ruse that we're a couple so no one guesses all of us are together.

The wind blows against my bare legs, making me huddle into Coop more. Red lights flash against the building as we step out into the front plaza. Coop draws me to the side as Blake and Seth go to talk to the first responders. Noah walks beside us as we make our way across the street.

The lights are bright, but someone shut the alarm off. A group of firefighters enter the front door and disappear into the lobby. Noah steps closer, blocking the wind a little but not touching me.

If I could, I'd pull him close and sandwich myself between him and Coop.

Seth runs a hand over his hair as he makes his way across the street to us. A flash of something dark catches my gaze, and I jerk my head to see someone wearing dark clothing disappearing down the side of the building that we came from.

A chill creeps over me. Maybe it was just a shadow. Maybe my imagination is getting the better of me.

Coop draws me into his chest. "We should have made sure you put pants on."

Seth stops beside us. "They don't think there's actually a fire. Blake is checking the computers, but it looks like a faulty wire. We should only be out here another hour while they search the building."

"I think I saw someone go down the way we came." I turn my face away from Coop's chest to meet Seth's eyes.

He jerks his gaze that way. "When?"

"A minute ago, when you crossed the street." What if this was all a setup? What if someone wanted to get in, and we gave them the whole building? "What if this wasn't an accident?"

Chapter 107

Strategy Meeting

Seth

Madison's eyes are huge and her face pale as she stares down the corridor between the buildings. I can't see anything now, but if she thinks she saw someone, we have bigger issues. Fuck.

"Give me a minute." I jog across the street and find the police officer we were talking to. "Officer Jones?"

He stops and turns. "Is there something you need?"

"Our assistant thinks she saw someone slip down the corridor between the buildings."

He glances over my shoulder and focuses on Madison in Coop's arms. His jaw flexes as he considers. "What's down that way?"

"The emergency exit stairs." I exhale. "The door would be unlocked to let emergency personnel in and remains unlocked until the security system is reset."

He nods and gestures to a few police officers standing nearby. "Wilson, Cox, go around back and check out the stairwell. We need to make sure no one comes or goes that way except for first responders. Take Nguyen and Mason with you. Two go in, make sure no one is on the stairs. The others watch the door."

"Yes, sir." They take off.

"It's not unheard of to trip alarms to empty a building out." Officer Jones pivots to face me. "Anything we need to know that they may target?"

I shake my head. "There are files on computers, but this seems like an extreme way to get to them." I glance at Madison, checking to make sure she's still there. "Our assistant has a stalker."

"Stalker?" He turns and regards Madison again.

She's huddled against Coop. The sweatshirt covers her sleep shorts, but her legs are bare. A cool breeze blows between the buildings. She shivers and burrows into Coop. She looks so small and vulnerable against him.

"Someone has been threatening her. Officer Bill Carr has been leading the investigation."

A woman walks toward Madison with a blanket. They talk for a moment before Coop takes the blanket and helps Madison drape it around her. The alarm forced us all out the back door, which not many people know about. Access to that stairwell is limited.

Fuck, is this all an attempt to get to her again? Or just to make her panic?

"I'll look into it. I need to get back." Officer Jones returns to help coordinate.

It could be someone looking to get into our system. We locked down the building over the weekend to keep access limited. We'll need to review the logs of who came in or tried to come in.

Blake joins me. His gaze follows Officer Jones. "What was that about?"

"Madison saw someone going around the side of the building."

Blake glances in that direction and narrows his eyes. "Stalker or the corporate spy?"

"Wish I knew. If they're inside, they'll have to pass the police to get out." I inhale and glance up at our building.

"Unless they hide."

Blake's right. The building is immense, and it would be easy to disappear and not reemerge until the morning when everyone is at work. Or wait until we're all asleep and then come out.

"Fuck. We're going to a hotel tonight." I'm not stepping a foot in that building until we have every inch inspected. I won't risk Madison that way.

Blake nods. "I'll let the officers know."

It's after one in the morning by the time we enter the penthouse suite at the hotel. It has four bedrooms, which is perfect for appearances but overkill for us. I don't think any of us want to let Madison out of our sight. Blake, Coop, Madison, and I walk into the living area, and I breathe a sigh of relief.

"Anyone want a drink?" Without waiting for a response, Blake moves behind the bar and sets four glasses out. He pulls a bottle of bourbon from the shelf and puts a finger's worth of liquor into each glass. Coop grabs two and hands one to Madison.

"Thank you." Her voice is quiet.

Blake hands me the other and lifts his into the air. "To a good night's sleep."

Like any of us are going to sleep after that. My mind keeps spinning around the facts. The fire alarms went off. We evacuated. The building had to reset, leaving it open. If Madison really saw someone going down the alley, they could be in there right now doing whatever they want.

Blake downs the drink like a shot while the rest of us take a sip. He sets his glass down and rakes a hand through his hair. "We need to figure this shit out. I need to sleep in my own fucking apartment, not a hotel room."

Madison drops the blanket on the couch and walks into Blake's arms. She wraps her arms around his waist and rests her head on his chest. For a second, he seems surprised by the affection. His hand drops to her back and the other strokes over her hair as his shoulders loosen.

There's a softness in his eyes as he looks at her. "We should go to sleep."

"We need to wait for Noah." Madison's voice is muffled in Blake's shirt.

Noah went to the drugstore to grab supplies for Madison and the rest of us since we didn't go back into the building. She offered to go with him, but he reminded her she was only wearing sleep shorts and sent her with us. Protecting her is a priority.

"Of course." Coop collapses on the couch and pats his leg. "Come entertain your future husband, sweetheart."

She rolls her eyes and a wave of affection flows through me. Could I imagine a future with Madison in it? Of course. Could I imagine a future with her without the others? No. What we have works because it's all of us.

But that doesn't work for the real world. For our business associates who would rather go with a subpar company than work with men with our unsavory reputation.

She takes Blake's hand and pulls him over to the couch before sitting down on Coop's lap. Blake settles beside Coop and they all look at me expectantly.

Fuck it. I refill Blake's glass and add more to mine before walking over to join them. I hand Blake his glass, and he gives me a nod.

"We need a list of suspects, princess." I lift her feet to my lap and take off her shoes.

"Like who I think might be the stalker?" Madison asks as she rests her head on Coop's and Blake's shoulders. She gives a small yawn. "Or everyone I've ever come into contact with?"

"Problem is, it could be someone she doesn't even know." Blake strokes his hand down Madison's hair and takes a drink of his bourbon. "Any list may not be complete."

"Don't stalkers try to insert themselves into your life?" Coop threads his fingers with Madison's, toying with the ring on her finger. It's a stake of his claim on her. It shouldn't mean anything, but it makes my gut tighten every time I see it on her finger. It's a reminder that we don't have a future with Madison. That all we have is right now.

The door makes a noise as someone inserts their keycard. We all straighten and wait. Noah steps into the room and sets the bag on the table.

"Why are you guys still up?" Noah strides across the room to Madison.

"We were waiting for you." She holds her barely touched bourbon out to him, and he takes it and downs the remains.

Setting the glass on the coffee table, he bends and lifts Madison into his arms bridal-style. She wraps her arms around his neck and gives him this soft, longing look. He lifts an eyebrow at me. "Which way, boss?"

Her gaze falls on me, and it makes my heart throb. Standing, I nod toward the primary bedroom. Noah heads that direction. Coop and Blake follow us. We have four bedrooms, but we'll make it work with the one bed.

Madison

Sunlight hits my eyelids from the crack in the curtain, and I wearily open my eyes. I'm alone in the bed that was crowded last night with all of us. The scent of coffee lingers in the air. I stretch across the bed and exhale.

I've gotten used to waking mid-orgasm or in someone's arms. It's weird being alone.

Fuck. Last night was another nightmare. I stayed calm during the evacuation because it was likely a faulty circuit or some other computer error. But then that shadow person appeared. Maybe it was someone, maybe it was my imagination. I roll to the edge of the bed and head into the bathroom.

I do the best I can with my hair and brush my teeth with one of the toothbrushes Noah bought last night. When I near the bedroom door, I can hear the guys talking. I don't hesitate to go into the living room.

"Security went through the entire building. If someone got in, they didn't leave a trace." Blake's voice is low. He glances over at me and gives me a small smile. "Morning, tiger."

"Were they able to do a locked-down sweep before anyone arrived for work?" Seth gestures for me to join them.

I head to the table. There's a seat open next to Noah and I drop into it. Noah puts his warm hand on my thigh and gives me a squeeze.

"Yes, and the police had the place on lock until the security team arrived."

"Did either of you see what Madison saw?" Seth turns to Noah and Coop. Everyone is dressed in the clothes they hurriedly threw on last night. Noah shakes his head. It was really dark with a lot of lights spinning around. I wouldn't be surprised if neither of them noticed the person.

"No, but I wasn't focused on the building." Coop sighs. "It's possible whoever she saw had no intentions of going into our building. They could have been leaving the area since the police were present."

"I'm pretty sure I saw someone, but it was dark. Even if I saw someone, like Coop said, it might not be related." I shrug and reach for the carafe of coffee to fill my mug, but Noah beats me to it and pours my cup.

"As much as I'd like to believe it's a coincidence, it's a little too perfect with the timing." Blake threads his hand through his hair. His green eyes are heavy with lack of sleep.

The urge to drag him back to bed is strong. Though sleep wouldn't be my only intention.

"I have a crew going through the lines to find out how the alarms both failed. Again, one alarm I might dismiss, but two going off? That's tampering."

"They didn't find anyone in the building." Seth leans back in his chair while he studies me. "That doesn't mean someone didn't try to get in though. Maybe they saw the police and thought better of it."

I nod slightly and take a small sip of coffee. It was late and dark. I was shivering and saw Seth. The movement out of the corner of my eye caught my attention. A figure dressed in black moved in the shadows and the swirling light from the emergency vehicles. I'm positive I saw someone, and they were sneaking.

"Madison."

I jerk at Seth's voice. "Yeah?"

"Are you okay?" His tone softens and his gaze roams over me.

I straighten in my chair and look around at the concerned eyes focused on me. "Sorry, still a little tired, I think. What did I miss?"

"Lunch today." Seth meets my gaze and holds it. "With William and Hunter."

Any appetite I have leaves at the mention of Hunter. I always knew telling William wouldn't change much. Especially if I worked there full-time. It would've just made Hunter sneakier. But I don't work for him. He's a client of the company I work for and therefore represent.

I force a smile. "Great."

"You don't leave my side for anything." Blake's voice is dark. "He may have his father convinced he's sorry, but I don't believe it for a minute."

Blake's green eyes fix on mine. We're in tune on this. "I won't leave your side."

<h1 style="text-align:center">Chapter 108</h1>

<h2 style="text-align:center">Punt</h2>

Blake

The morning flew by as I tried to sort through everything the security crew found. I also have a team reviewing the last few days of camera footage to make sure no one unusual was on the premises.

When I come out of my office for lunch, Madison stands next to her desk. Her smile is warm for me even as lines of worry crease her forehead. I'm not looking forward to this lunch.

Seth keeps dressing her and doing an awesome job. She has her blond hair pulled into a bun with little tendrils falling next to her ears. Except for those killer red lips, her makeup is light. Her blouse is a white satiny button-down, tucked into a black high-waisted pencil skirt. Her nylons are a sheer black, ending in black stilettos with red bottoms.

She's a knockout. If we had time, I'd bend her over my desk and make her forget all about Hunter Adams. Her cheeks flush pink as if she knows exactly what I'm thinking.

With all that's happened recently, the stalker, the corporate spy, I can't help thinking, why now? It's odd how everything seems to center on Madison. We didn't find out about the corporate spy until after she started. Coincidence?

Is she someone's pawn? Is this all one big manipulation? Have we accidentally let in a Trojan horse? I don't think she could tell me if she was. She seems so innocent and loving. Or is she really all she seems to be?

So fucking perfect for all of us.

Her blue eyes don't drop from my gaze, though her smile fades a little. I don't know what to think anymore. The moments we share are real, but something about last night just niggles at my brain like I'm missing something important.

"Are we ready to go?" Coop comes out of his office and looks between the two of us.

I don't know what I'm doing. But I know I trust Madison. I love her. "Yes, I'm ready."

Coop takes Madison's hand with that enormous ring he weighed it down with. That's something I can't even process. It's all a lie. Them being engaged. Them dating.

But when he flaunts her like she's his, it makes me want to claim her so she knows she's mine. Fuck, I want to fuck her in front of him to remind him who else she belongs to.

Seth and Noah join us as we head to the elevator. Coop draws Madison back against him and rests his chin on her head. He gives me a look like he knows I'm pondering something.

This whole lunch is a bad idea. Seth knows how I feel about it. If this were just my company, I would have terminated the relationship with Taylor's. Not tried to salvage it. But I get that Taylor's is a large account, and while Hunter is an ass, William is a good man.

"Who's Madison riding with?" Coop asks in the quiet elevator.

"I'm keeping Madison with me."

Her beautiful eyes lift to mine, and she gives me this little smile that makes my insides fucking buzz. That need to claim her is fierce. It will become a problem if I can't contain it.

"Would I really let my fiancée ride with two other men?" Coop's fingers tighten on Madison's hips, drawing her pencil skirt tight against her hips. She sucks in a breath.

"She's our assistant, Coop." Seth leans against the wall. *Not to mention she's fucking all of us, not just the pretty boy.*

The elevator stops at the garage level, and I hold out my hand to Madison. She steps forward and takes it. A rush of rightness flows through me. If someone put her in our paths on purpose, they could destroy us, because they know us better than maybe we know ourselves.

Wanting Madison is easy. Loving her is hard because I don't know what to do with my love. Especially when it's not just me she wants, but all of us. I don't think it would make the relationship any easier if it were just me and her though. In fact, I know I would have fucked it up by now if it were just me and her.

Besides, I'd never give up the relationship I have with my friends and business partners. Not for any woman.

We walk to the car and I open the door for her. She stops and looks up at me. When I meet her eyes, she blows out a frustrated breath.

"Hunter Adams is a lot of things, but sorry isn't one of them. This apology is to make his father feel like he's atoning. When he trapped me in that copy room, he said he'd be rough. He didn't care what I wanted." Madison's mouth tightens. "I don't want to feel that helpless again."

"He won't get a chance to corner you today." That I can promise her. My thumb traces her jaw. I can protect her. He won't get within arm's distance. This time I can make sure Hunter doesn't touch any part of her.

She nods and lowers herself into the car. Seth meets my gaze over the roof. We've discussed this. He knows where I stand on Hunter, but he makes the final call. That's why he's the boss. This whole deal could go sideways real quick if we aren't careful.

Madison

I spin the ring on my finger for the hundredth time since the car took off. I don't want to do this. Facing Hunter Adams is the last thing on this earth I want to do. I'd prefer to be back in that hallway with Jimi Alan.

Blake takes my hand and weaves his fingers with mine. My gaze fixates on our hands together. His large hand engulfs mine. He's been quieter than usual. Something weighs on his mind. Something I'm not sure I can help with, but I want him to confide in me. I want him to trust me with his innermost feelings. I hope someday he feels he can talk to me about anything.

The car comes to a stop at the restaurant. I exhale and follow Blake out of the car. Smoothing a hand over my skirt, I follow Seth inside. Blake stays behind me, flanking me. My outfit is my armor today, and my guys are my protectors. I'm safe.

We're the first to arrive, and the hostess leads us to a private dining room like before. My hands feel clammy as we sit at the table. Seth on one side of me and Blake on the other. My fingers play with the ring again.

Blake leans in and says in my ear, "Nothing will happen to you. I promise."

I lift my gaze to his. Fiery green eyes meet mine, blazing with need that makes my insides answer his call with a fire of my own. In his eyes, his fiercely protective side shines through. I'm safe today. I release my breath and nod.

Coop and Noah arrive with William and Hunter. We stand to greet them, but Seth and Blake don't move out of the way. No one can reach me to shake my hand.

"Ah, Madison, I'm so glad you joined us. I want to get this ugliness behind us so we can all move forward with our business." William steps forward but pauses as he realizes he can't actually take my hand. He reaches for his chair instead. "I'm sure you understand how this kind of thing happens."

Everyone sits down. I should have known nothing would happen to Hunter. That was the reason I refused to take the job at Taylor's. I would have rather tucked tail and gone all the way back to my parents' house than work with him. Guys like him always get rewarded rather than punished.

"This kind of thing?" Coop leans back in his chair, seemingly nonchalant. But anger brews under his cool facade. "You mean where your son assaulted my fiancée in your copy room? That kind of thing?"

William has the decency to look down as his cheeks redden. "I must apologize for my son—"

"He's here, so why doesn't he apologize for himself?" Blake asks as if he's asking Hunter to pass the salt. Like it's natural for him to call out another man to do the right thing.

I risk a look at Hunter's face. A muscle ticks in his jaw. His lips are pressed tight together like he wants to say something but was told to not stir the pot. Surprisingly, he's keeping his mouth shut. His gaze is fixed on the plate in front of him.

Blake's fingers touch mine under the table and I take what strength he gives me.

"We know things with Madison got out of hand—"

"William," Seth interrupts, "I know this must be hard for you. But this isn't a one-time thing with Hunter. And it won't end until someone either sues you or files felony charges against your son. I appreciate you have a business to run and you want your son to take over that business. But if he's going to continue to work with us, we need assurances that this type of conduct won't happen again. We won't risk sending our employees to your business until he gets some counseling."

"I'm not getting counseling," Hunter bites out. He lifts his angry eyes to mine.

My throat tightens at the fury in them. My pulse skips around like a predator has locked on me.

"Hunter." William's voice is firm and doesn't waver. He lets out a breath. He looks older when he lifts his gaze to Seth. "We've discussed proper behavior at work. We've all received a few days of sexual harassment training at our company and have a person who employees can discuss their situations with and file reports anonymously if they'd like."

His gaze turns to me and I feel sorry for him. He doesn't deserve a son like Hunter. "I know we failed you, Madison, and I don't know how many others. But going forward, our policy for new hires is to go through training and provide them with someone outside of me and Hunter to report their issues to."

Hunter drops his gaze back to his plate, but the rage inside him is obvious. His shoulders are tense and his fists are clenched. Someone is going to pay for all that rage he's bottling up. It won't be me, but I can't let it be anyone else.

I take a deep breath and meet William's gaze.

"I'm grateful you're making the workplace safer." I squeeze Blake's hand, needing his strength right now. "But you will always have a predator in your company with Hunter there."

I ignore Hunter's glare as I focus on William. My grip tightens more on Blake's hand.

"Counseling only helps people who want to be helped." My hand shakes as I reach for my water. "Your son made working for your company impossible for me. He didn't trap me in that copy room just once. And the last time, he had someone keeping a lookout so no one could stop him. He doesn't take no for an answer, and I don't know that you can fix that."

"Maybe if you weren't such a slut, I wouldn't have had an issue. You give it up to everyone else, why not me?" Hunter's words are harsh and unforgiving. "You think Derek didn't brag about fucking you?"

"Hunter!" William's voice is stern.

Blake's hand squeezes mine. I can't look at the other guys. Fucking Derek was a mistake. I never should have slept with a coworker at Taylor's. I realized that as soon as he stepped into my apartment.

"Maybe if she hadn't been such a whore—"

Seth stands and grabs Hunter's shirt, jerking him upright. My mouth drops open, but Seth's eyes are cool and composed. His face in Hunter's. "You need to watch how you speak—"

"Or what?" Hunter rolls his eyes as if Seth isn't being aggressive. His hands open and close though, ready to fight.

William stands with his hands up. "We should all calm down—"

"I'm not sure what you expected to happen here today, William." Noah stands and moves behind my chair. "Hunter doesn't regret what he tried to do to Madison. He doesn't want to change."

"Holy shit! I'm surprised I didn't see it before." Hunter laughs bitterly in Seth's face. "That's it, isn't it? You all use her like the whore she is."

Seth shoves Hunter away from him in disgust. Hunter staggers back against the wall and straightens his shirt. His smile is evil as he looks at me.

"We've heard the rumors about how the bosses at Morrigan Technology like to use their assistant for everything." Hunter's gaze roams up and down my body. "Figures this prude would put out for all of you."

"We're done here." Seth's words are cold and pointed. He turns to William. "I'm sorry, but we can't be involved with a company that lets a sexual predator run loose. And we won't stand for disrespect of our employees."

William says something, but I don't catch it around the buzzing in my ears.

Noah pulls my chair back, and Coop draws me into his side. I'm grateful for his support because my knees are barely holding me upright. Blake is right next to me on my other side. Seth leads the way out of the restaurant. My head is still spinning.

Seth chose me over their business. My heart pounds. A few weeks ago, I was afraid to speak up about their new client. I was terrified to tell them he sexually harassed me because a previous lover claiming the same had blackmailed them. Not only do they believe me, but they stood up for me.

They let go of a profitable new business opportunity for me.

I'm dumbfounded as they lead me to the car. Coop kisses the top of my hair before gently guiding me to Blake's side. As soon as the car doors close us in, Blake draws me into his arms. It takes me a moment to realize the wetness on my cheeks is my tears.

"We've got you, tiger." Blake's voice rumbles through me.

Seth takes my hand and kisses my knuckles. "I'm sorry I put you through that."

I lift my head and turn to him. "No. I'm sorry I didn't trust you in the beginning. That I didn't tell you who Hunter really was. I'm sorry you lost this business deal."

Seth cups my cheek and brushes away my tears with his thumb. "You're worth it, princess."

Chapter 109

Contract Frustration

Madison

It's been days since we fucked. Last night, Seth took me in his arms and kissed me before turning out the lights. I've gotten everything from simple pecks to soul-searing kisses, but nothing beyond that.

My pussy is no longer sore, my period is waning, and I'm hornier than ever. I've become accustomed to orgasms multiple times a day, and my body is starving for it. Tonight is my night with Noah. Last week it was a double feature two nights in a row with both Coop and Noah.

Just thinking about them taking me one after the other until we all passed out makes my pussy clench and ache. If someone doesn't do something soon, I'm going to find a vibrator and take care of myself.

"Madison." Seth's voice makes me jerk from the computer monitor where the numbers have blurred. "I need you."

Sighing, I grab my tablet and stand to follow him into his office. He doesn't *need* me. This is work time, so obviously he needs me to do my job. Even the underwear he laid out for me this morning was more functional than sexy.

Resigned to waiting until tonight to tempt Noah, I lower myself into the chair opposite Seth and lift my pen, ready to take notes. My gaze finds his expectantly.

"How are you today?" He leans back in his chair. His dark blue eyes roam down the length of me, keying me up. My nipples tighten and my pussy gets wet.

I don't think he wants to know how horny I am. "Good."

He makes this noise in the back of his throat like he doesn't believe me. "Come here, princess."

My eyebrows shoot up at his tone. That's the *obey me* tone, not the *let's focus on work* tone. I set my tablet on the chair next to me and round the desk to stand beside him. He slides his chair back and gestures to his desk.

"I'm still on my period." I feel it necessary to warn him. That, and my tampon will definitely get in the way.

"Bend over."

My insides buzz. I fight the urge to grin and do a little happy dance. I bend over the desk in front of him and wait.

The drawer next to me opens and closes. "Tampon?"

My cheeks flush. "Yes."

The flip cap to a bottle opens and the sound of liquid squirting out has me burning with need. Seth stands behind me and draws my skirt up around my waist. I bite my lip in anticipation of his touch.

He lowers my panties off my ass before sliding something supple but firm against my clit. A small click rings out in the office, and he leaves it there. He rights my skirt and pulls a tissue from the box on his desk.

"Return to your chair, princess."

I straighten, and the weight of the thing now pressed intimately against me is hard to get accustomed to. It rests between my lips, pressed against my clit, rubbing me as I walk to my chair. Just the feel of it firmly touching me arouses me.

Lifting my tablet, I sit and raise my gaze to Seth's. He studies me for a moment before he leans back in his chair.

"We need to go over a few files and get you up to speed for our Friday lunch meeting."

I cross my legs and give him my full attention. He runs through a few clients. I ask some questions when I need to. His fingers linger over the screen of his phone. I'm in the middle of writing what reports to print out when the buzzing starts and vibration hits my clit.

I gasp in surprise and lift my gaze to Seth. I knew what he put in my panties was obviously a sex toy, but I figured he'd wait longer to play with me.

"Do we need to stop, princess?" His finger hovers over his phone.

Biting my lip, I shake my head, feeling the pulsing against my clit like tribal drums. My insides turn to liquid heat.

"If you can't do your job . . ."

"I'm good. You wanted to go over Friday's business lunch."

Seth sweeps his finger up on the screen and the vibration increases. "What do you know of Stiner Enterprises' subsidiaries?"

I shift in my seat. As my arousal builds, the vibration makes it hard to focus. "They have thirty-three subsidiaries in ten different industries." The *-ies* goes up with the pulsing against my clit. I uncross my legs and recross them against the throbbing ache. "Right now, five different companies do their cybersecurity."

"Good girl."

"Fuck," I whisper at the shot of lust that pours through me at those words.

"Elizabeth wants to go out on Thursday."

I wish I could say that was like a splash of cold water over me, but the vibration has me so close to the edge that I groan my acknowledgment. Seth moves around his desk to stand in front of me.

"We've agreed to two dates a month for the next two months to see how things go and what public opinion is, since this is to help her image and mine." Seth sits against the edge of his desk.

"That makes sense," I bite out. Personally, I hate the thought of her near him at all, but my insides are burning so hot I can't focus on anything but my need to come.

"Set the tablet aside, princess." Seth gives me the voice that is meant to be obeyed.

I do as he says and look up at him, waiting, while I wind closer and closer to the edge.

"Does it hurt?"

I bite my lip and shake my head.

"Did you want me to fuck you last night?" He tips his head to the side considering me.

I must be a hot mess because my heart pounds heavy with the need for release. I nod and meet his heated eyes.

"Do you want me in your mouth or your ass?" His hand pauses on his belt.

Licking my lips, I think about what I want right now. I want to see his eyes as he comes for me. "Mouth."

Seth gives me a crooked smile as he undoes his pants and pulls out his erection. A burst of fresh heat washes over me. I spread my legs and lean forward to kiss his tip.

"Do you want me to do what I want? Or do you want control?" I trace a finger down the underside of his cock before lightly cupping his balls.

A knock echoes through the office. Before Seth can say anything, the door opens and Blake walks through. "I need to talk about the Lauder file."

Blake stops and looks up. His green eyes darken as he takes in my hand on Seth's balls and my wet lips. He shuts and locks the door, his hands already on his belt.

The vibration is too much, knowing they both want to fuck me. My mouth opens as an orgasm screeches through me. My eyes squeeze shut as wave after wave pummels my pussy with the unrelenting vibration.

"Did you just come?" Blake steps forward and strokes his hand over my hair.

Seth holds up his phone. "Vibrator against her clit."

He doesn't ease up on the vibrations as he sets the phone down. "She wants to suck my cock, but you could take her ass."

He passes Blake the lube from his desk. Blake takes it and gestures to the leather couch. "Should we?"

Helping me stand, Seth leads me over to the couch. Every step sends an aftershock through me. It's too much but I don't want Seth to stop. My panties are soaked through at the thought of taking both Seth and Blake.

Seth sits on the couch and helps me kneel before him. "Do what you want, princess."

Taking the phone from his pocket, he sits back and waits for me. Blake kneels behind me and tugs my skirt up. I bend over, sticking my ass out for Blake, and lick Seth's cock from his balls to his slit before closing my mouth on his tip and sucking.

Blake's zipper and the sound of him lubing his cock are the only warning I have before he tugs my panties down and his cock brushes my puckered hole. One of his hands presses the vibrator firmly against my clit as his cock sinks steadily into my ass.

I take Seth's cock deep inside my mouth as a moan buzzes through me. I swallow around his tip in the back of my throat while Blake strokes out slowly before pushing all the way in. My body convulses as I climax.

"Fuck, tiger." Blake hisses as he draws out and punches back into my ass. "You needed a good fucking, didn't you?"

Yes. Yes, I did. Do. We're far from done.

Moaning, I work Seth's cock, sucking, licking, bobbing, swallowing. Blake shifts the vibrator, rubbing it against my clit as he slowly withdraws before pushing in deep. Over and over. The room fills with the light buzz of the vibrator, their groans, my whimpers of need, and the slap of flesh against flesh. I tip over the edge again, moaning around Seth's cock as my orgasm shatters through me.

The vibration stops and I lift my eyes to meet Seth's. "Focus, princess. Make us come and I'll turn it back on."

I suck the head of his cock before taking him deep, pressing down on him as far as I can go. Following the rhythm Blake sets as he fucks my ass, burying himself deep inside me with each forward thrust. Until all I feel is them taking me, filling me, making me whole. My insides wind tighter and tighter, knowing that I'm going to fall over the edge even without the vibrator's persistent buzz.

Blake's fingers slip forward, beneath the vibrator, and press against my clit just as Seth's cum hits the back of my throat. I swallow, feeling my ass clench around Blake's cock, convulsing as I come around him. He groans his release, filling me with his warm cum.

I lift off Seth and breathe through the aftershocks. Seth tips my chin up, and our eyes lock. Blake's fingers draw away from my clit as the vibrator fires. My focus narrows on Seth's darkened eyes as I burst into another release. I cry out as Blake strokes in and out with his still-hard cock, prolonging my climax. My vision dims for what feels like an eternity. The vibrations stop and Blake withdraws, and all I can do is breathe in and out as I come down.

My body softens, and I rest my head on Seth's pants. After handing a washcloth to Seth, Blake returns behind me and gently cleans my ass and removes the vibrator from my panties. Little aftershocks buzz through me at Blake's touch as I watch Seth clean his cock before tucking it away.

Helping me straighten my clothes, Blake lifts me to sit on the couch next to Seth. He collapses next to me and takes my hand in his.

"You're good with the Elizabeth thing still, right?" Seth asks.

I arch my eyebrow at Seth. "You must be pretty worried if you waited until you had me orgasming to tell me about it."

He kisses me softly, lingering with his mouth pressed against mine. I sigh as I give in to the feeling that wells inside me at his touch.

Pressing his forehead against mine, he releases a breath. "It's for all of us, but mostly I'm doing it to protect you. Our reputation for being good businessmen may outweigh our sexual proclivities, especially as men, but I don't want to damage your career before you even get started."

His fingers play with the tendrils of hair framing my face. My heart feels too big for my chest as I meet his eyes.

"This works if we keep talking about this arrangement between you and Elizabeth. Don't hide what happens between you two and we'll be good." I can swallow my jealousy, knowing that while he seems to be with her, he'll come home to me. I'm the one he wants.

Chapter 110

Possession

Madison

It's almost three o'clock when the receptionist sends me a text stating someone is here to see me. I glance at the closed doors. Everyone's been busy this afternoon on calls or in meetings. The only time we really had were those stolen moments in Seth's office.

I open the group chat.

ME:

Reception says someone's here to see me. Going down. Won't leave reception.

I don't expect a reply. I can see most of them are in video conferences or on their phones. Taking my mobile, I go to the elevator and press the button.

A door opens behind me and Blake steps into his doorway. His fierce gaze is on me while he talks on his phone. He gives me a slight nod, and my chest floods with warmth. Then he puts his fingers to his eyes, telling me he'll be watching.

Some of the tension leaves me, knowing he'll still be watching on the camera feeds even if he isn't with me.

The elevator arrives and I step on. The lobby isn't as busy this time of day, but I don't see anyone familiar. I stop next to the receptionist and wait for her to complete her call. I'm not sure what I did to offend her. When she hangs up, she gives me a once-over.

I checked myself in the bathroom before leaving Seth's office. Nothing is out of place, and I know I look good in whatever he puts me in. So I just give her a smile.

"Over there." She jerks her head to the left before dismissing me.

Straightening, I head that way. As I round the corner, I spot Robert, my previous neighbor, standing against the wall. His face lights up when he sees me.

He moves forward quickly to intercept me. "Madison. How have you been?"

"I'm good. What are you doing here?" I'm confused. Why would he be here?

He holds out his hand and opens it. My grandma's bracelet. Fuck, with everything going on, I forgot he was bringing it.

I reach for it and lift it from his hand. "Where did you find this?"

The bracelet isn't fancy, but it's something my grandma gave me. Little charms decorate a simple chain. Each one is in its place. I'd thought I lost it in the move.

"The hallway." Robert moves closer, and I automatically take a step back. He doesn't appear fazed by it though. "The metal glinted in the light, and I remembered you wearing it. It must have dropped when those men came to move you out."

"Must have." But why didn't I notice it when Blake and I went back to look for it? What seems like ages ago. If it really was in the hallway, I'm sure I would have seen it.

While I'm busy thinking, Robert moves in closer, looking down at the bracelet. "You wore it all the time. Especially with that pretty floral sundress you loved so much."

Chills creep up my spine and I draw away from Robert. "Why would you mention that dress?"

I back away toward where people are, toward the receptionist. It can't be a coincidence, but it has to be. The guys said Robert isn't the stalker.

Robert's forehead wrinkles as he follows after me. "It's what you wore when I remember you wearing the bracelet. What's wrong, Madison?"

A metal trash can blocks my path, and it rattles as I run into it. "I have to go, Robert. Thank you for returning this to me."

"I saw a woman try to get into your apartment."

I pause with the trash can between us. It's distance, but not enough. "A woman?"

He nods and tucks his hands into his pockets. "She came by a few times. Tall brunette. Probably the high heels she wore made her look tall. I didn't get a good look at her face. She always turned away when I got to my door. I wasn't sure if you were subletting the apartment or if you had a new roommate after the incident with Valerie."

Brunette could be anyone, really. Courtney? Even Hope has brown hair.

Robert brushes a hand through his hair. "I thought you might want to know. In case, you didn't have anyone living there. I never saw them get into the apartment."

I step forward, grateful for the trash can between us. "If you see this woman again, could you text me?"

His dark eyes light up. "Of course. Do you want me to get her name?"

"No."

I don't want to tangle Robert up in this any more than I have to. I'll actually be glad to have him out of my life. While he seems like a nice guy, he still has that creep factor I can't shake off. Him "finding" my grandma's bracelet after I'd been to the apartment complex just seems odd and maybe too coincidental.

"You know, Valerie hasn't been by in a long time. It's probably safe for you to come back home." Robert has hope in his eyes.

I shake my head. "I don't live there anymore. I have a home."

For as long as they'll keep me, these men are my home.

"Oh." Robert steps back and looks down at his feet. "Okay, I'll tell you if I see that woman. If you need anything, I'm here for you."

———

When evening rolls around, I slip into my bedroom and set the bracelet in the jewelry box in the closet. Seth has it filled with gold and silver and gemstones. My dull gold bracelet looks lackluster beside it all, but it's mine. It's a piece of home that I carry with me.

My grandma was the only one who felt like home to me growing up. It's strange that I haven't thought about my parents much since moving in with the guys. I get a random text from my mother occasionally. Basically proof of life, I suppose.

When I close the drawer and turn to leave the closet, Noah stands in the doorway, watching me. I startle slightly and press my hand to my skittering heart.

"Noah."

He steps into the closet and closes the door behind him. That little taste of fear blooms in my stomach at his serious face.

"Is something wrong?" I swallow. Dread pours through me.

"No, kitten, but we need to talk." He closes in on me, and the moment his hand touches my cheek, my insides relax. This is Noah. He's serious sometimes and playful others. I've just seen him more playfully serious lately.

His thumb smooths over my cheekbone, and he gestures with his head toward the bench. We move to it and sit next to each other.

"What do you need to talk about?" I take his hand and raise it to my lips, pressing a kiss to his knuckles before lifting my eyes to meet his. Already they've softened to that warm brown that I love.

"I don't want to hold back tonight."

My brow furrows. "Why would you think—"

"You're on your period, and some women get weird about having sex during." He shrugs and his blond hair falls over his eyes, making him seem young again. "I know you played with Seth and Blake this afternoon."

"Do you guys keep a spreadsheet or something?" I smile, but my cheeks flush warm, thinking of everything that could be on that spreadsheet.

"This whole situation works because we communicate." Noah strokes his thumb over my lower lip. "It's not a competition. We tell each other everything."

"Including that we said *I love you* to each other?" My pulse pounds as my stomach knots.

His brown eyes are calming. "Not that, kitten. That's ours. I know you'll tell them you love them eventually, but until then, we can keep this one thing."

The knot in my stomach eases.

"You don't want to hold back tonight?" Butterflies erupt in my stomach thinking of what Noah might want to do to me.

He plays with my fingers, stroking them, rubbing them. "I want you tied so you can't move, like on the bondage horse."

Wetness gathers between my thighs, remembering.

His cheek brushes mine as he leans in to press his lips against my ear. "I want you open for me to use. I want to drive you so crazy with want and need you feel like you can't take any more."

I let out a harsh breath as my pulse quickens.

"If you leak all over the place, it doesn't matter. I want to fuck you hard and often."

Heat boils in me as he draws back until our faces are aligned. "I want you to give yourself fully to me tonight. Will you let me have you, kitten?"

His dark eyes search mine. My lips part and I wet them. "Anything, Noah."

When we walk into the living room, hand in hand, Seth glances at us from the kitchen. I squeeze Noah's hand and release it to go help Seth with dinner. When I stop beside him and look down at the island where he's chopping vegetables, I wait for him to tell me what to do.

He stops and I lift my chin. He kisses me softly, making me yearn for more, but he pulls away before I can do anything about it.

I breathe out before opening my eyes. "Can I help you with dinner?"

"Of course." He passes me a cutting board, a knife, and about half the vegetables left to cut up. We work quietly together. Noah disappears into the library where Blake works at the large table. I'm not sure where Coop is.

It's familiar and domestic. It's hard to believe I've been here only a few weeks. My heart is so wrapped up in these guys, it's going to destroy me when I leave them. Eventually, I'll have to. Being their secret won't last.

Either the truth will come out or it will weigh too heavy on my heart, watching them pretend.

The apartment door bursts open, startling me.

"Fuck!" Coop slams the door behind him and strides into the living room, searching the area until his eyes land on me. He makes his way toward me with determination in his eyes that melts my panties.

I don't even realize I'm backing up until I come up against the counter. He closes in on me and grabs the back of my neck. His mouth captures mine, and I cling to his shirt as he takes from me. I'd give him anything he needs. Always.

He lifts me onto the counter, never relinquishing my mouth. My fingers thread into his tied-back hair, not caring if I mess it up. The kiss goes on and on as he grinds his hard cock between my legs, pushing my desire to dizzying heights. His fingers dig into my hips, holding me still for him.

His lips leave mine to trail down to my neck, kissing, biting, sucking. I gasp in air. The world has been reduced to his mouth on my body, the press of his cock against my pussy, the need to feel him inside me.

"Fuck, I need you, sweetheart."

"Trying to make dinner here." Seth sounds mildly annoyed.

Coop gives him a haughty look and lifts me off the counter against him. I wrap my legs around his waist as he says, "Fine."

He strides across the apartment and kicks open a door. We're in the play room, but he doesn't turn on the lights. He rips the covers off the bed and drops me in the center.

"Wait there," he growls and stalks off to the bathroom. I draw in a breath.

Desire shivers through my veins. Coop can be playful, but I've never seen him fierce like this. Movement by the door captures my attention. Blake stands there with his arms crossed.

"You okay, tiger?"

Coop comes out of the bathroom before I have a chance to answer. "Go away, Blake."

He lays a couple towels on the bed before ripping off his shirt. Buttons scatter every which way. His golden muscles on display capture my attention.

"Coop," Blake warns.

"I'm fine, Blake." I quickly undo my buttons, afraid my beautiful blouse will be the next thing Coop destroys as he works on his belt.

"See? She's fine, Blake. Now fuck off." He whips off his pants and comes at me, naked and hard.

The door shuts, but when I glance over, I meet Blake's eyes as he sits on a bench.

"You want to watch?" Coop glances at him. "Fine, watch, but right now, she's mine."

Tingles course through me like I drank champagne. Coop reaches for me and jerks me upright. He's rough as he finishes undressing me, but he's gentle too. When I'm naked, he tosses me back on the bed and spreads my legs wide.

"Coop?" I'm about to mention the tampon when he grabs the string and draws it out.

"Sorry, if you're squeamish about such things, but I need to be balls deep in your pussy, right now." He dumps it in a trash can before climbing over my body. His cock lines up with my entrance and he slides all the way inside easily. I'm more than ready for him.

My breath catches as he gathers me against him. His mouth claims mine as he lifts my knees and spreads me wide. His muscles tighten against me as he pistons in and out of me, hard and fast, while his mouth devastates me.

It's hot as fuck the way he needs me. Tingles and sparks race through my body.

He lifts me against him and pulls my hair to tip my head back. His mouth trails down to my neck, biting, sucking, marking me.

"Say you're mine."

I bury my fingers in his hair, loosening it from the unraveling bun. "I'm yours."

"Scream it, so they all know it." He thrusts punishingly hard into me.

"I'm yours!"

His teeth sink into my neck, and I cry out from the twinge of pain.

"That's right. Mine. All mine."

I pull his hair until his lust-filled eyes meet mine. This goes both ways. "Say you're mine."

"Fuck, baby. I'm yours." He thrusts in so deep and rough, but I meet him thrust for thrust. I crave his aggression. Our bodies strive together, building something undeniable. My hips lift to receive him, welcoming him.

"Yours." The word is quiet as he whispers it against my lips before claiming them.

The impatience in his thrusts eases and his hold on me gentles. The flames building inside me reach an inferno, bursting. I arch against him as I come. His thrusts never slow, holding me suspended in my climax.

"Coop."

"Almost there, baby." His hand slides down between us and he strokes my clit, slow and methodical, pushing me closer and closer to the edge. He murmurs against my mouth, "Come with me this time. Drag me into the abyss with you."

The pressure builds inside me, a slave to his will. He leans his forehead against mine as our eyes lock. "Just a little more, baby. Can you feel it?"

I search his blue eyes. Our bodies are in sync, moving to a rhythm only we know, striving for just one more peak. This well of emotion I keep from him builds inside me, but this time I won't let it out.

"I'm yours," I whisper almost reverently.

"I'm yours." He thrusts deep and rubs my clit until fire blooms inside me setting off explosives through my veins. Pushing me even higher. "That's my girl."

My pussy convulses around his cock, drawing him deeper inside. Groaning, he comes inside me, hot and pulsing. His eyes lock on mine, showing every emotion so fast I can't catch them all. But I feel every inch of those emotions inside me as we collapse on the bed, breathing heavily.

Chapter 111

Corporate Securities

Coop

I bury my face in Madison's neck, breathing in her sweet floral scent and the smell of our sex. That need to claim her, to prove that she's mine, almost rears itself again, but she shifts below me. Her hands stroke through my hair, soft and gentle, like her.

Her touch settles me. I breathe her in and pull her tight against me, savoring this moment. Mostly alone.

"Yup, you two fucking is gorgeous." Blake's voice is tight, and I imagine he has a killer boner right now. Serves him right. "Dinner's almost ready. Clean up."

The door opens and shuts. We're finally truly alone.

Pulling my hair, she lifts my head so our eyes can meet. "Want to tell me what that was about?"

Her hands smooth down my face before curling around the back of my neck. Not taking my cock out of her, I shift us until I can stand, still hard, still inside her. Where I fucking belong.

She makes a little squealing noise as I jostle her into place with her arms and legs wrapped around me. Holding her ass, I walk us into the attached bathroom and start the shower.

Threading her fingers through my hair, she tips my head back again. "Are you going to answer me?"

She noticed that. Fuck. I grunt before walking us into the luke-warm shower. She practically crawls up my body to escape the cool water. Chuckling, I turn so it's hitting my back instead of hers.

"That wasn't nice." She pouts and I lean in to kiss her full lips.

My cock had softened, but with her slick body pressed against mine, it's only a matter of time before I'm hard again. She has that effect on me.

"We need to get cleaned up for dinner." I pull out of her and lower her to her feet.

She grabs a sponge and the soap I prefer. "What's going on?"

I do the same with her body wash and drag the soap over her breasts. Her nipples tighten for me, and her breasts grow fuller, making me want to claim her as mine again and again until I can feel it in my soul.

She clears her throat to get my attention.

I take a breath. "My mother called."

She stops. Sponge against my chest, mouth open like she's frozen. I pinch her ass, and she smashes the sponge on me.

"That"—looking somewhat horrified, she points to the play room —"was because of your mother?"

I cough to cover up my laugh. "That was in response to my moth-er's demands."

"She wanted you to fuck me?" She arches an eyebrow and I chuckle.

"She wanted me to be reasonable and break off our engagement," I admit. I won't use the exact terms my mother did, but that's the end result she wants.

Madison holds up her hand with the ring that is so perfect on her finger. Every time I catch sight of it there, I want to hold her against the wall and fuck her until she screams my name.

"Why don't you?" Her voice is soft as she looks up through her wet lashes. "We aren't really engaged. I get that you used it to make your ex jealous, but you succeeded. So why get all tangled up and make your life harder than it has to be?"

I crowd her into the wall as her eyes widen. "I enjoy being all tangled up with you."

Her eyes soften. Brushing a strand of her hair out of her face, I stroke my fingers down her neck.

"We don't need to be engaged to do what we're doing, Coop."

How do I explain this to her when I barely understand it myself? My hard cock presses against her stomach as I lean into her.

"I like staking my claim on you," I admit. "I like seeing you wear my ring like it's the most natural thing. I love watching you fuck my best friends, knowing that I'm the one who gets to say you're mine to the world. But that I choose to share you with them."

Her hands grab my shoulders as she arches her eyebrow at that. "You choose?"

I reach down and lift her by her thighs, spreading her open. "I choose to defile this body with them. To do nasty things to you and make you scream in pleasure. To know my cum is dripping down your thighs after I satisfy you."

My cock lines up with her cunt. Her hands dive into my hair, grabbing it by the handful as I thrust inside her.

"Coop," she cries out.

"I don't want to stop playing with you, goddess." I slowly slide out of her until just my tip is inside and thrust back in. She whimpers and tugs on my hair. "I want to fuck you all the time, even when you're bleeding. I wanted to fuck away your cramps, but I knew we needed to talk about it when you weren't in pain."

She smiles. "I would have hit you if you suggested that. My pussy was sore from taking all of you the night before."

"I know, but is it sore now?" I fuck her slowly, in and out. Watching her eyes and the ecstasy playing out on her face. She lets out little needy noises that make me want to go slow forever, but we need to get out to dinner before the guys come looking for us.

"Not sore now," she whispers and brings my mouth crashing

down on hers. Her hips thrust with mine until we're moving as one again.

She breaks off the kiss as she moans, coming all over my cock, drenching me in her cum.

Fuck, I love this woman.

The words flow through my brain, but quickly go away as I spill my release inside her, claiming her as my own. Fuck what anyone else thinks. If I can keep that ring on Madison forever, I will. Even if it means I have to marry her to achieve it.

———

Noah

Coop and Madison come out of the play room in towels. Blushing, Madison rushes off to her room while Coop strolls to his door. I caught the tail end of his move to take Madison off on his own. Blake followed, so I stayed out here.

Seth gave me a few looks while I finished helping him with dinner. It's probably written all over my face how much I love her. I don't really care anymore. They can believe I'm weak for giving in to my feelings. For not hiding what she makes me feel. But loving her makes me strong.

Even knowing she doesn't love just me makes me love her even more. Because while I know they won't always be stingy with their love, these three are broken and need more than just a feeling to believe in what they feel. But she loves them anyway.

I know she'll fill those holes in their hearts, if they'll let her.

I worry about Coop though. He collects pretty things, but he always lets them go. I just hope he isn't doing that with Madison because that could destroy her.

Coop comes out first and drops into his chair at the table. "Mother called."

I walk over with the plates and set them down. "Not happy about the engagement news or the potential grandchild?"

"Neither." He grins woefully and shakes his head. "You'd think she'd be happy to be a grandmother at last."

Blake sets a beer in front of Coop before he takes his seat with a beer of his own. "She wants to meet Madison?"

Coop's eyes lift to mine with a knowing look. "Of course."

I cringe. I've been to Victoria's meetings before. Even Leighton cried after dinner with Coop's mother. No one is good enough for her only son. While she puts him on a pedestal that no one could possibly reach, she makes him regret every decision he makes for himself by withholding her approval. He stopped trying to win her love long ago.

But she still has that hold over him.

"I'm not putting Madison through that." Coop shakes his head and drinks his beer.

"Are you calling off the engagement?" I sink into my seat across from him. I'm ambivalent about it either way. Their "engagement" won't stop me from claiming her as mine.

"Nope." Coop runs a hand through his wet hair. "We'll let the old lady stew for a little. Prove there's no baby on the way. Then maybe she'll be calm enough to handle meeting Madison."

"Who's meeting me?" She glides toward the table in a silky nightgown that barely covers her ass. Her hard nipples poke at the fabric, making my cock tighten. She's all mine tonight. I might leave on that nightgown. It'll be pretty bound against her body with rope.

"No one right now, sweetheart." Coop winks at her and her face flushes.

At least she got to come a few times already to take the edge off, because tonight, I'll punish her for letting them make her climax today. Torment her while filling her with my cum until she can't take it anymore and begs for release. Then maybe I'll give it to her. Maybe.

Her fingers trail over my shoulders as she passes me to take her seat. "You look pleased."

"I get you to myself later, kitten." I catch her hand and bring her knuckles to my lips. "It's been a while since we got to play alone."

Her eyes flare with heat. She'll be mine and mine alone tonight in my room. Locked tight.

Her breath catches as I release her hand. She takes her seat and presses her thighs together. Coop is right—she is a needy little slut. But she's *our* needy little slut.

"Is Victoria going to be a problem?" Seth sits at the head of the table next to Madison. He scoops dinner onto her plate first.

"No." Coop leans back. "She wants to meet Madison, but I can hold her off for a while."

Madison's eyebrows go up at that, but she doesn't say anything. None of us have really talked about our relationships outside of this one and maybe with a few of the women in the past. Our family lives are complicated.

"My mother would love you." I fill my plate. "Once she got over the fact that you aren't the woman she set me up with."

"We have that double date on Thursday." Madison picks a little at her food. "Will it disappoint your mother when you and Sara stop dating?"

I pause with my fork halfway to my mouth. There's a hint of bite in Madison's tone. Seth told her about dating Elizabeth today. Coop isn't willing to introduce her to his mother, even if she's his fiancée. And Blake hasn't said anything.

Fuck. Security is important. Almost as important as love.

"Protecting you is my priority. Sara and I might see each other for a while in public, just until the scrutiny dies down." I hate to hurt Madison more, but I won't lie to her. "We can all talk together on Thursday. Sara will assure you she doesn't want me that way, any more than I want her."

Madison finally lifts her eyes to meet mine. Doubt lingers in them. Of any of us to be jealous about dating, I should be the last one she worries about. I don't date much because the opportunity doesn't come up that frequently. Well, setups exist, but I don't want those women my mother pushes at me. They're all looking for a rich husband, not me.

Even the women we've tried this arrangement with before never really wanted me. I was just something they had to deal with to get to the one they really wanted. In college, women used me to get to Coop or Seth or even Blake. I stopped dating because it was easier.

Even when someone seemed genuine in their desire for me, I couldn't help wondering if I was a stepping stone. To someone better.

Taking Madison's hand beneath the table, I squeeze it gently before just holding it. Her eyes soften. I don't need to repeat how I feel. She knows I love her. Where her doubt stems from, I'm not sure.

But maybe tonight I'll work it out of her.

Chapter 112

Taking It All

Madison

Knowing what Noah has in store for me makes me eager to finish dinner and get started. The guys talk about work. About how to divide the Stiner project among the teams available. Taking mental notes occasionally, I can't help but worry this whole deal could blow up if Seth doesn't keep Elizabeth happy.

How she'll blow me up if he doesn't make her happy.

It's an axe waiting over my neck. The other one is Coop's mother. Was the "no one" Coop said I wouldn't be meeting right now his mother? She obviously upset him earlier, but when we talked, he didn't mention she wanted to meet me. But if she heard about our engagement, then why wouldn't she want to meet me? He seems determined to stop that from happening.

I'm not sure what to think. Is it because of me or because of her? My mother is logical and cold sometimes, but she can be loving other times. I'm just not a priority to her and never have been. Coop's family sounds frigid and unloving. I don't want to believe that though.

How could anyone who knows Coop not love him? He's fun, and

when he gets serious he gets so dark and . . . . Fuck, I can't even describe it in my own head. Growly, possessive.

"Princess?"

I lift my gaze to Seth, noting I'm the only one still at the table. Seth holds his plate and gestures with his head toward the kitchen. Fuck, I zoned out hard. I grab my plate and follow him.

I wait my turn to load the dishwasher, but Coop takes my plate and loads it. Blake spins me around into his arms before claiming my mouth. I rise on my toes as the kiss deepens, stirring the desire that always simmers under the surface.

It's hard to imagine going a single day without a kiss from every one of my guys. When this ends, I'm going to miss this part.

"Good night, tiger." His hard cock presses into my stomach.

I nibble on my lip, wanting to help with that, but knowing I'm Noah's tonight to do with what he likes. When I cleaned up after the shower, I didn't need to put in a new tampon. I'm done with my period and ready to play fully.

"Ready for bed, kitten?"

I glance at him from Blake's arms and give him a hopeful look. Maybe just a little sharing tonight? I've had them all today except Noah, but it's not enough. It's never enough with them. I want them all the time. It's an addiction, and I'm not sure I ever want to recover.

Noah closes in on my back, sliding the satin nightgown up over my hips. His body traps me against Blake before he whispers in my ear, "Do you want to be used by everyone, kitten? Fly off into subspace from being fucked so good?"

A burst of butterflies explodes inside me at the thought. I groan and rest my forehead against Blake's chest. The fire burns hotter, needier. Fuck, I want that.

"I could tie you to the bondage horse and let them all take you as often as they want. As often as I let them. You'll be all mine. I'll be in charge of your safe word. I'll be in charge of your pleasure. What do you say, kitten? Do you want to put yourself into my hands?"

"I—" My gaze lifts to Blake's.

His green eyes burn with desire. He brushes my hair off my cheek, sending sparks through me. Noah rubs his cock against my ass. Aching need shudders through me, but I want Noah to have what he wants. Not do what he thinks will please me and the others.

Turning in their arms to face Noah, I press back against Blake. His fingers trail over my neck and shoulders, brushing my strap down on my arm. Shivers ripple through me. I take Noah's jaw in my hand and tip his face so we're eye to eye.

"This is your night," I whisper.

His dark eyes are liquid pools of desire, making me want to sink into his darkness. His hand slides beneath my nightgown, and his fingers trace circles on my hip bone. Arousal churns hot and heavy inside me.

My lips part at how much I want him. That connection between us flows strong, and I take a breath before I admit, "I want to give you everything. Do with my body what you want. Take my safe word and make it yours. You decide when I've had enough. You claim my body and give it to whoever you like. Tonight, I'm yours."

Noah smiles darkly, lighting that fire in my belly that burns for him alone. "Let's play, kitten."

Noah

I know what my kitten wants and what she needs. She's toyed with the others today, but she wants all of us. I'm willing to give her what she wants. On my terms.

Dragging her into my body, I claim her mouth, squeezing her round ass cheeks in my hands tightly. She's given up control to me before, but not on this level.

We'll play with the boys for a while, but then she's mine to destroy and shatter before I put her back together.

Backing away, I hold her hand to bring her with me. My eyes locked on her dilated ones.

"She wants all of us." I glance at the others and nod toward the play room. I meet her gaze again. "She wants to be watched. To be played with. To come over and over again."

She shivers with my every word. Her nipples are hard peaks pushing on the satin of her slip.

"Same rules as before, kitten. No noise or you'll get spanked. This time with our hands." I jerk her through the door to the play room and flip on the dim lights. "Do you want this filmed?"

Biting her lip, she nods as heat flares in her eyes. "Yes, I want to watch you use me."

I glance at Seth, and he moves to set up the camera. We still haven't watched the one from the other night. I'm thinking a double feature this weekend while she rides my cock. I draw Madison into the room and to a bench.

"Sit."

She does as I ask but looks at me in question. I squat before her.

"I'm going to tie you a little different this time." Reaching out, I trace the peak of her nipple through the satin. "I'm going to bind your arms and breasts."

Her thighs press together, but I don't spread them open for me. Soon enough, she'll be at my mercy.

Coop brings a length of rope, and I uncoil it while she watches. Coop strips out of his shirt. That same dark energy pours off him as when he came through the apartment door earlier. He's done what he can to separate himself from his family. Dealing with his mother always sets him off.

Everyone is a little on edge. The stalker has remained quiet since the arrest, and all we can do is wait for the next message or the next attempt, making us all anxious.

I'm not the only one who needs to claim Madison.

"Arms behind your back, kitten."

Moving behind her, I guide her arms into position. Then I begin, drawing the rope around her torso. Binding her arms and her chest.

The act is soothing and almost meditative. The sounds of the others getting undressed is the only other noise in the room.

When I finish, I squat before her again. "Good, kitten?"

She nods. Her eyes are a little dazed, but she's still with us. Good, I want her to feel us inside her, using her. One after the other until she can't tell who or what, but just knows she needs it.

"Blake?" I stand before her and take off my shirt. Blake stops behind her. "Put her on the bondage horse."

He's only in his boxers. He bends and lifts her against his chest. She sighs at the touch of his warm skin against hers. Already sensitive to stimulation.

I follow him over as Coop helps position her on the bondage horse. Instead of putting her face down, she's face up. Her back arches with her arms tucked beneath her. Her head hangs off the edge of the center pommel.

Seth hands me a length of rope and I get to work. I bind her legs spread open and wrap the rope around her chest between her breasts to hold her in place. Tying the rope down through the tie points on the bench.

Stepping back, I admire her tied up and helpless for us. Her rapid breathing makes her breasts rise and fall. Her hair falls down like a curtain over the side of the bench. I didn't strip her of her nightgown or her panties.

"I'm going to cut away your panties, kitten."

She whimpers softly and I allow the sound without punishment. She doesn't like knife play, and I'll be careful not to cut her skin. I'll hold to her limits. Our eyes meet and I see the trust in hers.

Coop hands me the scissors. The cold, dull edge slides against her skin as I slip them beneath the edge of her panties. I cut them, and then the other side, and toss them into the trash, leaving her bare and open to us. No pad and no tampon string. She's so wet, I could slip inside her in a stroke. Coop takes the scissors away.

"You're done with your period?" I ask.

"Yes," she says softly.

Seth hands me a bottle of lube. Everyone is quiet, waiting for me to be ready, knowing this is my show. Knowing her pussy is mine right now. Her mouth is mine. Her ass is mine. I'll decide how much she gets and when she's had enough.

I slip my lubed hand between her ass cheeks and slide my fingers into her asshole. Her pussy clenches and I blow lightly on it. Her thighs flex as she tries to close her legs.

"Relax, kitten." I take my other hand and slide my fingers into her cunt.

She releases a breath but doesn't make a sound as I slowly pump my fingers in and out of her tight holes. So fucking wet and ready. Her hips try to move with my fingers, but she's bound tight. When the first flutters of her release pulse against my fingers, I pull them out.

"Wait here." Talking to the guys, I walk into the bathroom and wash my hands before getting undressed. I'll be the first to take her tonight. Everywhere.

Her eyes watch me as I stride to her. The others stand to one side, studying her body as they stroke their dicks. I grab her hair and thrust my hard cock past her lips, deep into her mouth. She jerks a little at the intrusion, but a soft moan is all she lets out.

I glance at Blake. "Three, as a reminder."

When I draw out of her throat until she can suck on me, he circles to her ass and spanks her three times. She sucks through the spanks, drawing hard on my cock. Getting her tied up and ready to be used has me so hard it won't take much to come.

Blake presses his fingers into her ass. I don't need to tell him not to fuck her yet. She's mine to do with what I want, after all. I reach forward and pluck at her nipple through the satin. Her breath catches around my cock. Holding her head back by her hair, I rock my hips, slowly thrusting my cock in and out of her mouth while teasing her nipple.

Blake continues to fuck her ass with his fingers but rubs her clit with his other hand. Her breathing is harsh around my cock. I pinch her nipple and order, "Suck."

Her cheeks hollow out around my cock as I piston in and out. Her body tightens as she comes. She draws on my cock as I thrust a few more times. My release fills her throat. I rub her nipple to tease her as she swallows around me.

Stepping away, I nod to Coop. He walks over to take my place. His fingers tease her other nipple while he cradles her head in his hand.

"Open like the good little slut you are," he says in a low voice.

She opens her mouth and he slides his cock inside. My cock hardens again as her lips spread for him, as he presses in deep, and she gags a little around him. She's so beautifully helpless. At our mercy.

When Blake moves out from between her legs, she whimpers in need. I trail my hand down her spread leg as I round to where her pussy and ass are spread open for me. I meet Coop's eyes, and he nods as he pulls almost all the way out of her mouth.

"Three for whimpering, kitten. Next time will be five." I smack her ass twice before smacking her right on her pussy.

She moans around Coop's cock. He gives me an evil smile as I spank her four times on her other ass cheek. Then once on her wet pussy.

Her body tightens as she comes, but she doesn't make a sound. I slide my cock into her cunt as it continues to convulse. Coop and I fall into a rhythm of thrusting and withdrawing. Him in her mouth. Me in her pussy. Long and hard until Coop groans his release.

Seth hands me a metal butt plug as he crosses to take Coop's place at Madison's mouth. I wait until he's at her mouth and holding her head. As he slides into her mouth, I slip the plug between her ass cheeks and press it inside her asshole.

For a second, we stay still, both buried inside her and her ass stuffed full. We draw out of her slowly and methodically as we take her together. Seth tweaks both of her nipples as she writhes between us. With the bindings, she can't move much.

Teasing her clit with my fingers, I tug on the plug, making the wide base stretch her opening. Her legs tremble as she arches against the ropes. A flush blooms on her neck and chest as she comes. Her throbbing cunt grips my cock in a stranglehold, drawing me into my release.

I groan as my cum fills her.

Withdrawing, I use my fingers to press my cum back inside her pussy while teasing her ass with the plug. Seth thrusts deep in her throat and groans. She swallows him down. Running his hand along her jaw, he backs away.

"Words, kitten. How do you feel?"

Her pussy pulses around my fingers. "Good. Green."

I thrust my fingers deep inside her pussy before lowering my mouth to taste and tease her sweet clit, sucking it into my mouth while I fuck her with my fingers. Blake moves to her head, caressing her hair before grabbing a fistful of it.

"Open, tiger."

Her pussy clenches around my fingers as he slides his thick cock into her mouth. I torment her clit with my tongue and thrust my fingers in and out of her pussy as Blake takes her mouth. When my cock hardens again, I tug the plug out as I suck her clit.

She groans around Blake's cock as she shatters. Lifting my mouth, I guide my cock to her asshole and press in while she's still climaxing. She's tight and hot around me.

I love fucking every inch of her. She's mine to do with what I like. Blake and I fall into a rhythm. My fingers in her pussy follow his thrusts while my cock alternates. When he pulls out, I push in.

She writhes beneath me. Little helpless, needy noises escape her. I won't punish her for them. Not this time.

I pull my fingers out of her cunt to grip her hips so I can thrust harder and deeper into her ass. Blake bellows as he comes down her throat. He steps away, and her harsh breathing reaches me. Each breath punctuated by my hard thrusts into her.

My cock pistons in and out of her ass as I stare down at her pussy, open and rosy, wet from her arousal, my cum, and my mouth. I thrust deep and fill her ass. As my cum fills her, she comes with a throaty moan.

Still hard inside her ass, I smack her ass four times. When my hand comes down on her pussy hard, she cries out as she shatters again.

I rub her pussy softly as she comes down. "Good kitten."

Chapter 113

Bandwidth

Madison

My breath shudders in and out of my lungs as I come down from my orgasms. I can't help but want more. Noah eases the ache of slapping my pussy by rubbing it. I want to moan and whimper at the building pressure inside me, but as much as I enjoy the pain, I don't want to be spanked again. My ass is sensitive from the spankings already.

My arms are bound tight beneath me. They haven't fallen asleep yet. I can't focus on my arms though. All of my attention has shifted to my pussy and Noah's cock filling my ass.

I can't move as Noah draws his cock out, leaving me empty. His cum leaks out of me. Nothing I can do about it. My legs are spread wide, baring my pussy and asshole to them all. My head hangs down, waiting for the next cock to fill my mouth.

Someone steps between my legs, and a cock nudges at my entrance. Then I feel the cool metal against my asshole and the plug slides in. It's wider at the base, wider than even Blake. It's almost like having another cock inside me that doesn't move until they tug on it.

And when they do, delicious ripples course through me.

Hands stroke beneath my nightgown and over my belly as he slides his cock inside me. Coop. He thrusts slow and steady into my pussy while he tugs on the plug randomly, lighting me up even more.

Seth cradles my head, holding his cock at my lips. "Open, princess."

Arousal flows hot and heavy through me as I wet my lips and swallow before opening for his cock. Hands massage my breasts, but all I can see is Seth's legs. Coop rubs my clit as he fucks me. This isn't the almost brutal claiming of earlier. Whatever demon rode him then has calmed.

The rope circles my breasts and holds me in an arched position. It's uncomfortable, but relaxing knowing I don't have to hold myself just so. The ropes will keep me exactly where my men want me.

Fingers slip beneath the satin to touch my nipple, and I explode at the brush of skin against me. My climax rocks through me.

"Fuck, keep doing that," Coop says, harshly. "She's coming around my cock like the good little whore she is."

Blake chuckles and pinches my nipple, sending jolts of desire down to my pussy.

Seth's hips rock into my face, taking my throat with his cock. Coop pulls out the plug and shoves it back in as he thrusts in my pussy. I don't know that I'll be able to come again without a sound, and I can't hold back much longer. It's welling in my chest, needing release.

Groaning, Seth explodes. Hot jets of cum fill my mouth with his salty taste. I swallow as much as I can, taking it all inside me. When he pulls out, Noah is there. His cock thrusts into my mouth, and I gag a little around him before swallowing.

Coop curses as he comes inside me. He jerks out the plug, and I can't stop myself from shattering more. I'm not sure if I'm actually coming down between orgasms or just having one long continuous climax at this point.

"How are your arms, kitten? Moan, if you feel any tingling." He slides his hand under me and touches my fingers. They aren't tingling so I don't make a sound.

A cock presses against my asshole, gliding in easily even though he's thicker than the rest. Blake. Something cool presses against my entrance and slides into my pussy until it fills me. A part of it rests on my fluttering clit.

Noah continues to drive his cock into my mouth, taking me a little rougher than before, but I love it. Suddenly the object moves on my clit and vibrates inside me. Blake slides in and out of my ass, bumping the vibrator with his hips.

It's too much, and I'm back over the edge, shaking with the intensity of my orgasm and unable to come down with the vibrator still pulsing against my clit. A part of me wants to fight the sensation, but then I give in to it.

I ride the waves as they continue to fuck me. Suck when I can and know that's about all I can do in this position. Noah bellows as he comes down my throat. Blake fills my ass with his hot cum and steps away.

Another cock slides into his place, and another hand takes my hair. I fall into the sensation, the movement, the need, the ache, the desire.

Noah

The moment Madison gives in to subspace is beautiful. Her body relaxes as Coop fucks her mouth. Seth's cock slides into her ass while he fucks her pussy with the vibrator. Sweat glistens on her skin as she moans around Coop.

Seth gives her five spanks on her ass as he thrusts into her. She moans harder as it tips her over the edge. I step forward and tease her nipples through the satin nightgown.

"Do you like being used by us, kitten?" I don't get an answer but I don't expect one. "I want this body to be so used, cum spills out of you all night on my bed."

"Fuck." Coop comes at the image I paint. He withdraws, but I put my hand up before Blake can step into place. She moans and thrashes as she comes again, drawing Seth into another orgasm.

When Seth draws out the vibrator and his cock, she whimpers.

"Need, kitten, or sore?" I unbind the rope holding her torso to the bench and help her sit up, letting the blood rush out of her head. Her dazed, hungry eyes watch me as she licks her lips.

"Blake, will you hold her up while I get her legs untied?"

He holds her against him as I slowly unwind the ropes from her legs. Coop takes her freed leg and massages the muscles.

I wind the rope into a loop. "Seth, I want three cocks in her. I give you the option of telling us what to do or being the third cock."

He steps forward and captures Madison's jaw in his hand before trailing his thumb over her lower lip. She sucks in a breath as her passion-blown eyes follow him.

"I'll direct." He steps back. "As long as I get to fuck the princess one more time after."

I nod in agreement. "Her arms stay bound."

I check her hands, making sure the color is still good and the ropes aren't cutting off circulation. Satisfied, I step back.

Seth purses his lips and strokes his chin as he searches the room. He gestures to the chaise-like bench. Perfect.

Blake lifts Madison against him, and her mouth finds his shoulder and sucks. He shifts her in his arms until his cock slides into her cunt.

She gasps against his skin and trails her tongue along his tight neck muscles.

"Blake on the bench, leave your cock buried in her cunt until everyone else is in position." Seth rearranges the video camera.

"Yes, boss." Blake straddles the bench and lowers onto it while he leans against the back, holding her upright by the ropes.

I climb behind her before Seth can say anything and take the ropes, tugging them tight against her body. She moans softly. Seth sighs from behind the video camera.

"Noah, take her ass. Coop, take her mouth." He gestures toward where we're already positioning ourselves.

I wait until Seth has the video recording before I lower Madison toward Blake, holding her suspended above him with the rope. She sighs and moans against the sensation of the rope digging into her flesh.

While Blake carried her, I stroked lube over my cock. I could take her mouth again, but I want to feel the fullness of her ass and pussy being pounded at the same time.

Easing the head of my cock into her puckered hole, I take my time, pulling out and pressing back in, just the tip, until she shudders and comes all over Blake's lap.

"Fuck, she drenched me." Blake thrusts up into her and she moans louder.

Grabbing her hair, Coop tilts her head toward him and follows my lead, pressing the tip of his cock between her lips before withdrawing. Together, we keep doing that. Teasing her, torturing her until she's a hot, whimpering mess between all of us.

Coop meets my eyes and I nod. On the next thrust, we both press deep into her. She shatters around me, and I bite my lip to keep from coming. She's glorious when she comes, and I want to make it happen over and over until I take it all away.

I tug her up against me, changing the angle of Blake inside her. The noises she makes almost make me blow. I bite the back of her neck and feel her convulse around me and Blake, tightening around us, pressing us together with only that thin membrane separating us.

"Do you like being stuffed full of cock, kitten?" I whisper in her ear as I pull out and thrust in deep at the same time Coop does. Seth steps up on the side opposite Coop. He strokes his cock. "Turn and take the boss into your mouth, kitten. Make him feel good."

When Coop releases her, she turns. Her hair is a mess from us pulling on it. Tears roll down her face, and her breathing is heavy and fast. Seth grabs her hair and thrusts his cock deep into her mouth. She moans around him.

"Do you like the boss's cock deep in your throat, kitten? Swallow around it."

Seth's groan tells me she did exactly what I told her to.

When I tug on her rope, she moans. "Lift your hips, kitten. Give Blake a ride while I fuck your hot, tight ass. Don't forget Coop."

Coop and Seth tangle their hands into her hair and alternate fucking her face while I help her grind and ride Blake's cock. Blake lifts her hips and lowers her on him. We all move together fluidly. One seamless machine hell-bent on getting our girl off.

Her ass and pussy begin to flutter around us.

"You're getting close, kitten. Can you hold off? Can you hold off until we're ready too? Or are you going to come all over us and draw us into our release?"

She whimpers as she moves between Seth's and Coop's cock.

"Maybe you should just come. That way we can take you as rough as we like until we finish. Would you like that, my little slut? Feeling us pounding into your tight little body?"

It's like a freight train blasts through her. Her whole body pulses as she comes. Coop releases down her throat before turning the reins over to the boss.

Seth fucks her mouth like a man on a mission. Blake raises her higher before thrusting back in, and I take her ass as rough as I promised. The whole time she's moaning and coming around us.

We find our release and fill her with our cum again. Her body draws on us, wanting it, needing it. We're one rough-breathing mass as we slowly relax. She lets me take all her weight as she comes down.

I draw her against me and lift her off Blake to carry her into the bathroom. Coop joins me. I let him take her as I unbind her arms and chest. She releases a sigh as the rope slips from her.

Tipping her chin up, I search her eyes. "Green, kitten?"

She nods as she leans against Coop. He has one of her arms while I take the other, rubbing it to bring sensation back. Coop slides her nightgown up over her hips, letting it glide against her sensitive skin as he drags it off her. She shivers, her darkened eyes watching me.

I take her into my arms while Coop starts the shower. He gives me a questioning look, asking if this is private time or if he can share.

After this, I'm ready to have her to myself in my bed, but for now, I nod. I don't think either of us are going to be doing much in the shower with her besides cleaning.

But she needs to wind down and be held. That's easier with two of us.

We step into the shower with her and take turns cleaning her. We try to be fast and efficient. Though my cock isn't the only one stirring, we get her out of the shower and into a towel. Coop gives her a long lingering kiss.

"Good night, sweetheart."

She cups his cheek and presses her lips to his. "Good night, Coop."

I cradle her in my arms as I head through the play room. Seth and Blake are in their boxers with wet hair when we enter the living space. I set Madison on her feet, and they each give her a good night kiss.

"You're beautiful, princess." Seth presses a kiss to her forehead before meeting my eyes. His are fierce and protective, but he knows I'll treat her right.

Taking her hand, I lead her into my room and lock the door behind us. She takes in a breath and looks at me over her shoulder, her blue eyes beckoning me forward. We're not done yet.

Chapter 114

Accountability

Madison

The shower helped me come out of subspace and regain awareness. That and the kisses wishing me good night. I felt a little self-conscious not wearing anything but a towel in the common area, but before I can dwell on it, Noah closes in and lifts me in his arms.

He lays me on the bed and climbs over me, tossing both our wet towels onto the floor. "Now you're all mine."

I run my hands through his thick hair and tug lightly on it. "I'm always yours."

He comes down over me and kisses me, slowly exploring my mouth like it's the first time and not the hundredth. His skin scorches mine, stoking the fire for him. I follow his lead as I cup his jaw, finding his tongue, chasing it back into his mouth until he sucks on my tongue.

My pussy pulses with aching need again. I swear I can't get enough of these guys. And Noah's thick, heavy erection against my thigh tells me he can't get enough of me either.

He takes my hand to one side and something soft wraps around it. Before I can emerge from the kiss, he locks my other hand in place. The material is silky and wide.

He lifts his head to look down into my eyes. "I told you I wanted to use you over and over again tonight."

Tracing his thumb over my lips, he drags it down the center of my chin, down between my breasts, over my belly button, until he slips his thumb between my legs and runs down over my clit to my entrance and slides inside. The fire always burning for him erupts into flames.

"You aren't sore yet. Are you, kitten?" His eyes watch mine carefully.

"No, Noah," I whisper as he pushes his thumb in and out of my pussy. I spread my legs for him, giving him full access.

"Hmm." He draws his thumb out of me and trails back to my asshole before pressing in. "Here?"

My lips part as need pulsates within me. I shake my head. He kisses me before skimming his lips over my jaw and down my neck. He leaves a trail of kisses across my chest until he sucks my nipple into his mouth. His thumb thrusts in and out of my asshole.

"Noah," I breathe out as a slow rush of sparks travels through me, lifting me higher, slowly building to a crescendo.

"Do you remember what I said, kitten?" He kisses his way to my other nipple before sucking on it, flicking it with his tongue.

My hips move with his thumb, trying to reach the edge again.

He draws his thumb out and lifts off me, walking into the bathroom. I close my legs around the ache pulsing between them. The water runs and then shuts off. The air is cool against my heated skin. Slowly, the sparks fizzle in my veins.

Finally, he comes back out. He lifts my hips and lays a towel under my ass before tossing a towel next to me.

"Noah?"

"Yes, kitten?" He sits beside me on the bed but doesn't touch me.

My brain struggles to drown out the haze of desire. He wanted to use me tonight. Until I couldn't take any more. "What are you waiting for?"

"I'm going to fuck your tits until I come all over that beautiful chest and neck of yours, but I don't want you so close you get off too." He reaches into a drawer and pulls out some lube.

"So you want to use my body." A sharp tingle races through me. I liked it when they used me before. "But not make me come?"

He pours some lube in his hand and rubs it between my breasts, slicking it over my nipples. I inhale harshly as need crawls inside me. "Exactly. I want you to feel pleasure, but I don't want you to come. If you do—"

He rolls my nipple between his fingers and tugs. It pinches slightly, but it also makes my pussy ache. I whimper, wanting more.

"If I do?" I whisper.

"I won't use your body to get off. I'll come all over you and leave you tied to the bed all night, covered in my cum." A spark is in his eye like he doesn't mind that outcome at all.

I consider him, hovering over me, stroking his long, hard cock in his hand, imagining watching as his cum spurts all over me. My pussy gets wetter and I squirm against the sheet.

Heat flares in his eyes. "Behave, kitten. Trust me, you'll prefer I use your body than the alternative."

Setting the bottle on the nightstand, he runs his lubed hand over his cock. It glistens in the low light the lamp gives off, making his cock shine. I want him any way I can get him.

"Ask me to fuck your tits, kitten." He slides his hand over the path his cock will take, and my insides heat.

"Please fuck my tits, Noah."

He glides his hand over my breast and pinches my nipple. "Try your own words, kitten."

His dark eyes meet mine and I press my thighs together against the building ache.

"Please slide your cock between my breasts and come on my neck, Noah."

He grabs a pillow and stuffs it behind my head so my chin is almost on my chest.

He squeezes my breast before he rises and straddles me. The ties keep me from reaching for him as he clutches my breasts together around his cock. His hips thrust, shuttling his hard cock through my breasts as his fingers circle my nipples.

"Did you enjoy having so many cocks service you tonight, kitten?"

I lift my gaze to meet his before returning to my view of his cock. Licking my lips, I nod. "I like being fucked."

"Do you feel empty now? Do you need a cock in your cunt and ass and mouth?"

The thought of that makes me gush with need. But I don't need anyone else in this moment. "Some other time. I enjoy being with just you. Being able to focus on exactly how you make me feel."

Our eyes meet and that connection we always have flows between us.

"Open your mouth, kitten."

I do as he asks, and he slides his cock up to my parted lips. I flick my tongue out to lick the precum from his tip.

"Fuck. You make me want to do dirty things to you."

A shiver rolls through me. I lift my head a little and suck his tip into my mouth, licking him like an ice cream cone. He pushes in and out of my mouth a little before settling back between my breasts.

"What do you want to do to me?" I whisper, wanting to hear everything.

"I want to play Coop's game of hunt in the dark. I want to hold you up against a wall with my fingers around your neck while I fuck you. I want to keep fucking you until we finally burn through this attraction and it just becomes comfortable, but I don't think you and I will ever be 'comfortable.' The fire between us rages too hot."

"Do you think it will consume us?" The words are breathy as my arousal overwhelms me. My eyes lift to his before returning to watching his cock work between my breasts. He plucks at my nipples, and I cry out at the shot of lust that flows to my pussy.

"I would let it consume me if it meant I could have you. I would burn for you, my love." He arches above me, his head tipped back, his abs tense as he squeezes my breasts tight around him. His cum jets out across my chest, over my neck, and even onto my lips.

He's beautiful in his release. I want more.

Ripping the pillow from beneath my head, he spreads out over me and kisses me, not caring about the cum currently coating me. I'm hot and needy. I open my legs to cradle his hips as he consumes my mouth.

We kiss each other until his cock twitches against my pussy. My breath catches as he grows hard against me and then slides inside me. He sits back on his knees, putting his arms under my knees to lift me and spread me open for him.

"Don't come, kitten. Or I'll come all over that smooth belly of yours." He plows into me, thrusting deep into my hot, wet core.

I bite my lip to keep myself from coming. He pauses and searches my face. My pussy flutters all around him, so close to coming.

"Not enough of a threat, kitten?" He thrusts slowly in and out a few times. "I'm sure Coop wouldn't mind joining us and coming all over you so you can feel like a good little slut covered in our cum."

Oh, shit. Oh, shit. Oh, shit. I'm so fucking close, and I don't think I want that, but it's making me combust on the inside imagining it. I bite my lip as I meet Noah's eyes.

"Fuck that. You're my whore tonight. Coop can come all over you tomorrow."

He begins to fuck me in earnest. He's not doing anything but shuttling in and out of my pussy. It shouldn't trigger my orgasm, but it's building whether I want it to or not.

He pulls out of my pussy and flips me over. I let out a startled cry as my arms cross, but it's not pain. There's some slack in the ties, so my arms aren't stretched out, just above me. He lifts my ass up in the air and thrusts back inside me deep and hard. His hands hold my ass cheeks, pulling them apart as he fucks me.

"We're going to end up on a messy bed tonight, aren't we, my love?" His hand slides around to my clit and pinches it.

I cry out as I come. I couldn't stop it if I tried as wave after wave crashes over me. Noah pulls out and his warm cum falls on my back. My pussy is still shuddering as his fingers press inside.

"I'm going to cover you in my cum, kitten. You'll be sticky from head to toe."

"Yes, Noah, please. Just make me come." My head rests against my arms as I push back against his fingers, trying to get more, trying to come again. Fuck it. I want it all.

His mouth closes over my clit and I'm lost. I might have screamed my release, but I'm too busy feeling this overwhelming explosion happening to hear it. His cock thrusts deep into my pussy, and the feeling spirals out of control.

"All night, my love. All night."

Blake

Madison walks off the elevator at nine. She's dressed and presentable looking, but she also has dark circles under her eyes. Noah got here on time for once, but not my tiger. She looks a little worse for wear.

"My office," I call from the doorway before backing in.

She breezes past me, soft floral scent wafting in the air. "My alarm didn't go off."

"Maybe because you left your phone on the island." I reach into my desk drawer and pull out a stiff paddle.

She groans and closes her eyes. "If you knew my phone was out there, why didn't you try to wake me up?"

When she opens her eyes, she meets mine and I just smile at her.

"And spoil my fun?" I sit down on the couch and pat my lap. "Five for being late and five for Coop making the coffee."

She crosses her arms and taps her foot. "Shouldn't Coop get to dole out the five for having to cover my duty?"

"Don't worry, sweetheart, I plan to watch." Coop grins from the doorway and gestures toward me. He blows across the coffee cup in his hand. "Stop wasting time and get your punishment over with so we can get on with our day."

"We'd be getting on with our day if I didn't have to submit to punishment," she mutters as she walks toward me. Her dress flows around her legs as she moves. I never forget that she's beautiful, but sometimes the way she moves stirs this well of emotion within me.

She looks at my lap and then down at her dress. "I don't want to get wrinkles."

I stand next to her and gesture to the couch. "Kneel on the couch. Face the wall. Put your hands on it."

She gathers her skirt and kneels on the couch, doing exactly what I want.

"Coop." I gesture toward her skirt.

He strides over to her and lifts her skirt, showing her thong underwear. Her ass cheeks are pale and smooth. My cock is hard just thinking of slipping between them. Fuck. Focus.

"Count, tiger."

I smack the paddle against her ass cheek.

"Ow." Her hand goes to her ass, but she remembers to count. "One."

I let that one slip because she looks exhausted. She puts her hand back on the wall and looks at me. This time when it lands, she flinches slightly, but only says, "Two."

Coop leans in and rubs her ass. He whispers loudly, "Don't worry, sweetheart, I'll make sure your ass feels real good tonight."

"If you don't mind." I gesture with the paddle for him to get out of the way.

"Of course." He moves to the side again.

She takes the rest of the spanks like a champ. Counting them off until the last one. Coop sits next to her on the couch now, still holding her skirt up. I rub her reddened skin and she hisses.

The temptation to pull her panties to the side and thrust into her wet cunt is almost too much. Instead, I smack her ass gently.

"Go on. You have a lot to do today." I pick up the paddle and walk behind my desk.

She watches me with a raised eyebrow. "That's it?"

I smirk. "Yes, tiger. That's it. Go get to work and stop wasting time."

Her lips press together in a firm line. She glances at Coop who stands and smacks her ass lightly before leaving my office.

She stands and straightens her dress before she heads to the door.

"We've got a client lunch today. Review the client file." I'm already sitting and pulling up files on my computer.

"Yes, sir."

I can almost hear her eyes roll from here, but I let it go. Today is a busy day, and as much as I like to play with Madison, it's time to get some work done.

Chapter 115

Responsive Design

Madison

The day drags on. I don't think there's enough coffee in the world to make me feel perky today. Not even my morning spanking woke me up.

Last night, Noah kept his word. Kept me tied to his bed all night as he used me over and over again. He might have wanted to keep me from coming originally. Instead, after passing out from so many orgasms and only an hour of sleep, I woke in desperate need of a shower to him untying my hands.

He didn't completely cover me in cum, but it was pretty much everywhere. Not once did I consider using my safe word to make him stop. I didn't want him to stop. I stripped the bed and threw the sheets in the washing machine before coming upstairs. The only good thing about this morning is my period is definitely done.

The landline rings on my desk.

"Morrigan Technology Group, this is Madison. How may I help you?"

"Madison, this is Anna Beck." Her voice is bright and cheerful.

But I don't know why she'd be calling me. Maybe she wants to talk to one of the guys?

"Good morning, Anna. How may I help you?"

"I wanted to see about that lunch."

That's right. At the benefit Anna said we should get lunch. I completely put it out of my mind, not just because of the attack, but because I figured it was just something she said to everyone. That whole "we need to get together" line but then no one ever does anything about it.

"Lunch?"

"Yes." Anna laughs lightly. "Lunch on me. We didn't have a chance to catch up at the benefit, and what you went through—"

Her voice cuts off and I hear a sniff. I didn't realize Anna cared that much about me. I loved working for her. The kids were easy. But at the benefit, she treated me like a long-lost friend.

"I'm fine. Yes, lunch would be nice. Maybe this weekend?" I glance up as Coop comes out of his office and leans against my desk.

"I'm so glad you're okay." She takes a breath. "This weekend works. How about Sunday?"

I glance at Coop and he raises a curious eyebrow. "Sunday lunch sounds great, Anna. I can't wait to catch up."

"Fabulous. Let me know your cell number so I can text you the time and place."

I give her my new number, and she texts me right away with her name. Coop continues to watch me with a confused expression.

"I'll see you Sunday." Anna once again sounds happy and then ends the call.

I set the phone in the cradle. "Did you need me, Coop?"

"Always, sweetheart. Anna . . . ?" He glances at the phone.

"Anna Beck. Patrick's wife. I used to babysit for their kids." I smile, thinking about their children. "It was fun, but not the type of experience I needed during college."

"Hmm." Coop doesn't get up to leave or tell me what he wants.

Noah steps out of his office and we both look at him. "You ready for our lunch?"

Coop smirks. "Of course. This time she's riding with us."

I squirm in my seat. They don't always play with me on the way to client lunches, but sometimes they do. Both their fiery gazes roam over me, heating my insides to the boiling point. Fuck, they're a potent duo.

"Grab your stuff, kitten." Noah pulls my chair out from under the desk.

Standing, I bend to grab my purse. When I straighten, I turn to them and they both have their eyes on my ass. I shake my head and smile.

Noah catches my look and smirks as he holds out his hand. "Come on, kitten. Maybe we can arrive early to lunch for once."

He leads me to the elevator with Coop hot on our tail.

"Shouldn't we wait for Blake and Seth?" I turn to look at their doors when the elevator announces its arrival.

"They get plenty of you." Coop enters the elevator and leans casually back against the wall. "Come on, sweetheart. Let's take advantage of the long ride down."

"It's not that long," I protest as I follow him.

Noah presses the button. When the elevator doors close, both of them turn to me. I raise an eyebrow as my panties dampen and my pulse races.

"Can I help you?" I back up against the wall. Not quite feeling cornered, but definitely feeling hunted. I don't hate it.

"I should have taken a picture." Noah leans back against the wall opposite me.

I tilt my head, confused. "A picture?"

"Of you naked on my bed covered in cum. Passed out from fucking too much. You just couldn't stop coming last night. Even after we used you in the play room. Every touch wound you up and made you orgasm."

My cheeks flush, from desire not embarrassment. I'm not

ashamed of what they do to me. Coop tips my chin up. Fire burns in his eyes, holding my gaze, making my knees weak. My breath catches.

When he speaks, he's not talking to me though. "Did you make her taste it?"

Coop licks his lips, sending a shiver of awareness through me. My gaze focuses on his mouth. The curve of his lips. The things he does to me with that mouth. I release my breath.

"And reward her for her misbehavior?" Noah chuckles. "No, but it probably got in her mouth on more than one occasion."

I lick my lips, remembering when he came on my neck and face a second time. He'd stroked his cock as his other fingers were buried in my pussy and his thumb teased my clit. His body hard all over as our eyes held. When he came on me, I shattered on his fingers.

Coop's fingers trace my dress's neckline. "You're red all the way down here, my little whore. Did you miss the taste of his cum?"

His hand curves around my breast, and my lips part as his blue eyes still hold mine. "Did he fuck your tits?"

His thumb circles my tightened nipple. Nodding helplessly, I can't speak as desire thickens my throat. The elevator stops moving, and I glance at the doors, but they remain shut. Noah's hand is on the Stop Elevator button.

"Answer me, slut." Coop's hand trails lower and he cups my pussy through my dress.

Air rushes out of me as his face lowers to get in mine.

"Did you miss his cum dripping out of your sweet pussy? Or was mine enough to keep you satiated through the night?"

My head rests against the wall. Searching his blue eyes, I wet my suddenly dry lips. His other hand presses on the wall next to my head. "Yes, I missed him filling me with his cum. But all of you filled me so full before that."

He rubs my pussy through my dress. For a moment, I worry about it staining. But as my desire consumes me, those thoughts drift away.

"I think she needs to remember what you taste like, Noah. Our little slut is hungry for more than lunch." His hand leaves my pussy throbbing. He catches my chin in his grip and rubs his thumb over my lower lip. "She needs to remember what it means to be owned by us."

His eyes glow with this inner fire as he releases me and steps back. Both he and Noah undo their belts. My mouth waters. I'm so addicted to these guys.

"Hands and knees?" Coop asks Noah as casually as if he were asking him to pass the salt shaker.

"No, make her stand and take it." Noah steps up to me and grips the back of my neck as he strokes his cock with his other hand. Our eyes lock. "I wouldn't want to mess up her knees before a client meeting."

Coop circles behind me and lifts my skirt, exposing my ass. His fingers trail over my sore ass cheeks. He lets out a low whistle.

"Blake marked you like a good little slut, but he didn't let you get off." He presses against me, his hard cock against my bare ass. "Maybe if you're a good little whore, we'll get you off. Would you like that?"

I bite my lip and nod.

Noah chuckles. "Such an eager little slut."

"I bet you're soaking wet for me, little whore." Coop yanks my panties to the side and his cock slides against my clit. "Wet and eager for it. Bend over."

I press my ass back against Coop as I bend over between them.

"Take me deep, kitten." Noah's words nearly make my knees crumple. I wet my lips before taking his cock deep into my throat. Coop sinks into my pussy at the same time, making my insides burn with need.

I tremble between them. This needy thing. This object they use to fulfill their desires. And I love every second of being their little slut.

Noah caresses the back of my neck as his thumb massages my jaw. "Do the work, greedy slut. Get me off and maybe we'll let you come."

Moaning, I suck on him as I bob my head over his cock. Coop

kicks my feet farther apart with his hands on my hips and his cock deep inside me. He just stays there, buried in me while I lick and suck on Noah's cock. My pussy pulses around his thick erection.

Coop draws almost all the way out before sliding back in again. I moan around Noah, taking him deep into my throat so he can feel the vibration.

"Fuck, kitten." His hand clenches on my neck before his other hand slides along the front of my throat, down beneath my gaping top to my breasts. "Do you remember how good it felt to have my cock slide here?"

His fingers slip under my bra and circle my nipple. "You have the best breasts. They're perfect to suck and tease, and so fucking sensitive." He tugs on my nipple, and I whimper at the shot of arousal that soaks me and Coop.

"How did she look covered in cum?" Coop thrusts harder into me until he's shoving my mouth farther onto Noah's cock.

"Like a goddess. Like a whore. Like she's mine. Like she's ours." Each phrase is punctuated by both of them thrusting into me. "She wouldn't stop coming."

He tweaks my nipple, making me moan as he rolls it between his fingers.

"I edged her once, but now when our little slut wants to come, she can't seem to control herself." Noah tugs as one of Coop's hands rounds my hip.

"No control?" Coop glides his fingers over my clit, and my brain goes fuzzy as my body burns. "We'll have to teach her better."

"Come for us, kitten." Noah strokes my nipple while thrusting into my throat as Coop plays my clit like his own personal instrument. His cock thrusting in and out of me. It's all too much.

I shatter, hurtling off into an orgasm that draws both of them with me. Their cocks jerk inside me as they find their release. Cum fills my mouth and my pussy. It's just what I need and triggers an aftershock. My knees go weak. I would've slumped to the ground, but Coop slides his arm around my waist, supporting me.

"What a good little whore," he whispers in my ear.

For these two? Yes. As often as they want me. An alarm sounds. Noah steps away, using a handkerchief to clean himself before releasing the stop. The elevator jolts into movement.

Coop pulls out but shoves his fingers inside me. Thrusting a few times to send aftershocks coursing through my system. He pulls his fingers out and presses a cloth between my legs.

"Be a good slut. Suck my fingers clean."

Coop slides his fingers between my lips, and I suck on them while meeting Noah's hungry gaze. Tasting Coop and me along with the taste of Noah. While I suck, Coop finishes cleaning me up and moves my panties back into place before straightening my skirt.

He draws his fingers out of my mouth and spins me against the wall before taking my lips with his. He kisses me like he's parched and I'm the only drink for miles. The fire inside leaps to attention, wanting more. I give him all I have in that kiss.

Coop pulls away and Noah slips into his spot, claiming me with his kiss. Showing me who I belong to and why I'll never be able to fully give him up.

They both make me weak for them. I want to stay in their arms all day and all night.

When the elevator dings its arrival, he pulls away and brushes my hair out of my face. "Good kitten."

Chapter 116

Strategic Planning

Madison

Lunch was pleasant and the afternoon was busy. So busy I barely saw the guys. They didn't really leave their offices until the executive meeting.

I'm finishing the final setup in the conference room when Seth comes in. He runs a discerning eye over my outfit for the day. It almost feels like he can see every piece he set out for me.

"How are you after last night?" Seth sits at the head of the table and pulls the tablet I set up for him over.

I fill the glasses on the table from the water pitcher. "Good."

"We weren't too rough?"

I lift my gaze to his curious blue eyes. "No, sir."

There's a slight twitch of his lips at that. I give him a small smile.

"Do you want me to stay and take notes this time?" I pause beside the chair I would use. They don't always need me in the Wednesday meetings. Most of the time it's just catching each other up.

"Yes." Seth gestures to the seat. "Please."

Sitting down, I open my tablet and bring up a notepad. Blake notices me when he comes in and sits next to Seth. Noah and Coop come in together. Both give me a smirk that makes my blood boil and my face hot.

As soon as everyone sits, Seth clears his throat. "We've gotten nowhere on the corporate spy. Every lead sends us down another rabbit hole. Sometimes the potential client receives a text or email. Other times it's an anonymous call. Sometimes a man and sometimes a woman."

"We've been looking at collusion." Blake leans back in his chair and looks over everyone. "But that makes it easier for the perpetrators to cover for each other."

"What about a honey trap?" Coop looks at me with a glint in his eyes when he says that.

I lift an eyebrow at him.

He smiles slowly. "Not an actual honey trap, but get a fake client in to see if someone calls them."

Seth leans his elbows on the table. "It's not a bad idea. It might give us more information if nothing else. Jason Harper gave us everything he gleaned from the person who contacted him. No one else has offered more, but that doesn't mean they weren't contacted."

"Are there any similarities in the companies they do contact?" I sit back and tap my pen against my pad. "There has to be some correlation or they would contact everyone."

Noah smiles. "Madison's right. If we can find a correlation, it would help us set up the perfect honey trap. If they don't have a system, it won't matter because if they contact everyone, they'll still contact our honey trap. But it will make sure they target the right one."

A little burst of pride glows from my insides. I love being part of this team. I love the sex, but it's not just about that. Each of these men gets me. They understand that I'm as driven as they are.

The rest of the meeting goes smoothly.

"Princess, order us some dinner tonight. We'll be working late." Seth meets my eyes and I nod.

"Of course." I head to my desk to pull up the online ordering and get the guys their usual from the restaurant downstairs. I just hit send when I notice someone behind me.

"Just because we have work tonight doesn't mean we can't play, sweetheart." Coop's voice is dark in my ear, sending thrills through me.

I don't turn as his hands massage my tense shoulders. Shivers race through me. "What did you have in mind?"

"After we finish our work and everyone goes downstairs for the night, I've left you an outfit on my bed to change into." Coop's lips brush my ear, sending sparks through my veins that make me weak as he whispers. "We'll play out a little fantasy of mine."

Desire pools hot and heavy in my stomach, but I draw in a deep breath. "What if I don't want to play?"

Coop's hands lift from me, taking his warmth with him. When I spin around in my chair, he's leaning against the wall. "We don't have to play if you don't want to, sweetheart."

"You won't tell me what it is?" I cross my legs, and his heated gaze tracks my movement. A pulse of desire races through me.

"I don't want to ruin the surprise. I know your limits, goddess. I'll stay well within them." The sparkle in his blue eyes intrigues me.

I definitely want to play. Role-play, besides the one night with Noah and Coop, hasn't really been a thing. And I really enjoyed it that night.

"After work?" I arch an eyebrow. "Just us?"

His smile grows wide. His eyes sparkle with a dark light that sets my pulse fluttering. "After work. Just us."

***

Coop

"Any common variables?" Seth leans back in his chair.

We've been going over files for hours, each of us taking a stack. Madison and Noah cleaned up our dinner leftovers hours ago. Glancing at my watch, I notice Madison stifling a yawn.

I glare at Noah. He kept her up late, and it better not fuck up my night with her.

Noah's barely paying attention, so he doesn't notice my glare. He's probably just as tired as she is. Madison's gaze lifts to mine. She wets her lips as her eyes drop to my mouth. A pulse of heat goes through me. Maybe we won't get to play long, but we'll definitely get to play.

"Medium-sized companies that may not make a huge difference to our bottom line." Madison stretches as she says it. Her breasts press against her dress. I'm more of an ass man while Noah is the breast guy, but I still love them. Soft and supple.

Of course, everything about Madison is fantastic.

"It's not much to go on, but it's a start." Seth runs a hand through his hair. "Do we think there's a link between Madison's stalker and the corporate spy?"

"You know how I feel about coincidences," Blake says. His sleeves are rolled up, showing his forearms. No matter how many weights I lift, I can't get big like Blake does, but my arms aren't exactly small.

"The simplest answer is usually the solution?" Madison asks. "We believe multiple people are working together on the corporate espionage. But we only believe one person is behind the stalking."

"The stalking is personal, and so is this. But the targets are different." Seth shakes his head and puts his hands on the conference table. "We know Madison's stalker has been watching her, maybe since she arrived in New York. We also know the corporate spy has been working on our clients for a few years. That means it's likely two separate entities, because Madison just entered our lives."

"We can only bait one trap at a time." I fold my hands behind my head and look around at the other tired faces. "We need to either locate or create a medium-sized company for our spy to contact. I've got some equipment that may track them down. Theo is the fastest hacker I have."

"Can we trust him?"

Seth's words give me pause. That's part of the problem with both situations. Who do you trust? Who *can* you trust? Someone we already put our trust in is working against us.

"I've known him for years. Yes, in this case, I think we can trust him." I lean my elbows on the table. "My equipment is good enough that we'll get a location and maybe a number. But with Theo, I'm confident he can get even more information."

Theo liked to hack as a teen. His computer skills are top-notch, and he's never let me down. Plus, as far as I know, he's happy with his career track and Morrigan Technologies.

"We have a list of current employees on the suspect list," Blake says. "As well as a list of former employees. There's not a long list of people who would be mad specifically at us. So we've narrowed the list to a few employees who were fired. And of course Andrea."

That bitch just never seems to go away. That was a fucking mess.

"What about Courtney?" Madison leans forward. "Hope said she wanted my job, but you guys keep passing her up."

"She was friends with Andrea." Blake rubs his jaw. "She's been on the list since day one, honestly. She does her job, but she seems disgruntled."

"If she wants to work with us so badly, why would she sabotage the company?" Noah lifts his gaze from his computer and looks around. "She hasn't been on every job that got the call. But she's definitely a possibility."

"Have you worked out your suspect list, princess?" Seth's tone softens when he speaks to Madison.

"I've been working on it." She looks down at her hands. "But no one really stands out. Professor Alan made sense. I ignored his advances. He knew me from school. He had some opportunity. But this person had access to me before. My school, my apartment, even here."

Her eyes flash up to mine. I wish there was something I could do. But my money only goes so far. There just isn't enough evidence. Besides, she's safe here with us.

"Val and Jeff haven't reemerged." She shakes her head and then stops. "Fuck, Robert."

Who the fuck is Robert?

"What about your neighbor?" Blake asks.

Ah, the reclusive neighbor. Not another fuckboy like that guy she banged at Taylor's.

"He came and gave me my bracelet back. He found it in the hall. But he said a woman tried to get into my apartment a few times. Brown hair, but that's all he caught." She straightens. "When Robert found the bracelet in the hallway, it was after Blake and I had been there."

"So is Robert back on the suspect list?" Blake asks, clearly not pleased with this turn.

"I don't know." Madison shakes her head. "I mean, you guys said he wasn't one because he didn't leave his apartment when I was trapped in the file room. But the bracelet. And while he didn't have access to my apartment, he has been inside it."

"He was in your apartment?" Blake's expression clouds with anger.

"He always talked to me when I got home, and one time he followed me in." Her eyes lock with Blake's. "That's it. It took me a while to get him out of the apartment, but otherwise, he was never welcome."

"Is it possible Valerie would have let him in when you weren't there?" Blake asks.

Madison leans back and looks up at the ceiling like she's looking for the answers. "Valerie didn't really like Robert, and he steered clear of her. But when she was strung out, who knows what she'd do? It's possible."

"I think we need fresh brains for this." Seth pushes to stand, and everyone closes their laptops or tablets. "Come here, princess."

She moves into his open arms and he hugs her to him, kissing the top of her head. I get it. Someone is trying to take Madison away from us. Someone else is trying to take down what we've worked to build.

Even if the stalker wants Madison, he's going after what's ours. And we won't let that stand.

As she steps out of Seth's arms, Blake draws her into his. Each of us has lost a piece of ourselves to this woman. Maybe not lost, but given. Freely. Because she gave us something we didn't know we needed.

When Blake finishes, Noah engulfs her in an embrace that shouldn't make me jealous. I love Noah like my brother. I want him to be happy. He makes her happy, which makes me happy, but they have something I'm not sure I can ever give her.

My heart is cold and hard and not worthy of someone like Madison. But Noah's is, and that's what I'm jealous about. I can keep her in luxury above and beyond what all my friends can, but I can't give her the one thing she needs.

As she pulls away from Noah, she turns to me. She doesn't hesitate to step into my body and put her arms around me, leaning her ear over my pounding heart. I close my arms around her and shut my eyes as I rest my chin on her soft hair.

For a moment, I can pretend. Pretend I deserve her. I'm not willing to give her up, though, so even if I don't deserve her, I'll still keep her and try to be what she needs. Something the others can't give her. What that is, I'm not sure yet.

Chapter 117

Corporate Imagination

Madison

It's weird walking into Coop's room without him. He keeps it immaculately clean, almost like a fresh hotel suite. On his neatly made bed is a silver package wrapped in a red ribbon with an envelope on top.

I sit down on the edge of the bed next to it. The envelope is made of thick, crisp white paper. Opening it carefully, I pull out a white card with *Cooper Graham* in a gold scrolling font at the top. In bold black handwriting is simply:

You're failing sex ed and need to convince your professor (me) to help you pass.

I scrunch up my face. I've never failed a class in my life. Pulling the ribbon on the box free, I lift the lid and find a barely there pleated, plaid skirt and a white button-down shirt. The fabric is nice, not at all like a costume for Halloween.

Beneath the outfit is a pair of knee-high socks and black Mary

Janes. And the most innocent set of silky white panties and a push-up bra. My eyebrows rise. How long has he had this fantasy?

Okay, so failing sex ed because what? I'm a virgin and I'm supposed to prove to my professor I deserve an A by seducing him? It's up to me what my backstory is. I could play it innocent or I could go the other way . . . I've skipped class because I'm already well-versed in sexual education and willing to prove it to him?

Shaking my head, I stand and take off all my clothes. This won't go well. I'll probably get through two minutes before I laugh with either scenario. But I'm willing to try for Coop. The clothes fit me well, but the skirt barely covers my ass. I walk into his bathroom and brush my hair into two low pigtails.

I untuck and unbutton the bottom of my shirt and tie it into a knot, revealing my midriff, and unbutton the top until the lace from my bra just shows. The choices of lip color are between a soft pink and a dark red. If I try to play the seductress, I *will* laugh. It's unavoidable. But I might get him to lead more if I play the virgin.

Grabbing the pink lipstick, I put it on. Some light eye makeup completes the look.

The full-length mirror almost makes me laugh. I'm a few years too old for a schoolgirl's uniform, but it's quite sexy. I can see why Coop would go for this. Does that mean he'll be dressed as my professor?

For a second, my mind stalls. Professor Alan isn't and wasn't ever my fantasy. He implied a lot of things without coming out and actually sexually harassing me. I didn't want or seek his attention.

But this is Coop. The knot in my chest eases. Yeah, if Coop were my teacher in high school or college, I would've crushed hard on him. Besides, Professor Alan accosted me at a charity event, not in his office. Because I was smart enough to avoid his office hours.

Drawing in a breath, I shake off the bad feelings just thinking about that asshole brings to the surface. I won't let him stop me from enjoying my man's company and trying to give Coop his fantasy.

Ready to play the schoolgirl, I walk through the bedroom, grabbing my badge on the way. I could have walked out into the hallway, but I didn't even think as I went into the common space. A low whistle fills the room. My gaze goes to Blake on the couch.

Heat fills my cheeks as I walk toward him. "How do I look?"

I look ridiculous and hot at the same time.

"Like a high school fantasy brought to life." Blake's hungry eyes devour every inch of me. "Come here, tiger."

"I don't know if I should." Trying to look shy even as the fire of desire burns within me, I bite my lip intentionally. "I'm supposed to go talk to my teacher. I wouldn't want to be late."

Blake smiles devilishly. His green eyes sparkle in the light. "I won't make you late, love."

I raise my eyebrow and give him a shy smile before making my way over to him, swinging my hips a little more than usual. When I stand before him, he leans back and pats his lap.

Arching my eyebrow, I twirl my ponytail around my finger and cock my hip. "Do you want me to call you Daddy?"

Blake chuckles darkly. "Daddy doesn't do it for me, love. Sit on my lap or I'll have you across it."

I lower myself delicately onto his lap. His warm hand grabs my thigh to help position me. Anticipation makes me wet. I'm down for whatever he wants.

"Now what exactly is the costume for?" Blake leans back. His hand strokes lightly up and down my bare thigh. I fight the urge to open my legs, grab his hand, and put it where it will bring me the most pleasure.

"I'm failing sex ed and need to beg my professor to help my grade." I arch an eyebrow at the silly scenario.

His hand slips beneath my skirt. Parting my thighs, he rubs my pussy through my panties. "You want another scenario, tiger? I owe Coop a little something you could help me out with."

I meet his mischievous green eyes and smile, knowing I'm so going to get spanked for this, but I can't resist. "Whatever you want, Daddy."

I knock on Coop's office door. My outfit now includes a black silk tie that hangs down over my belly button.

"Come in."

My nerves flutter in my stomach. I'm not exactly an actress, but this is all in fun. I push open the door, trying to be a student on the verge of failing. Trying to feel what it would have been like to fail at something and be desperate to bring my grade up. No matter what.

"Professor Graham?" I step into his office and leave the door slightly ajar behind me. I pluck at the hem of my too-short skirt. "You wanted to see me."

"Yes." He looks up from his desk. He's wearing a pair of wire-rimmed glasses. Fuck, that look definitely does it for me. His button-down shirt sleeves are rolled up, showing off his tight, corded fore-arms. My panties were already damp, but hot damn, Coop is like a fantasy all on his own. "Of course. Take a seat."

He gestures to the chair in front of his desk. I walk around it and sit with my legs crossed, straightening my skirt, careful not to show anything. Not that the skirt really gives me that luxury. His gaze rakes over me. His eyes pause on the tie. It wasn't part of his outfit.

"I can't afford to fail your class. Is there any extra credit I can do to help me pass?" I lean forward, and his gaze dips to the lace of my bra and my cleavage.

He rubs the side of his mouth as he leans back in the chair. "I don't know, Miss Harris. You've failed all the written exams. It's not like there's a practical exam for sex education."

"I'll do anything. If I fail, I'll lose my scholarship." I lean forward farther to give him more of a view down my shirt. "Please, Mr. Graham. Ask me anything. I'm sure I can figure out the answer. I just get so nervous during the exams."

Sitting back in my chair, I stroke my hand down the tie.

Coop sighs and digs through a stack of reports on his desk. He pulls one out and licks his finger to turn to the page. Seriously, I'm not sure what makes him even hotter as a professor, but this actually might work for me.

"Your answers are ridiculous. It's like you haven't even seen a cock."

Ah, he was hoping for the virgin backstory. I almost grin, but I keep my cool.

"I haven't." I pout.

Coop widens his eyes as he side-eyes me. "You're what? Eighteen?"

"Yes, sir."

"And you've never watched porn?" he asks incredulously.

"No, sir. But I swear I'm a fast learner. It just gets all jumbled in my head when I read it." I scoot forward to the edge of my seat and give him my best innocent look. "What if I can prove to you I can learn anything?"

He shakes his head. "I don't know. Maybe you should just retake the class in the fall."

I shoot to my feet. "Please, Mr. Graham. I'll do anything. Reading isn't helping. Maybe you can show me."

I pluck at the hem of my skirt, and his gaze falls to my hand.

He stands and puts his hands on his desk, shaking his head almost regretfully. "I need to get back to grading papers."

"Please." I twirl my hair around my finger and look up at him through my lashes. I'm sure I look silly, but his eyes flare with heat which encourages me. "I'll do anything you want."

He looks contemplative for a moment before he sits back in his chair. "Fine. Come here."

I walk around his desk and stand in front of him. He grabs my tie and slides it between his fingers. Shivers race through me. Hopefully, he doesn't decide to get inventive and use my prop against me. I couldn't exactly walk in with a rope.

"What have you learned so far?" He drops my tie and sits back in his chair. His hungry gaze devours every inch of me, keying me up even more. My insides quiver in anticipation.

"That sex is between two consenting adults."

"Or more." He runs his finger across his lips. A bolt of lust strikes between my thighs. "You've never seen a cock?"

"No, sir. May I see yours?" I drop my gaze to his erection pressing against his zipper.

"As long as it's educational." A light twinkles in his eyes like he knows how cheesy this is.

It's like a really bad porn scene, but I'm not worried. Things will heat up nicely, but not exactly the way Coop has planned. I just need to get him in a compromising situation.

"Of course." I try for innocent, but there's a hint of laughter in my voice. "Purely educational."

He reaches for his belt and undoes his pants, freeing his cock. I get even wetter at the sight of his raging erection. So many things I could do with him. To him. And I want to do it all.

"Oh my, Mr. Graham." I lean into the stereotype of the innocent. "Are they all that big?"

"No, they aren't." He strokes his hand down it with a cocky smile.

I step closer and bite my lip, reaching out tentatively. I lift my gaze to his. "May I touch it?"

He arches his eyebrow and slides back into his professor role. The fucking tease. "I don't think that's a good idea."

"You're probably right." I lean back against his desk and run my fingers down my tie, cocking my head to the side as I watch his hand stroke his cock. Pressing my thighs together against the growing ache watching him pleasure himself creates, I lick my lips, already tasting him.

"You don't want to ask me how *hard* it feels?" He stresses the word *hard*, and I almost laugh as he wiggles his eyebrows.

I purse my lips. "I really think I would get more education if you let me explore your cock, but I'm worried you'll try to touch me, and I'm not ready for that."

"I can keep my hands to myself." He puts his hands on the arms of his chair.

I give him a doubtful look. "I'm not sure . . ."

My hand goes to my tie and he finally gets the hint. "What if you use your tie to bind my hands?"

I smile like he's the most brilliant man on the planet. "You're so smart."

Coop smiles and cocks an eyebrow at my overacting. Before he can think better of it, I pull my tie off and then go around to his back. He gives me his hands willingly, and I use the double knot Noah taught me to bind his hands and tie them to the chair to keep him there.

I sashay in front of him. The short skirt barely covers my panties. I drop down in front of him and spread his knees apart. My gaze lifts from his throbbing cock to his blue eyes.

"Does it hurt like that?"

"You want to kiss it better?" He gives me a cocky smile.

"Would that help, sir?" Precum leaks out of his tip. Pretty sure I know the answer to that.

"Yes, it would help a lot." He shifts in the chair.

I lean forward and take his tip into my mouth, wrapping my hand around his shaft.

"Fuck, Madison. Just like that. Take it deeper."

"Nah, tiger. Why don't you stand?" Blake's voice fills the room.

Chapter 118

Proxy Battle

Blake

Madison stands and hops up on the desk facing Coop. She grins back at me. "Oops."

Coop's brow scrunches. "What's going—"

"Love, take your panties off."

Madison slides off the desk and shimmies out of the panties Coop wanted her to wear. When she holds them up, I close and lock the door.

"Stuff them in his mouth." I raise an eyebrow at Coop, wondering how much he'll protest this interruption or if he'll go along with our new game.

Madison glances over her shoulder and throws me an air kiss before she straddles Coop's lap. "Open."

For a second, he looks like he's going to protest. But then he opens his mouth for her, and she leans in and sucks on his lower lip.

"Good boy." She puts her panties in his mouth. "I got a little *education* of my own before coming up here."

His eyes flare with heat. He's loving this side of her, and I can't say I blame him. She's taking charge, but only as far as I let her leash out.

"Come here."

She grabs his chin and kisses his nose before standing in that obscenely short skirt. Her hips swing as she walks my way, and Coop's gaze never leaves that skirt.

I tip her chin up so she looks at me. "Who do you belong to, love?"

"You . . ." Her smile turns mischievous. "Daddy."

My cock twitches. I'm going to spank her good for that, but I spin her around so her back is to me and Coop can see her face. My hand goes between her legs, and I thrust my finger into her pussy.

"Oh!" Surprise colors her tone as she leans against me.

"And this pussy?" I lean down to speak directly in her ear. My gaze meets Coop's. Her pussy grows wetter around my finger. "Who does this pussy belong to?"

"You, Daddy." She squirms against me. Her words less of a taunt as her breath quickens.

"Whose cock do you want in my pussy, love?" I stroke my finger in and out, never dropping my gaze from Coop's. His, though, looks at where my hand works her under her skirt. I make sure he can see her wetness running down my finger before I thrust it back into her.

"Yours, Daddy," she whimpers, clutching at my sleeve. Her pussy is so fucking wet, the noise of my finger sliding in and out fills the room.

"Hands on his knees." I draw my finger out of her and suck it into my mouth.

She moans as her gaze follows my finger. I arch an eyebrow at her and swat her ass, sending her into motion. She stands in front of Coop and bends to put her hands on his knees. She lifts her face to look in his eyes.

"Our girl likes to take orders." I open my fly and pull out my cock, stroking it as I walk over to stand behind her. I smooth my hand over her ass, lifting her skirt that barely covered her throbbing pussy.

She lets out a breath and widens her legs without me having to tell her.

Coop arches an eyebrow at me.

I rub the head of my cock over her wet pussy, sliding it down to her clit and up to her entrance.

She moans low.

"She's all of ours, and we're all hers." I thrust deep into her dripping wet cunt, and she groans. I grab the back of her neck. "Let Coop know exactly who you belong to, love."

She meets his eyes as I draw out of her, holding her hips still. "You, Daddy."

I punch back into her, making her cry out. "What happens when someone's a dick about claiming you in front of me?"

Coop's eyes narrow on mine as I pull out and punch back in.

"You'll claim me in front of him to prove who owns me." Her head droops as I withdraw again.

"Tell Coop whose pussy this is." I pick up the pace, thrusting into her tight little cunt, making her breasts sway in that tiny shirt.

"It's yours, Blake. Fuck me harder. It's yours." She moans as I fuck her hard. "Oh, fuck. Blake!"

She comes around my cock, drawing me deeper, squeezing me tighter.

Her knees weaken, and I hold her hips upright as I continue to pound into her, riding her hard. Her breathing becomes pants, and she makes little incoherent sounds as I push her over the edge again.

"Suck his cock, tiger. Give him a taste of what's mine." I pull out of her greedy cunt without coming.

She sinks to her knees and takes Coop into her mouth while I stroke my cock. Her pretty pink lips stretch around him. She hollows out her cheeks and sucks him deep into her throat. He groans around her panties, and his hips buck up, trying to go deeper into her throat.

"That's enough, tiger."

She comes off his cock with a pop and waits for my next order.

His chest rises and falls rapidly as precum gathers on his tip. Staring at it, she licks her lips.

"Sit on his lap."

She turns and sits on his lap, wrapping her legs on the outside of his. His cock pressed against her bare ass. I move in front of them and wink at Coop.

"Suck my cock, tiger."

Leaning her hands on his knees, she accepts me into her mouth. She takes her time and sucks and licks every inch of me, taking me as deep into her throat as she can until I can barely hold back.

"I understand how much you love to claim our girl, but just be aware, this is going to happen when you do. I'm going to fuck her in front of you and make you watch. That will help you understand how it feels to watch your best friend claim the woman you can't."

Coop's eyes flare hot as she wiggles her ass against his cock.

"Turn around, tiger. I want to come in your sweet pussy."

I step away so she can resume her position, facing Coop with her hands on his knees. I thrust into her and she gasps.

"Good girl." I stroke my hand over her hip as she moans.

"Please, Daddy." She pushes back into me, and I know what she wants.

Even if I should punish her for using Daddy, I cave because her pussy is tight and perfect on my cock.

"Take him in your mouth, love. Take him as deep as I take your pussy."

She wets her lips and slides her mouth over his cock. She follows my rhythm as I chase my release. I wrap my hand around her hip and slide my fingers over her clit. Rubbing her until she comes all over me. Her pussy convulses around my cock, drawing me into my release. Coop moans around her panties as he comes in her throat.

I smack her ass. "That's for calling me Daddy."

She glances over her shoulder at me. Still buried deep inside her, my cock twitches at the look in her eyes. "You like it. Just a little."

Chuckling, I pull out of her and put my cock away. I grab her ass and spread her cheeks. "I'd stay and fuck your ass too, but I have some work to do tonight."

My fingers slide into her cum-filled cunt. I thrust a few times before moving them to her asshole, spreading my cum around her opening before thrusting my fingers inside. She moans as she grips Coop's knees.

"Just making sure you're prepped to play with your toy, tiger." I lift my gaze to Coop, whose gaze is locked on my fingers fucking Madison's ass. I draw them out and turn her to face me.

"Give me a kiss, tiger."

She stretches up to kiss me, flashing her naughty bits at Coop.

Leaning down, I whisper in her ear. "Make him beg for it."

Madison

Blake swats my ass one more time before leaving, closing the door behind him. I turn and study Coop, who looks at me expectantly.

"You don't expect me to untie you, do you?" I straddle his lap and reach between us to run my fingers over his hardening cock. I give him a mocking sad face. "See? I don't really get a chance to play like this."

He mutters something, but I just shake my head.

I trace my finger over his lips. "Blake has the right idea. I'm happy to use you as my toy for once."

I climb off his lap and walk to his desk drawers. Bending over, flashing him my goodies. Searching the drawers until I find what I need, I glance over my shoulder.

"For a guy who swears he's all work in the office, you have an awful lot of toys in here." I grab the lube and a beaded dildo with straps on it. Pretty sure I know what to do with this one, but I might need a little help.

Straddling Coop's legs again, I meet his eyes. "So this attaches to your cock, right?"

I hold up the dildo with the straps. He nods.

"This goes around your cock and this one goes around your balls?" I wait for his nod of confirmation.

When he mumbles something, I narrow my eyes. "Is this important?"

He rolls his eyes and nods.

"Fine. Open." I reach for his mouth and he parts his lips. I draw out the panties. "Speak."

"If you untie me, I'd be more than happy to show you how to use that." He nods to the toy.

I pretend to think it over, but then shake my head. "Open."

"Madis—"

I shove my panties back into his mouth. "Be a good boy and sit still while I figure this out."

It takes lube and a few experimental fittings before I have it on solidly. By the time I stroke his cock with my hand and consider how to take this, I'm soaking wet just thinking about how fucking him and the toy will feel.

I give him a look. "I'm going to take out the panties again, but you better behave. You can use the red-light system if you need me to stop for any reason. Are you going to behave?"

He nods and opens his mouth.

I take my panties out and drop them to the floor.

"Good." This won't work on the chair very well. Scooting off his lap again, I round to the back of the chair. I release the tie from the chair, but keep it knotted around his wrists. "Sit on the couch."

I follow him to the couch, and he settles on it. I love how small this skirt is. It doesn't get in the way as I straddle him and lean against him above his cock while I figure out the best way to take both his cock and the toy in me. He leans into my breast and puts his mouth over my shirt and bra, scraping his teeth against my nipple.

Backing away, I tip his chin up to look at me. "Did I give you permission?"

"What are you going to do? Punish me?" The challenge in his eyes makes me bristle.

I stand. "Turn over."

He gives me a wink before he turns over. His pants still cover his ass. I draw his pants down over his hips and spank his firm ass once, kind of light. Not really confident in what I'm doing.

"Harder, sweetheart."

My cheeks flush and I smack his ass harder.

"Fuck," he groans like he likes it. "More."

I smack him three more times on his ass cheeks until my hand stings. "On your ass, Graham."

He shifts back on his ass. His cock leaks precum, and I lick my lips. I want to take him so many ways, but first . . .

"Behave, so I can figure this out."

"I don't know, baby, I think I might be a bit of a brat." His blue eyes sparkle with laughter. "I like it when you spank me."

"I'm not sure I'm very good at being dominant," I admit. My hand still stings a little. Next time I'm finding a good paddle.

"You're doing great." He wiggles his eyebrows.

"Thanks." I straddle him again. I hold his cock steady against my entrance as I lower down, making sure the tip of the toy hits my puckered hole. Slowly I lower, taking his cock inside me while the toy slides into my ass.

It takes me lifting up then sliding farther down a few times before I have both Coop and the toy completely inside me. I sit on his lap with my hands gripping his shirt as I breathe through the fullness.

"It feels different than when you and someone else are inside me." I blow out a breath.

Coop's darkened eyes meet mine. "Watching you take my cock is incredibly hot. When we get to bed, I want you to queen me."

"Queen you?" I lift a little and sink back onto him. A moan works its way out of my throat.

"Sit on my face and ride my tongue until you come all over me."

I whimper as I rise and fall, taking his cock. Fuck, I want that. He leans in and captures my mouth. I give in to him, feeling a surge of lust building within me as his tongue penetrates my lips. He tastes me, teasing my tongue with his.

"Untie me, goddess. Let me worship you properly."

Biting my lip, I hold his face and search his light blue eyes.

"Next time I want to play longer."

"You can tie me up anytime you want to, sweetheart. Fuck, if I didn't want to come right now, I could wait and let you play. But you in that outfit . . . Fuck, Madison. I need to fuck you so fucking hard." He captures my lips again, and I fumble to untie the knot behind him. When the tie loosens, his arms wrap around me and he lifts me against him.

I cry out in surprise into his mouth. He lowers me onto the floor and follows me down. His cock and the toy remain deep inside me.

He brushes the hair out of my face, then reaches between us and pulls open my shirt.

"So many things I wanted to do to my naughty little schoolgirl." He tugs my bra out of the way and takes my nipple into his mouth. Sucking and licking, making my whole being light up like a winning slot machine.

I grab his hair and hold him to my breast. "Suck harder."

He does and his hips draw back, pulling out slightly before he crashes back into me. I cry out at the sensation. Each bead rubs at my sensitive nerves as it comes out and goes back in.

"Fuck me, Coop." I pull his head off my breast and up to my mouth. My kiss claims him as he moves inside me, slowly at first, feeling how the toy moves with him, experimenting until I'm squirming beneath him.

Each thrust sends me higher and higher, until I'm gasping into his mouth, pleading with him to go faster, harder. Craving that feeling of ecstasy that's just out of reach.

Arching, I explode around him, tugging on his hair, feeling every inch of him and the toy inside me as my body pulses around both. He pulls out and I whimper at the loss. He shifts and I can tell he's doing something with his hands. After a moment, he lifts my knees up and out before I feel his smooth cockhead against my asshole.

He presses inside, filling me so full as he captures my moan with his mouth. My fingers cling to his hair, keeping us locked in this kiss as he fucks my ass, picking up speed with every thrust. Our tongues tangle together.

He tears his mouth from mine and rears up, watching his cock disappear into my ass. He sucks his thumb into his mouth and then presses it against my clit, rubbing it until I can't do anything but breathe, and I'm barely doing that. My ass clamps down on him as I scream my climax.

He pushes harder, faster, chasing his release. Aftershocks ripple through me, and he roars as he comes, each pulse of his cock shuddering through me as he fills me.

We collapse in a heap on the floor. Our chests rise and fall together. Our breathing chaotic. His weight feels good. I don't think I have the energy to move from this spot. Pretty sure I'll just have to lie here forever.

Lifting onto his arms, he hovers over me, still a part of me.

"I've never felt like this about anyone else." He brushes my hair from my face. His blue eyes are bright and uncertain. "You mean something to me, Madison. But I'm not like Noah. I don't know how to give you my heart."

My heart fills my chest. Sliding my hands to his jaw, I rub my thumb over the stubble there. I love him, but the words terrify him. When I slipped before, I saw his fear. But I can ease this worry. "I don't need you to be like Noah. I just need you, Coop."

Chapter 119

Below the Line

Madison

It's date night and I'm getting ready. Well, date night for everyone except Blake. Though technically it's his night to have me. I can't help but feel a little bad for scheduling it this way. He sits on the bench in my closet, watching me with those possessive green eyes.

Of course, he interrupted Coop's night, so I guess I can't feel too bad. I still get shivers when I think about last night. With him. With Coop.

How did I get so lucky to have these men in my life?

"Did he pick that out for you to be seen in public?" The "he" being Seth. Blake's frown is even more pronounced. "Maybe I should go with you guys."

The black dress is formfitting, stretchy fabric with holes cut out over the hips on the sides. There's no wearing panties with this outfit without lines, so I'm going commando. The neckline is high and would be modest if it weren't for the plunging back that nearly shows my ass crack.

As I look in the mirror at my curled hair and diamond necklace and earrings, even I can't help but wonder what Seth was thinking.

The look is more sex kitten than double date with my fiancé, and my fiancé's best friend and his date.

"You can't go. That would be weird." I slip on the high heels Seth set out.

"It's weird going out with two of the guys you fuck on the regular when one of them is on a date with another woman."

Turning, I glare at Blake. He holds his hands up.

"Sorry. I heard it." Blake looks chagrined. "Just hoping they won't keep you out late."

I step into his space and put my arms on his shoulders. "Tonight, I'll slip out of this dress and into bed with you. I promise."

"Just *don't* call me Daddy." He lifts an eyebrow as his hands settle on the bare skin of my waist.

A mischievous grin crosses my face. I give him an innocent, wide-eyed look. "You didn't like that, Daddy?"

His fingers dig into my side. "If you weren't going out, I'd spank your ass until it was red so you'd remember not to call me Daddy. But I'll save your punishment for tonight."

His spicy cologne makes my knees weak. My thighs rub together at the thought of Blake's punishment. Him bending me over and spanking me before fucking me. His eyes flare with heat. His hands slide down over the curve of my ass.

"Leave the dress on when you get home. I want to remember why you need to be punished." He smacks me lightly on my ass and moves into my space. My breasts rest against his chest. Tipping my chin up, he turns my face from side to side as if checking my makeup. "Flawless."

I just shake my head. My hand smooths over the stubble on his jaw. I let out a low purr. "Keep this."

He tugs my hips into his, pressing his hard cock against my stomach. He rubs his rough stubble against my neck, sending sparks chasing through me. His lips press against my ear as he drawls, "Want me to mark up those thighs for you tonight?"

I suck in a breath as desire pounds through my veins. "Are you going to make me beg for it?"

He draws back until his mouth hovers over mine. His breath is hot against my lips, and I part them, waiting for his kiss.

"I'm going to show you exactly how I want you to submit to me. The positions I want you to hold for me." His nose rubs against mine slowly. His hands squeeze my ass. "You'll get your punishment, and then you'll get fucked. Hard."

I bite my lip as I meet his green eyes. I want him to take me now. For a second, his resolve looks like it's going to break.

"Are you ready?" Coop's voice comes from outside my door.

Blake and I turn. I suck in a breath. Coop in a tux was spectacular. Coop in a suit, ready for a date, is perfection. He straightens his cuffs, his black cuff links glinting in the light as he looks at me and Blake. Coop's long, dark hair hangs loose around his shoulders. His blue eyes lock on mine, and I swear my knees get even weaker.

"Fuck, Madison. Maybe we should just stay home." His eyes trail over me from head to toe, taking in every inch in between. "Seth dressed you in that to go out?"

"Yes, and I promised Sara we'd do this." I run my hand down the front of Blake's dress shirt from work. His hard muscles twitch beneath my touch.

Blake releases me and smacks my ass as he moves away. "Don't worry. I helped get her nice and ready for you."

Coop raises an eyebrow at Blake and shrugs. "I guess we'll have time to fuck on the way to the restaurant."

"I'm not ruining this dress." I run my hands over the soft fabric that fits like a second skin. Seth could have made a career as a stylist. The clothes he chooses for me are exquisite. Every detail well thought out.

Thinking of Seth, my heart sinks. I don't want to ask, but I can't resist. "Has Seth left yet?"

"He was walking out the door when I came down to change." Coop invades my space. His hand slides to the back of my neck, holding me while he searches my eyes. "Disappointed, sweetheart?"

I take in a breath and let it go. Seth is doing this for me. The purpose of his date tonight with Elizabeth is so no one realizes I'm with them all. Right now, no one is pushing that particular button, and we don't need the additional stress.

"It would have been nice to see him before he left," I admit but smile for Coop. I straighten his collar and brush down his lapels. "But I've got all the eye candy I need right here."

"Is that all I am to you?" he teases, drawing me closer. "Eye candy?"

My breasts brush against his chest, and a pulse of need flows through me at the look in his eyes. My fingers play with the ends of his hair. "You are gorgeous."

"Not as beautiful as you." He trails his other hand down my bare back, pressing me in closer to him until our hips are flush. "This dress makes me want to do dirty things to you, goddess."

"Get in line," Blake scoffs as he heads out the door.

Warmth rushes to my cheeks. Fuck, I never had a high libido until I met these four. I'd go months between lovers. Using a guy to scratch an itch. But not these guys. I can't help but want more from them. All the time.

"Always happy to line up for you, baby." Coop tips my head back and lowers his lips to brush against mine. "Especially when you're tied up and helpless. I love using you, filling your cunt, ass, and mouth with my cum."

He claims my lips. Our bodies flush against each other as he takes his time to explore every inch of my mouth. Desire consumes me. I clutch at his lapels to keep him against me and to keep from falling. I could stay right here in this moment with Coop for as long as the world would let me.

When he pulls away, he releases a heavy breath. Heat fills his blue eyes. "Fuck, baby. Let's just lock the others out and spend all night exploring each other's bodies."

"While that sounds amazing"—Noah's voice breaks the moment —"if we don't leave in five minutes, we'll be late."

"I bet I could make Madison come in five minutes." Coop's eyes twinkle. Heat pulses through me. Pretty sure we wouldn't need the whole five.

"Coop," Noah chastises.

Coop draws me in for a quick kiss, and then spins me in his arms to face Noah. "Look at my date for the night and tell me you don't want to fuck her."

Noah and I take each other in. He's dressed in a suit that is perfectly trimmed to him. His blond hair falls over his dark chocolate eyes. He looks incredible. We both just stand there looking each other over.

Coop wraps his arm around my waist, drawing me back against him. His fingers slide up and down my exposed side, lighting sparks beneath my skin. He rests his chin on my shoulder and says in my ear, "You should tell Noah all about last night."

Heat floods me. After we made it to Coop's bed, I rode his face. His tongue thrusting up into me while I pressed down on him. I'm not sure he could breathe during all of it. I came so hard I almost passed out. Then I rode his cock before he rolled me to my back and fucked me slow and methodical until I stopped counting my releases.

Just thinking about it has my pussy pulsing with aching need.

Noah raises an eyebrow at me. "Good night?"

Melting against Coop, I press my lips together. "Mm-hmm."

Noah leans against the doorjamb. His gaze never leaves my eyes. "I'd hate to mess you up before your date, but that dress is amazing on you."

Coop slides his hand down my stomach to the hem, pulling it up. "No panties either."

His hand slips between my thighs and strokes over my pussy, paying close attention to my clit. My heart clatters in my chest as I forget to breathe.

"So fucking wet, goddess," Coop purrs in my ear. His finger thrusts inside me and I moan, needing so much more.

"We could just fuck all night." Noah steps into the closet with his hand on the door.

Fuck, I don't want to be the strong one. "Sara is waiting for us."

I close my eyes as Coop twists his fingers inside me. I'm on the edge, but we need to go.

"Please, Coop—"

"Please fuck me?" Coop curls his fingers, pressing on a spot that makes me see stars.

"That sounds about right. Isn't that so, kitten?" Noah closes in, and my willpower wavers. I reach out for his lapels, needing something to hold on to.

"Want me to make you feel good?" Coop whispers before taking my earlobe between his lips and sucking.

"Coop?"

His fingers work harder now, rushing me to the finish line whether I want to get there or not. I can't help but fall into the waves, letting him draw me deeper and deeper.

"Yes, sweetheart." He kisses my neck as Noah's hands work to lift my skirt.

"The car's here." Blake's authoritative voice fills the space. "If you're going to make her come, hurry."

Noah grins before he takes my lips with a kiss designed to destroy me. I moan into his mouth. He strokes his hand over my breast and tugs at the nipple through the fabric. When my lips part on a gasp, he slides his tongue inside, fucking my mouth in time with Coop's thrusts.

The pressure builds until it explodes in a burst of white-hot heat. I cry out into Noah's mouth as Coop strokes me through my orgasm.

"You guys need to head down. I expect her to be returned in the same shape she's in now." Blake's voice makes me blink.

"Well fucked?" Coop chuckles as he carefully extracts his hand from between my legs. He sucks his finger into his mouth. "Almost as good as when you come on my tongue."

Noah helps me straighten my dress, smoothing it over my hips.

"Just keep her safe." Blake shakes his head, but his hot gaze meets mine.

"Don't worry so much, Blake. We're on it." Coop smiles as he draws me into his side.

I step away from him and trail my hand over Noah's freshly shaven jaw before walking over to Blake. Stepping into his space, I draw his face down to press my lips against his. Drawing in a breath, I lean my forehead against his and meet his eyes.

"I'll be careful." Knowing I'm about to be a brat, I try to keep my smile from showing as I add, "I promise, Daddy."

Chapter 120

Incentivize

Seth

This is a mistake. My gut roils as the car pulls up in front of Elizabeth and Gloria's house. I don't want to be here. It feels wrong all over. But I also know if I don't, the shit will hit the fan.

We're not in any shape to deal with the consequences, so here I am. Giving in to the demands of a woman I can't stand.

Reluctantly, I get out of the car, straighten my suit jacket, and cross the drive to the front steps. I knock three times and wait. I'm tempted to give her three minutes total before leaving and calling it a night.

She opens the door, though, and smiles like the cat that caught the canary. "Seth. A pleasure as always."

"Elizabeth." I don't smile or even give her name a specific tone. I'm here under duress and she knows that.

"Do you want to come in? I've made reservations at the best restaurant for being seen." Her dark eyes smile like this is an actual date. She's wearing a fitted black dress with a loose skirt. Her dark hair is piled on her head in some sort of updo.

She's gorgeous and could get any guy if she didn't have the personality of a snake.

"I'd rather get on with our evening." I gesture for her to join me.

She steps out and closes the door. Her fingers dig into my arm as she takes it. "Remember, people might be anywhere, and we need to show a united front. Or do you want your little crush to hit the press?"

"So lovely of you to remind me just what a treacherous snake you are. I'm sure we'll have a great evening out." I pause before the car door, waiting for her to release my arm.

"If you don't make this look good, I won't hold up my end of the bargain."

Lifting her hand from my arm, I squeeze her fingers tight before bringing her hand almost to my lips. I press a ghost of a kiss to her knuckles before lowering and releasing her hand.

"Of course, my dear." I open the door and offer her my hand to help her in.

She arches an eyebrow, but takes my hand and slides into the car.

The car ride is quiet. Elizabeth told the driver which restaurant as I walked around to my side. I don't care where we go. I just have to fake it until the end of the evening. Fake like I actually want to be with this woman and she doesn't make me angry enough to throttle her.

We pull up in front of the restaurant, and I don't bother waiting for the driver to open my door. I just want this night over with. Dinner and then home. Where I'll check on Madison and go to sleep alone.

I open the door for Elizabeth and pretend she's Madison. Pretend I'm the one who gets to show her off to the world as mine. Not keep her hidden from everyone.

It's not Elizabeth's hand in mine. My smile is for Madison, picturing her in the outfit I selected for her, knowing she'll look stunning in it. If she even made it out of the apartment. She's temptation incarnate, and I wouldn't blame the guys if they canceled their night out to stay home with her.

"That's not so hard," Elizabeth says through her teeth as she smiles.

My smile fades a little, but I push Elizabeth back to the background and lead Madison into the restaurant like I have every right to. We get stalled along the way by well-intentioned people wanting to talk to Elizabeth or me, but they're just extending the evening.

We're shown to our table where we order drinks and look over the menus.

"The integration team has been in touch." Elizabeth smiles like we're discussing something other than business. But she's smart enough to realize small talk will just frustrate both of us.

"Good. We're hoping to get in quickly." Our drinks arrive and I sip my scotch. "We plan to have everything settled by the end of the month."

Elizabeth reaches over to put her hand over mine. My fingers twitch with the need to pull away, but I keep them there. Her smile widens. Instead of scheming brown eyes, I imagine blue eyes the color of the sky and blond hair swept up, showing off the long column of Madison's neck.

I turn my hand in hers and let our fingers tangle, imagining she's Madison. It's the only way I can get through this evening without looking at Elizabeth as if she's the disgusting blackmailer she is.

"We should discuss how long our romance should last." Elizabeth takes a sip of her wine. "After all, we need a nice long relationship to get the most benefit from it."

My fingers twitch on hers. I give her a fake smile. "You're the one with the leverage."

For now.

The company that does our background checks is currently looking into Elizabeth. I'll only be beholden to her for as long as it takes to find something to use against her. I won't let her destroy

Madison's future. Elizabeth could come at me and I could take the hit, but I won't let her take Madison down.

Elizabeth laughs delicately, though her fingers tighten on mine. Her nails dig into my skin, but I maintain my expression. "Don't be a bore, darling."

"I didn't guarantee entertainment, my dear." I take my hand from hers and look around the restaurant. Not paying attention earlier might bite me in the ass because Noah and Sara walk through the dining room to their table, followed closely by Coop and Madison.

Fuck.

The dress looks better on her than I could have imagined. It clings to her curves and shows flashes of her pale skin perfectly. Her legs are long, and the heels make her ass look fantastic.

"What a coincidence." Elizabeth's words capture my attention. She doesn't seem surprised at all. "The very object of your desire walks in, and you're mesmerized by her. If you don't want the rest of the restaurant to believe you want your assistant, you'd better pay close attention to me."

I'm not naive enough to believe this is a coincidence. Elizabeth planned this. Backing me into a corner where I have to make up for whatever perceived attention I throw Madison's way. What a fucking bitch.

Taking my glass, I drink the remains of the scotch and hold the glass up as our waiter walks by. He nods, and within a few minutes, a fresh glass of scotch is in my hand.

"Coop and Madison are engaged. It doesn't matter what or who I look at." I swirl the scotch in the glass. "I'm here with you to prove a point. Am I right?"

"You should give up on the girl, Seth. You and I understand each other." Elizabeth leans forward as she talks. "Yes, I'm hard and driven, but so are you. That's what made us perfect in college. My mother's plan was always Cooper, but you were always mine."

"You had me fooled back then." I shake my head and take a drink. How stupid I was to think she loved me.

"Not really. You enjoyed that I was willing to submit to you. I'm still willing to do that." Elizabeth trails her hand along my forearm. "You and I could rule the business world with Morrigan and Stiner together. No one could compete with us. Our children would have the best of both worlds."

I nearly choke on my scotch. *Children?* I raise my glass to her in a faux toast. "You're determined if nothing else. Delusional, but determined."

"Don't tell me you love her," Elizabeth scoffs. "You're too smart to let your heart lead you. This is just another business transaction. A way to secure your future. Our future."

"Children are a business transaction?" I set my empty glass down.

"Why not?" Elizabeth shrugs as she takes a sip of her wine. "I was. It worked out for my mother. Knowing you though, I wouldn't expect you to not be a part of their lives."

"Fuck," I breathe out. This was all a mistake. I rub my temples. "This won't work."

Elizabeth laughs like I said something hilarious. "We don't need to be too hasty. We have time to plan and arrange things. Maybe you could even carry on an affair with your lovely assistant while we're married. We all have our vices, after all."

"How desperate of you." This evening is going to be a shit show. Before I even left home, I knew it would be, but I'd hoped to make it through. For Madison's future.

I care less and less about burning down my future, but I can't be what stands in Madison's way. She deserves the world, and if I can make that happen for her by taking one for the team, I will. Even if that "one" is Elizabeth Hartfield.

She can have my time for now, but not my future.

"I will reiterate, I'm not looking for a wife of convenience nor poor, unloved children. You and I would never survive a relationship together. Please stop bringing it up. I'll do my time and act like the devoted boyfriend, but I'm not looking at this long-term. And I won't change my mind on that."

The waiter chooses now to bring our meals. We sit in awkward silence while he places our food before us. "May I get you anything else?"

"Another scotch." I hold up my glass. He nods and walks off.

"Maybe you should slow down," Elizabeth says quietly. "We don't need you drunk."

I wink at her. "If I have to spend the evening listening to you, then yes, being drunk might be the answer."

Because being sober isn't working.

Madison

"Oh my god, your dress is gorgeous." Sara pulls me into her arms and hugs me like we're already best friends. It's weird and awkward, but I pat her back.

"Thank you." When she releases me, I take in her almost fifties-style dress with a flared skirt and tight waist. "You look amazing."

"Thanks." She takes my hand and pulls me into a sitting room. Noah and Coop follow us. When we sit on the couch, the guys take chairs. "I wanted to talk to you all before we head to the restaurant tonight."

Which is why we were inside her house, instead of on the way to the restaurant. Coop assured me the restaurant wouldn't give away our reservation. He said it with the knowing smile of the rich.

"What's this about, Sara?" Noah sits relaxed in the chair.

She sighs. "Okay, so the guy—" She turns to me. "Noah told you about the guy, right? The one I'm trying to get to notice me?" When I nod, she continues, "He'll be there tonight, but he's on a date with another woman. I told Noah he probably wouldn't notice if I had sex with another guy in front of him."

My cheeks heat, thinking about how many times I've had sex

with someone else in front of my guys. Sure, they were all in on it, but they definitely took note or joined in.

"Okay? Why are you telling me this?" I understand she's trying to get someone's attention, but why the cloak-and-dagger routine?

She looks at Noah before her gaze comes back to mine. She glances at Coop briefly. "Uh, Kayla said something might be going on with you and Noah. And Noah said he had someone. And if there is something going on, I didn't want you to think I'm after him. Trust me, I have enough man problems to deal with with this other guy."

"Uh . . ." What do I say to that? The engagement ring is on my finger. It's not like I've said anything to make her believe I'm with them both. Plus, there's the NDA.

"It's okay, Madison." Coop sits forward. "There are enough pieces of the puzzle for Sara to figure out you're with us both."

Noah leans back. "It's not public information. Obviously, we don't want this getting out because it could hurt Madison's future."

Sara nods and turns to look at me again. Her hand rests over mine. "Seriously, it's okay. I'm not planning on spilling the beans to anyone else. I want to be friends. I need more friends in my life. My brother's friends think I'm their responsibility, but that also means they scare away my friends."

This I understand. Well, not the brother's friends part, but definitely about making new friends. "It's not like I'm just fucking around with them."

"I love Madison." Noah doesn't hesitate to spill that information. My heart trips in my chest. My gaze darts to Coop who doesn't look shocked at all. His blue eyes meet mine, and it's a silent acknowledgment that it doesn't bother him.

Sara beams. "That's awesome. I'm so glad you have two guys who love you."

I automatically open my mouth to deny that Coop loves me, but Coop speaks first. "But it's an unconventional relationship that most people wouldn't understand. It's important to keep it to ourselves."

"Of course." She leans into me. "And I'll have plenty of questions to ask you later."

"We should go." Noah stands and straightens his jacket.

"This is so romantic." Sara grabs Noah's arm and turns back to me. "You get to go out with both your guys, and I get to be part of it."

"She's definitely lucky." Coop reaches a hand down to help me up. His blue eyes meet mine, and he gives me a small smile. "After all, she gets to be with two men who love her."

Chapter 121

Conversion Rate

Madison

I'm in shock. The entire way to the restaurant, the conversation swirls around me while I sit there replaying what Coop said on repeat.

She gets to be with two men who love her.

Was he just saying that to reiterate what Sara said? Or does he mean it? Does he love me?

"What would you like to drink, miss?"

All eyes are on me at the table. I've been running on autopilot. But we're in a busy restaurant surrounded by other diners. I snap to attention.

"A glass of your best Riesling, please," Coop answers for me and squeezes my hand.

I turn to him. Does he love me? It seems impossible.

The waiter leaves the table. Coop leans in close to me.

"Are you okay?" His thumb strokes over the back of my hand, sending little shots of awareness through me.

Fuck. I don't think asking if he loves me would be a smart move currently. We're engaged and out with another couple. Just because I love him doesn't mean he loves me.

Besides, it makes sense that he would say he loves me. It's just part of the cover story.

As much as I want him to love me, that would be ridiculous. Someone like him would never love me. Desire me, yes. Love me?

"I'm fine." I touch the side of his face and smile. "Everything's good."

He doesn't look convinced, but he presses his lips to mine and the world fades for a second. Even if he doesn't love me, I still love him. And every moment I have with him is precious to me.

He presses his cheek against mine as he whispers in my ear, "Another minute of you zoning out and I would have taken you somewhere more private to wake you up."

Heat flushes through me. He draws back, and his eyes tell me he's aware of what he does to me.

"He's over there." Sara leans across the table to tell me. Ah, something else to obsess about. Sara's mystery man. "Wyatt Hawkins. Dark hair, dark eyes." She sighs. "He's wealthy and my brother Tom's best friend."

I glance over at the table she points out. A sinfully handsome man sits with a voluptuous blond. She's curved into his side, whispering something in his ear. His dark gaze flicks to this table for a hot second. He doesn't see me looking at him because his focus is on Sara.

The second Sara turns back in his direction, it's like a switch flips and he's totally into the blond again. Interesting.

"So where does Dante fall into this?" I place my napkin on my lap, happy to dwell on something that's not about me for a while.

Sara's face burns red, and she gets really interested in her napkin suddenly. "Dante thinks he's protecting me. But I think he's just keeping me away from Wyatt. He's also my brother's friend."

I've spent too much time with my guys because I kind of want to say that it seems like she's interested in both, so why not have them both? But just because it works for me and my guys doesn't mean it will work for Sara. Besides, it's not like we're out about it.

I'm currently engaged to Cooper Graham, while Noah is out with Sara, and Seth is out somewhere with Elizabeth. We're keeping it a secret.

"Oh, isn't that your boss?" Sara tugs at Noah's sleeve.

I freeze. I don't want to look. I don't want to know. He wouldn't bring her here. That's just cruel.

Noah turns to look. When he turns back, his gaze locks with mine. "Our boss is out on a date."

"That woman? Again? Gah, she's the worst." Sara straightens her napkin on her lap. She freezes when she sees my face. "Are you feeling okay, Madison? You look a little pale."

Forcing a smile, I refuse to look in that direction. "I'm fine, just a little warm."

I take a sip of my water. Coop threads his fingers through mine and holds my hand. He leans into me and whispers, "He's doing this for you. Not her. You. Remember that."

Glancing at Coop's blue eyes, I smile and nod. Logically, I know that, but inside . . . it feels like someone's digging out my guts and throwing them in my face. Their relationship isn't real, but once upon a time, they were real. What if being with her stirs up those old feelings?

"I'm not sure what Seth sees in her. Must be one hell of a business deal to put up with that woman." Sara sighs. "My brother had a girlfriend like that. Real vapid and not at all friendly. I was so glad when they finally broke up."

"What does your brother do?" I need the distraction. Anything to keep me from looking at Seth and Elizabeth. Even if he says they don't fit, they do. And it twists my insides into knots thinking about it.

"He and his best friends run an accounting firm. They're basically the partners of it and oversee everyone else." Sara sighs and glances at Wyatt. "Tom gets to see him every day, plus they all share an apartment."

"By best friends do you mean Dante and Wyatt?" I'm grasping at straws, trying to make conversation so I won't look.

"Mmm." Sara puts her water down. "Them and Finn Lawson."

She gives a little shiver and her cheeks flush with color. Okay, that's interesting. Or maybe my situation colors how I look at hers. After all, before my guys, I never would have thought being with four men at the same time was honestly an option. For the time being, our situation works because we all desire each other, but without love, it can't work long-term.

But Sara likes Wyatt, so maybe he's the focus of her attention. When my gaze falls on Noah, he smiles. Noah loves me, but could I be with just him and watch the others find love without me?

Coop squeezes my hand. I can't picture him with anyone else. I can't honestly picture myself with anyone but all of them. Am I just being greedy? Wanting them all because I've had them all?

"Oh, Kayla said she'd be in town the week after next. We should all go out for drinks." Sara pauses as the waiter sets our drinks in front of us.

"What can we get for you tonight?" he asks.

I look at the menu while everyone else orders. I pick something at the last minute. When I lift my gaze to smile at the waiter and hand him the menu, my gaze stalls on Seth and Elizabeth.

My heart pounds. He's smiling with his glass of scotch raised to his lips. His fingers are tangled with hers on the table. My breath catches.

He's smiling.

He's smiling for her. A lump forms in my stomach and sears the back of my throat. I have to get away.

"If you'll excuse me, I need to powder my nose." I push back from the table and quickly head for the restrooms.

I duck into the women's bathroom and take a deep breath while leaning my hands on the counter. I'm so pathetic. He's doing this for me. I meet my own eyes in the mirror, noting my pale face. *He's doing this for me.* I need to grow the fuck up. This is just part of being in a relationship with these guys.

Appearances mean everything in the business world.

Drawing in a breath, I look up to stop the emotions from spilling down my face. Blowing out my breath, I try to let go of this hot, burning feeling welling inside me. It's okay. It's going to be okay.

"Are you okay?" Sara closes the door behind her and steps up to the sink next to me.

"Yes, I'm sorry. I just . . ." How do I explain I'm jealous that one of my men is out on a date when I'm out on a date with two other men? While another of my men is at home waiting for me?

Unfortunately, I can't, so I shrug.

"You can talk to me if you need to. If I know anything, it's how frustrating men can be." Sara opens her compact and takes out her lipstick. "I mean, it's one thing to have a crush on my brother's best friend. It's another for his other best friend to flirt with me constantly. And then the third one to try to run my life like I'm his responsibility. So yeah, men, *pfft*, who needs them?"

"They're good for some things." I lean against the counter and watch her apply lipstick.

"I think Kayla has the right idea. Her girlfriend sounds amazing." Sara slides her lipstick back into her purse and smiles before blowing out a breath. "If only I didn't like cock."

She sighs like that's a tragedy. I can't help the laughter that escapes me. Sara grins.

"Look who I'm talking to. You've got two cocks." She lowers her voice. "Seriously though, what's that like?"

Both bathroom stall doors are open, and there's no one else in here with us. "Amazing. Like seriously, amazing. When Coop and Noah decide to take me together? Panty melting."

Sara's eyes light up. "Seriously? Together? Like both at the same time?"

I blush and nod. It's nice to be able to share at least that much.

"Fuck, I thought that only happened in books." She shakes her head and then gets serious again. "Are you okay? Do you want to sit in here and talk for a while, or should we head back to your men?"

I draw in a deep breath and release it. "I think I'm ready to go back out there."

Seth

Our dinner arrives, and Elizabeth has been droning on about whatever crosses her mind. I give up trying to have a conversation when Madison reappears at the table. Fuck, why did I put her in that dress?

Practically every man in the room watches her walk by. I sip what's probably my fourth scotch. But it makes the evening a bit more tolerable. Madison laughs at something someone at her table said.

I wonder if fucking her on the table in front of everyone would be too caveman-like. Would she get off on it? Having everyone watch her get fucked?

"If you don't stop staring at her, people are going to talk." Elizabeth's voice cuts into my thoughts. She sets her fork on her plate.

"Would you rather I stare at you?" I narrow my eyes at her, feeling belligerent. It's my own damn fault we're in this situation. I never should have taken Gloria's bait. I lift my scotch glass and see it's almost empty. It's probably time to switch to water. Fuck.

"I would. After all, we're out on a date." She straightens and leans forward. "We could put all that pent-up sexual tension to work. You could hate fuck me. I don't mind being used."

I chuckle and push the drink away. Definitely time to switch to water. "I believe in this situation I would be the one being used."

"It doesn't have to be this way, Seth." She runs her hands over her skirt. "We used to be good together."

"Until you tried to fuck my friend." My words might have been a little louder than I intended. A couple next to us turns and stares at me. Fuck.

"Are you trying to ruin both of us? That's ancient history," Elizabeth hisses. She leans in closer and smiles. "If you don't want me to run my mouth off to the press, you'll kiss me right now."

This isn't worth it. But then I think of Madison's future plans. Every time she makes a move, this whole thing will be brought up, dug up. Not just about me wanting her, but how it seems suspicious that she lived with all of us. Then, the older story about Andrea will rise from the dead.

It could crush her future. It could crush her.

I picture her blue eyes over Elizabeth's brown ones. This is beyond fucked-up, but this is damage control. It means nothing. Just a quick peck.

"I'm sorry," I whisper and lean in and kiss her.

Chapter 122

Broken Interface

Madison

I laugh at something Coop says, feeling much better about the situation. Our food has arrived, and we've kept the conversation light. I've kept my gaze from straying to Seth. But each time it slides his way, he looks bored out of his mind and my heart settles a little more.

Coop sucks in his breath. I glance at him and then follow his line of sight. Seth is kissing Elizabeth.

Fuck. He's kissing her. My breath freezes in my chest. For a moment, everything moves in slow motion. His hand is on her face and his lips are pressed to hers. A fist closes around my heart, squeezing it so hard.

I gasp and stand, needing to get away. I don't think, I just go. Bursting into the bathroom, I push the door closed behind me as if to ward off the evil that's trying to sink into me. To stop my eyes from seeing what they saw. To keep my heart from shattering into a million pieces.

How is *that* for me?

A tear slips down my cheek. I fall back against the wall and slide down to the floor, needing to protect myself. I can't get the image out of my head. Why would he kiss her? What purpose would that serve? He has to have a reason, right?

Someone knocks on the door. I shake my head but don't say anything. I can't. What even could I say? I don't want Sara to come in here, because how do I explain *this*? My boss kissed the woman he's out on a date with and it's breaking my heart.

I want to curl up and forget this night even happened. Wash my eyes of the image of him smiling at her and kissing her. Her! The woman he used to love. Maybe he still has feelings. Maybe he didn't realize it. Maybe spending time with her—

The door opens and Seth steps into the bathroom. His eyes are frantic as he looks around. Then those devastating blue eyes find me. My torn-apart insides ache. He pushes the door closed and engages the lock.

My hands shake as I swipe at the tear on my cheek and wait.

For him to say something.

Anything.

I don't know what will make this okay. He kissed her. Hot pools of jealousy swirl in my stomach, threatening to pull me under and drown me.

He pushes his hand into his blond hair and stares at the ceiling for a second. "Madison—"

"You kissed her." The accusation rips out of my soul. I want to be the woman who is sophisticated, but the man I love just kissed another woman in front of me. My heart is bleeding all over this floor. It hurts so bad.

"Fuck." His voice is soft, but the anguish catches my attention. He drops to his knees in front of me. His blue eyes capture mine. "She brought us here, knowing you'd be here. Knowing she could use you against me."

He reaches up and grabs his hair like he wants to pull it out. "The only way I could get through tonight was to imagine she was *you*. That I was showing *you* off. Holding *your* hand. Kissing *you*."

When a tear slips down my cheek, I swipe at it. The ache in my chest won't go away. But I'm listening, because I want to believe him. I want him to be mine, but then the image of him kissing her rears its head. I close my eyes, but it remains there, playing on an endless loop.

"Tell me what to do to fix this, princess. Because I'm dying inside." He moves closer until his knees bump into my feet. I don't have the energy to pull them away. "Help me, because I can't see you like this. I don't want to hurt you."

"You kissed her." The words tremble on my lips, holding back a floodgate of tears.

"Not her, Madison. Never her." He reaches out and brushes a rogue tear from my cheek. Those sparks between us don't fail to rise at his nearness, making me long to lean into his touch to let him comfort me. "I could never—"

He draws in a breath and rubs his fingers together, spreading my tear over his skin.

"You could never . . . ?" But he did. I saw it.

His gaze lifts to mine. "I don't want to hurt you, but I need to protect you. I can't do both. I can't protect you without going out with Elizabeth, and being with Elizabeth hurts you. Please tell me what to do because I can't lose you. I can't—" He closes his eyes. When he opens them, they're filled with determination. "I love you. Only you."

My heart pounds fiercely with his admission as another tear slips from my eye. I don't know what to feel. He loves me. He doesn't want to hurt me, but he did. But he did it to protect me. This is so fucked up.

"Please tell me what to do." His eyes shimmer in the light, and I can't hold myself back from him any longer. I need his comfort. To feel safe.

I launch myself into his arms. He catches me, draws me into his arms and onto his lap and holds me close to him while I cling to him.

"I love you, Seth," I whisper so no one else will hear. I need him to hear it, to feel it, to know why I'm so distraught seeing him kiss her.

"I love you, princess." He moves to capture my lips, but I stop him with my fingers over my lips.

"I can't." Those lips have touched hers. I can't kiss him after he kissed her. It may make me the biggest hypocrite in the world. I literally kiss three other guys besides him, but he can only kiss me. That's the rule we agreed to.

He reaches up and grabs a paper towel from the dispenser. He rubs his mouth, wiping away any residue from her. Crumpling up the paper towel, he pitches it at the trash can before grabbing me and capturing my lips with his.

Sparks light up my insides. My heart feels like it's going to burst. He trails kisses over my cheek to my ear and whispers, "I love you."

A knock sounds on the door. My eyes widen. I'd forgotten where we are. Oh, fuck, I'd forgotten where we are!

"You can't be in here," I whisper, but I don't move away. I want to linger in this moment, in his words as they help to patch up my heart.

"Noah's watching the door for us." Seth brushes my hair out of my face and looks me over. He presses his forehead against mine. "I wish we could stay here, but we have to go back out there. I have to go back to her. Just for now."

"I know." I clutch at his suit jacket. I don't want to let him go. I don't want him to leave me.

"We'll talk at home. Okay?" He presses his lips to mine. "We'll figure this out."

"I don't want you to have to date her." I meet his eyes steadily. My heart pounds. "It hurts too much."

He nods and blows out a breath. "We'll find another way."

Standing, he helps me to my feet. We both straighten my dress before he draws me in close. "You look magnificent tonight."

I cup his cheek with my hand and smile sadly. "You look very handsome."

He presses his forehead to mine and then leaves me. Unlocking the door and slipping away before I can do anything else. I draw in a deep breath and a laugh slips out. He broke my heart and then told me he loves me.

I want to curl up and fly at the same time. I doublecheck my makeup and outfit in the mirror. When I feel like I'm ready to face whatever will happen out in the dining room, I take a deep breath and step out into the hall. Instead of Noah, Coop leans against the wall opposite the door. His hands in his pockets as he looks me up and down.

"Let's go home, sweetheart." He holds out his hand and I take it, grateful I don't have to return to my seat and pretend I don't see Seth with her. I can't handle it anymore. Just seeing them together weighs on my soul.

Coop pulls me into his side. His warmth surrounds me, drawing me in. I lean against him, craving more.

"Noah and Sara went to get the car."

Elizabeth rounds the corner and stops when she sees us. My breath catches in my throat. Her eyes widen and then grow calculating. "If it isn't the happy couple."

"If it isn't the cold-hearted bitch." Coop slides his hand possessively over my hip.

Elizabeth tsks Coop. "Is that any way to talk to a client?"

Her gaze slides to me dismissively. She smooths a hand over her skirt.

"When you're the client, yes." Coop moves to walk past her.

"You should remember your place, Cooper." She turns to look at him with her cold eyes.

"And what place is that exactly, Elizabeth?" Coop bites out. His fingers dig into my skin a little. The level of his hatred for her has always been obvious. He doesn't hide it, and right now, I'm glad for it because it means I don't have to pretend to be nice to her.

"You don't run Morrigan Technology. Seth does. And when Seth and I are together, I'll make sure you're the first person we let go unless you decide to play ball." She pauses and looks at me with a disparaging smile. "Well, the *second* person I let go."

My hackles rise, and I've never wanted to slap anyone as much as I want to slap her.

Coop laughs. "Oh, fuck, and I thought you had an actual threat of some sort. Yeah, good luck with that, lady. I'm sure it will go just as well as crawling into my bed at night and begging me to fuck you."

"I did not beg." She straightens like she's mortified, but a little pink tinges her cheeks.

Coop leans into her space and says in a feminine tone, "Please, Coop. I need it. I want it. Only you can give me what I really want. Please fuck me." He straightens and his voice returns to normal. "As I recall, I said you could go fuck yourself. How's that going for you? Or are you too much of a cold-hearted bitch to get yourself off?"

Her eyes narrow into a glare, but Coop doesn't wait for her to say more. He leads me around her and out to the car. Helping me in next to Noah before sliding in beside me. Both guys' thighs press tight against mine.

Sara leans forward to take my hands. "Coop told me you got sick. Are you doing okay? Do you need anything? I feel terrible about having to cut the evening short, but I'm sure these guys will take good care of you."

I squeeze her hands, grateful for the guys' quick thinking. "Yeah, I'm sure I'll be better soon."

The car takes off. Sara and Noah talk about a book they both read. Coop holds my hand in his, keeping me warm.

I suddenly remember the purpose of our evening. "Did the guy notice you?"

Sara blows her hair out of her face. "When he and his date left, they stopped by our table to say hello. You were in the bathroom, so it was just me and Coop at the table."

"He was pretty stiff." Coop turns the ring on my finger. His ring. "Like it was an obligation to stop and say something."

Sara sighs. "That's pretty much all I get from him. I wish I could just forget about him, but he seems to be everywhere in my life. Tom brings him and the others to everything. Like he's adopted them."

"Maybe it's part of his bro code? Leave the sister alone? That's a thing with siblings, right?" I offer. Did no one else notice his heated gaze on Sara? It wasn't just that one time either.

Her green eyes widen. "Do you think?"

"I don't know. Maybe." What did I know about men? I have four of them and I'm still trying to figure out where I stand. I lean my head against Coop's shoulder, and his words from earlier still swirl in my head.

She gets to be with two men who love her.

What if he meant that? Should I confront him or just be happy he said it in passing?

What if they all loved me? Where would we go from here?

Nowhere? They've made it clear that a relationship with all of us would be detrimental to their business and to my future.

Would love be enough?

If I remained their dirty little secret?

Chapter 123

Square the Circle

Coop

The car stops in front of Sara's house.

"I hope you feel better." Sara takes Madison's hand and squeezes it.

"Be right back." Noah steps out of the car and holds his hand out to help Sara.

Madison's hand tightens on mine as Noah offers his arm for the walk. Sighing, she looks down. It eats her up inside seeing us with other women.

At least I don't have to keep up a charade. Unless one counts going out with just one woman a sham for me, which normally it would be, but not with Madison. She's all I need.

She turns to me and clears her throat. "Did you mean what you told Sara before dinner?"

Yeah, knew that wouldn't slip by her. I smirk to hide the pounding of my heart.

"That I like red wine better than white?" I know what she's talking about. It wasn't a slip of the tongue or some ruse to keep up appearances. It's the best way I have of describing what I feel for her. But I don't know how to express myself in a normal way.

Her mouth drops open like she can't believe I just said that.

I chuckle and lift her chin with my finger to close her mouth. Drawing her to sit sideways on my lap, I tip her chin up so that our eyes meet.

"I'm not good with emotions." I swallow, hoping I don't put my foot in my mouth. "Growing up, emotions weren't nurtured, they were looked down upon. My parents didn't show their affection, and whether they loved me or I was just a necessity to continue their line was up for debate."

"Coop—" Her soft eyes want to give me an easy out. I'm not here for that. Not this time.

"No, it's true. So do I know what love is?" I shrug. "I would do anything for Blake, Seth, and Noah. If they need me, I'll drop everything and come running. I'll fight for them. Stand up for them. Is that love? They'd do the same for me. So is that because we need people in our lives or is that love?"

She doesn't answer. Her fingertips trace my jaw. Red rims her eyes from crying over Seth. I want to punch him for hurting her, but she wouldn't want me to. Everything about her is better than I deserve, but I can't help but want to own some part of her heart. It's selfish, but I don't give a fuck.

"You make me feel wanted, needed, and a part of something so good that we'd be fools to let you go. When you smile, I want to smile. When you cry, I feel this ache deep inside me. I need to protect you and care for you. I want to fuck you with my friends and without. You are part of my life. So if that qualifies as love, then I'm all in."

Madison's eyes tear up.

"I didn't say it to make you cry again." I brush the stray tears off her cheeks.

She rises on her knees and tugs her skirt up so she can straddle my lap. When she captures my face between her hands, she searches my eyes in the dim streetlight.

"Coop, I love you. And I would do anything for you." Her words are fiercely spoken. "I can't imagine my life without you in it."

"Good, because you're stuck with me. I love you, goddess." I capture the back of her neck and kiss her, needing to feel this connection. With one hand, I work on my pants, needing more. Needing to solidify what she makes me feel.

She reaches down and helps me free my cock before she sinks over me, taking me into her body. We groan into each other's mouths at the feel. Our tongues tangle as she rises and sinks on me again.

"How long was I gone for?" Noah asks as he slides into his seat and closes the door.

"Not long enough, obviously." I grin at him before dragging Madison's mouth back to mine. She grinds down on me, but it's not enough.

I shift with her in the seat until I lay her back with her head on Noah's lap. Drawing her leg up onto my shoulder, I thrust in deeper. Her moan fills the car. Fuck, I could spend eternity listening to her make all those noises.

Noah brushes her hair out of her face and slides his hand down along her neckline. "What's the occasion?"

"Coop told me he loves me," Madison pants out as I thrust deep into her welcoming cunt, taking long strokes, wanting to draw this out. She trembles beneath me.

"Finally." Noah arches an eyebrow at me.

"Fuck off, Noah. Not all of us can be in touch with our feelings like you." I stroke her clit, rubbing the hard nub. Her moan makes me want to fuck her harder. "Besides, I figure if I'm going to marry the woman, I ought to love her."

"We're not really engaged." Arching against the seat, Madison rocks her hips in time with me. I rub circles around her clit and she sucks in a breath.

"Tell that to my mother."

When her eyes widen, I wink at her. Noah leans his head back against the seat as the car pulls away from the curb.

"You might have to actually ask her to marry you, if that's what you want." Noah meets my eyes before dropping his gaze to watch my cock thrusting into Madison's pussy. He reaches over and teases her clit with me. She tightens around me and arches her back. So fucking close.

"Fuck, I just told her I loved her and now you want me to propose to my fiancée?"

Noah laughs.

Moaning, Madison shatters. All my attention focuses on her. Her body arches beautifully as I thrust deep inside her, quickening my pace, feeling her walls clench around me, dragging me into my release. My cock jerks as it fills every inch of her, claiming her, marking her as mine.

I lower her leg and lean over her to claim her lips. I want to spend all night exploring her, but tonight isn't my night.

When I come up for air, Noah reaches over into the console and pulls out a few wipes, handing them to me.

Madison's satisfied eyes meet mine as I draw my cock out and push my cum back into her with two fingers. A little aftershock ripples around my fingers as I thrust them deep. She sighs and looks up at Noah.

"We need to talk when we get home," she says.

Those words make my gut clench, but I clean both of us up and help her sit upright.

"Seth?" Noah asks.

Her eyes turn glassy, but she doesn't cry as she nods. She rests her head on my shoulder and takes both of our hands. "I can't watch him be with her."

I meet Noah's gaze over her head. Both of us are on the same page. Sure, there will be repercussions from us announcing we're all dating, but I don't think it will hurt Madison's future as much as Seth and Blake think it will. Besides, we don't need to really announce it. We just have to live our lives the way we want to.

Which means Madison is ours.

"We'll figure out something." Noah threads his fingers through hers.

My heart still feels swollen from her telling me she loves me. It's euphoric and makes me believe we're capable of anything, but even I know not to be too hasty. There are other factors at play here, and all we can do is plan how to go forward from here.

Blake

I gave up pacing about fifteen minutes ago and settled for waiting on the couch. The TV is on, but the volume is low. I can't focus, but I also don't want to disrupt everyone's evening out with what my buddy told me.

The door opens and Coop, Madison, and Noah come in. They're subdued as they walk into the main area. I stand and take a step toward them.

Madison looks back at Coop before they all head toward me.

"How was dinner?" I need to get the pleasantries out of the way.

"Eventful." Noah sits on the couch and draws Madison down to sit next to him. Coop sits on her other side.

"We need to talk about Seth's situation." Coop takes Madison's hand and brings her fingers to his lips, kissing them lightly.

I sit on the ottoman across from them. My brows furrow. "Seth's situation?"

"Elizabeth needs to be dealt with." Madison's glassy blue eyes lift to mine.

"Everything okay, love?" I put my hand on her knee, wanting to comfort her.

When she shakes her head, a tear slips free. I don't know what happened, but I know she needs me. I hold out my arms. As she slides over to my lap, my arms wrap around her and she curls into me. Her hands clutch my t-shirt. A sob racks her body, making me hold her tighter.

What the fuck happened?

I glance at Noah and Coop, but they just watch her.

"Hey," I say gently, rubbing her back. "Hey, tiger, what's wrong?"

She shakes her head against my shoulder as her tears dampen my t-shirt. That instinct to protect her against everything makes me want to punch these two for upsetting her. Or was it Seth?

Kissing the top of her head, I look to Coop. "What happened?"

"Elizabeth and Seth were at the restaurant acting like a couple out on a date." Coop swallows. His gaze never leaves Madison's shaking shoulders. "He kissed Elizabeth in the restaurant."

"Fuck." I run my hand down Madison's back and squeeze her against me. Seth wouldn't do something like that unless he felt there was no other choice. "He had to have been backed into a corner."

Noah nods and walks into the kitchen to grab a couple of tissues. "Elizabeth picked the restaurant on purpose. She knew we'd be there. That Madison would be there. She used Madison against him."

When he returns, he hands me the tissues. I give one to Madison. She dabs at her eyes and meets mine. "He said he couldn't protect me and not hurt me."

I want to burn Elizabeth down to the ground. She already tried to mess up our lives once before. We survived that, but this time her target seems to be Madison, and that won't stand.

"We started a thorough background check on her. We'll find something to hold over her head so she won't go forward with telling the press about you and Seth." I tip her chin up and use a tissue to wipe the tears from her face. "This is what Elizabeth does. She's only out for her own gains."

"Seth can't play into them though." Coop clears his throat. "Tonight, Elizabeth played her hand perfectly and got exactly what she wanted."

Madison rests her head against my shoulder. One arm drapes around my neck while I hold her other hand in her lap.

"We won't be able to fix anything until Seth gets home. We'll

need to discuss our options." I clear my throat. "There's more information on Madison's case. My buddy at the station called."

Both Noah and Coop lean forward. Madison's fingers tighten
around mine.

"They found Valerie's body."

Madison sucks in a breath. "Her body?"

"She overdosed in a trap house they raided yesterday. They're
still trying to identify her remains. But they're confident it's her." I
run my hand down Madison's back.

"What about Jeff?" She lifts her head. Her eyes are no longer
glassy.

"They've got a lead on the drug dealers who ran the house. They
think he may be with them." I take a deep breath. "I have guys lined
up to go through her room at your apartment tomorrow."

She nods while looking at our hands. Her wide eyes lift to mine.
"I didn't want her dead."

"I know, love." Drawing her head back to my shoulder, I say, "I
don't know if we would have learned anything even if they caught
her. We'll see if there's anything useful in her apartment and then
give it to the police for when they track down her next of kin."

"Should we stay up for Seth?" Noah stretches his arms over his
head. "Or deal with it in the morning? He seemed a little tipsy after
he kissed Elizabeth."

"He'll want to know about Valerie." I know that, but I'm also not
sure what time he'll get home, and that could make things awkward
for him and Madison. What if he's out for another couple hours? "We
can text and see when he thinks he'll be back."

I'm not about to let Madison go to grab my phone. Understanding
my dilemma, Coop pulls out his and types a text.

The door opens. We all look up as Seth enters the apartment.

Chapter 124

Crime and Punishment

Seth

Madison's eyes are the only thing I see when I walk into the apartment. It nearly destroyed me to see her crying over something I did. She still seems upset over it. Fuck. I don't know how to make this right.

Blake holds her in his lap while they all look at me. I disappointed them all tonight.

I run a hand through my hair and walk over to the couch to join them.

Blake's eyes burn into me. Obviously, he knows what I did. The drinks definitely didn't help my decision-making, and I regretted it the moment my lips touched Elizabeth's.

"Even though it seemed like a good plan, obviously caving to Elizabeth's demands was a disaster." I slump against the back of the couch and loosen my tie. Drawing it out from my collar, I wrap it around my hand.

"You did it to protect the company and Madison." Coop understands the necessary evils in this world better than most. His parents raised him to look for ways to make the public perceive him at his best. Not that he followed that advice or even put much stock in it.

"How did you get out of the date so early?" Noah asks.

"Food poisoning." I give them a half smile. "Maybe alcohol poisoning. Either way, she didn't want to be around me for the rest of the night after I fouled up her bathroom."

"Nice." Coop grins. It was definitely effective.

"How are we going to deal with her?" Blake's hand rubs down Madison's back.

Her eyes meet mine, and my heart beats a little harder. I might have been slightly drunk to make it through the evening, but I remember every word we said to each other in that bathroom.

Not exactly the best way to tell a woman you love them, but I couldn't hold it in any longer. She needed to know the truth.

"Elizabeth has something she's hiding. I just have to find it. Preferably before our next date." I rub the back of my neck. "I can't keep this up. She's not happy just to have me there. She wants a full-blown relationship, not just a few dates. I refuse to give her any more of me."

"I'll see what our team has dug up." Blake sighs. He kisses the top of Madison's head. "My buddy called. They found Valerie's body yesterday."

I blow out a breath. Even if I wished her dead, I didn't really want it to end that way. "Jeff?"

Blake shakes his head. "They have a lead though."

"Good. Though that leaves some unanswered questions." It would have been good to know if Valerie gave someone a key or access to the apartment. That information might have helped us track down Madison's stalker or at least narrow down the suspect pool.

"I don't want you to go out with Elizabeth again." Madison straightens and meets my eyes. "You don't have to protect me that way. If it's for the reputation of the company, that can be your decision, but I don't need you to take this on for me."

I run a hand through my hair. Fuck it. "I don't know where we go from here. But I know we have to figure out what this"—I gesture to all of us—"is and I can't do that with a guillotine dangling above my neck. Elizabeth holds some cards for now. We'll deal with her. I promise. I'll find an excuse to put her off while we figure out what will stop her."

Resting her head against Blake's shoulder, Madison takes a deep breath. "I'm done. Can we swap nights? I'm not going to be much fun. I feel like I've been through the wringer."

My chest aches to know I'm the reason for that.

"Can we just all sleep together, and then tomorrow night Blake and I can have our time?" Madison strokes her hand down Blake's cheek and looks into his eyes. Even though I love her, there isn't an ounce of jealousy over seeing her with my friends. She wants them as much as she wants me. And I know she loves them as much as I love them.

"I'm okay with that, tiger. Whatever makes you comfortable."

Her gaze lifts to me.

"Even me?" I've been stupid and blind, juggling too much, and almost dropped the most important ball. I almost lost the one thing I could never get back.

Madison stands and straightens her dress. She holds out her hand to me. "Even you. I don't believe in going to bed angry or putting someone in the doghouse. You're all mine, and I need you to be with me tonight. To sleep near me so I know you're still mine."

I take her hand and pull her to stand between my knees. "I will always be yours."

Resting my head against her stomach, I inhale that rich floral perfume laced with Madison's unique scent. Her arms wrap around my shoulders.

"You don't have to sacrifice yourself to save me, Seth." She presses a kiss to my head. "You just need to be mine and let me be yours."

"I think Blake should punish Seth the way he punished me," Coop says.

I raise an eyebrow at Blake and look up at Madison. "Is that what you want?"

She bites her lip and glances toward Blake. She thinks about it for a moment. The guys and I talked about Blake's interruption of Coop's night. We talk about everything. Though none of us have admitted our feelings for her to each other.

Nodding her head slightly, she makes her decision. Her sky blue eyes meet mine and she smiles softly.

"Yes. You know how to stop or pause this, right?" She takes my hand and unwinds my tie from it.

She's absolutely stunning tonight. I need to fix what I broke and will go to any lengths to get back to where we were. I nod. "Green, princess. Whatever you want to do. I just want your forgiveness."

Her fingertips trail over my shoulders while she walks behind me. "Hold out your wrists."

Coop and Noah get comfortable to watch the show while she wraps my tie around both my wrists, binding them behind me.

Madison moves in front of me, sliding her hand along my shoulders, leaving a trail of sparks beneath her fingertips. When she kneels before me, she reaches for my belt and slowly opens my pants.

"This doesn't seem like much of a punishment," I admit as she frees my hard cock.

Leaning over, she takes it deep into her mouth before coming off it. She smirks at me before going back to where Blake stands.

"You're lucky she's not wearing panties. Blake had her gag me with them." Coop's eyes heat. That fucker loved every minute. Meanwhile, I'm over here wondering how to get untied.

I don't like the feeling of being out of control. It's the reason I like to test myself with Madison. Though lately I've been failing. My desire for her overwhelms my control.

Blake inches up her skirt until it's barely covering her ass. He reaches between her legs and thrusts his fingers inside her pussy. Okay, this kind of punishment I can take, though my cock aches with the need to be touched.

"She's already wet and ready, Seth." Blake tips her head to the side and kisses her neck. "She's aching for release. Aren't you, love?"

"Yes, please." Her lips part and her eyes dilate. She needs this. Fuck, she wants all of us and our fucked-up little games. She's never denied us anything we want to do, and she gets off on it. She's so fucking perfect.

"I love you, Madison." The words flow off my lips. Once said, it's so much easier to repeat. I don't know if anyone else in this room feels this way about her. Maybe Noah, but I don't give a shit.

She deserves to hear *I love you* every day for the rest of her life, and I'm more than willing to promise her that. If she'll have me.

Her eyes soften. She mouths, *I love you.*

Blake watches me with unreadable eyes. His fingers thrust in and out of Madison's cunt while she leans back against him. Her wetness drips down his fingers as her breath works in and out of her lungs, faster and faster.

"Do you know how good your pussy feels around our cocks, tiger?" Blake whispers loudly in her ear. "When you come around us, making us need more and more. Hot and tight and all ours."

She whimpers as he draws his fingers out. "Blake?"

"Hands on Seth's knees, love." Blake smacks her ass.

She gives him a heated look over her shoulder before sashaying my way. Her hips are hypnotic in their swaying. Still not sure how any of this is punishment, but if this is the way to be forgiven, I'm all in.

Her darkened eyes meet mine as she bends over and puts her hands on my knees. She blows out a breath over my straining cock, making me groan at the ache radiating through me. Her eyes lift to mine with a hint of mischief in them. Fuck, I love this woman.

Blake steps behind her and undoes his pants, releasing his cock. With one thrust, he buries himself inside her. Her head drops between her arms as she moans.

"I punished Coop because he was being a possessive dick with our girl." Blake pulls his hips back and thrusts in deep again.

Madison's breath works in and out, and each time she releases her breath, it bathes my cock in warmth, fleeting and not enough to make me come. Her breasts sway with every thrust. My fingers itch to cup them and pinch her nipples, but I'm bound tight.

I'm understanding why this was torture to Coop. I may love to watch, but right now, I ache to participate. To stir her up the way she does to me.

"This punishment is from Madison." Blake rubs her clit, making her hands tighten on my knees as she pushes back against him. Her eyes are passion laden when she lifts them to meet mine.

"I'm yours." She closes her eyes and whimpers in need as Blake picks up the pace. "I'm all of yours. But that means you can only be mine."

Those blue eyes open as she pants out, "No one else's. Not even to save my reputation. Those lips are mine and only mine."

She squeezes my legs as she moans through her release. Blake thrusts a few more times before he finishes inside her. I need her tight, wet heat surrounding me.

Blake lifts her chin so I can see her satisfied eyes. "Don't break her heart."

As Blake steps away, he nods to Coop. Coop strokes his cock as he steps behind her. He gathers the cum on her thighs with his fingers and presses them deep inside her cunt. An aftershock makes her gasp and clench on my thighs.

"We're going to fill you so fucking full of our cum, sweetheart."

He pulls his fingers out before thrusting his hard cock deep into her. When she moans, he brings his fingers to her lips.

"Taste it."

She takes his fingers into her mouth and sucks on them. My aching cock weeps at the pleasure on her face in profile. Her darkened eyes watch me as Coop fucks her cunt. He pulls his fingers out of her mouth.

"Taste the boss." He holds her hips while he thrusts deep inside her.

I don't know if I'll last if she sucks on my cock. My balls tighten as she licks her lips. When she lowers her mouth to hover over my cock, her tongue darts out and sweeps through my slit, gathering the precum leaking out. Sucking in a breath, I resist the urge to thrust. If my hands were free, I'd grab her hair and thrust in deep. Push my cock into that warm mouth and claim what is mine.

"Not too much, sweetheart." Coop grabs her hair and lifts her head as he pounds into her pussy. Her hands tighten as she cries out her release. Her eyes are open and locked with mine. That spark of desire races between us.

Coop pulls his cock out of her pussy and nudges at her puckered hole before sliding inside. Her mouth opens in a silent scream as she pushes back against him, taking him as deep as possible.

"Fuck, goddess, your ass is like a vise clamp on my cock. Relax, sweetheart, let me fuck your ass so Seth knows how to do it next time." Coop winks at my glare.

"Fuck me harder, Coop," she bites out. Her gaze finds mine. I don't know how I didn't say it before now. How much I love every inch of her. Crave her like no other. How her pleasure is more important to me than my own.

Coop rubs her clit in circles while he fucks her ass. "Come on, my little whore. You know you want to come again. Drip all over my fingers and beg me to do nasty things to this body."

Her face tightens as she moans. I could watch her come all the fucking time. It doesn't matter if I'm the one doing it, as long as I get to see her.

"Coop. Ah, fuck." She drops her head against my thigh as she keeps coming.

"That's right. Don't stop, sweetheart. Your ass is so fucking tight around my cock. I won't last much longer. Can you feel every inch?" He pulls almost all the way out before slamming back in.

She rocks forward from the force, crying out her release. That's it for Coop. He thrusts deep into her as he groans, filling her with his cum. Fuck, I want to stroke my cock. I want to cup her face and kiss her as she comes down from her climax.

Madison turns her head and licks up the side of my cock, making me groan with need.

Coop pulls out and smacks her ass. She sucks in a breath.

"Noah, you're up." Coop heads to the bathroom.

"Turn around, kitten." Noah stands and pulls out his cock. "Sit on the boss's lap and push back until your ass cradles his cock."

"Fuck," I hiss out as she follows his orders. Such a perfect little submissive. Her legs spread to either side of mine, dripping cum and her own slick on my lap and cock. Her ass cheeks cradle me perfectly.

When he approaches her, she leans forward with her hands on my knees. The black dress bares her back almost down to her ass crack. I long to lean forward and taste her skin. She takes Noah's cock into her mouth and wiggles against me.

Fuck. This *is* torture.

Noah gathers her hair and holds it in one hand. "Let me have control, kitten."

Madison stops moving, and I can feel her muscles relax against me. Noah meets my eyes as he thrusts deep into her mouth. She moans around his cock.

"You made her cry." His dark eyes narrow on me.

"I know." My heart aches remembering her tears, how broken and fragile she looked on the floor. The betrayal glistening in her eyes.

"The only tears she should cry are from fucking or happiness." Noah thrusts in deep and holds her there. I feel a tear hit my thigh before he pulls her back.

Her ass cheeks rub against my cock, and I fight not to come all over her beautiful dress.

"I know." Everything I did was wrong. I shouldn't have let Madison talk me into going out with Elizabeth. Elizabeth told me her end game at the benefit. I thought she'd given up, but she wants me for life. She thinks blackmail will keep me tied to her.

Noah pulls out of Madison's mouth. "Turn around, kitten. I want to come in your sweet cunt."

She turns, and tears streak down her cheeks as she meets my gaze. Noah slides his cock deep and her eyes close, but then open to hold mine.

Our gazes lock as Noah fucks her. When she tips over the edge, her breath comes out in quick pants as she digs her nails into my legs. Her face is flushed with passion as Noah slips out of her and backs away.

"Show the boss what he'll miss if he doesn't shape up, tiger." Blake's voice is commanding.

She lifts upright and straddles my hips before lowering her tight, wet heat onto my cock. I bite back a curse, knowing I won't be able to control myself this time. She has all the power as her hands settle on my shoulders.

"Do you want her?" Madison asks, meeting my eyes but not moving her hips.

"No, never. I only want you." I try to shift to a more comfortable position for my arms and, honestly, to get a little friction from her tight pussy wrapped around me.

"No more dates. No more blackmail." She lifts and falls on my cock.

"Fuck. No more." I couldn't go through with anything else if I tried.

"If it comes out, we'll deal with it." She lifts. "Together." She falls, taking me completely inside her. Her breath teases my lips and I want to taste her.

I would swear anything to her in this moment. In any moment.

"Yes, princess, together. Always together."

She cups my face and searches my eyes. "I love you, Seth."

"I love you, Madison."

She takes my mouth as she rides my cock. I don't know how to stop from coming at this point. It's too much. She tightens around me and moans into my mouth. When I open my eyes, Blake is behind her, and I can feel his cock inside her ass through the thin wall.

Her whole being tightens as she cries out and comes around both of us. I can't hold back and I don't want to, so I let go with her, letting her lead me into my release.

Blake groans as he fills her ass.

She tips her forehead against mine and whispers, "Mine."

I press a kiss to her lips. "Mine."

Chapter 125

Product Testing

Madison

A brief kiss on my forehead wakes me up. Warm bodies surround me. The sun hasn't even risen yet. Last night, after a quick clean up, we all fell into bed. I snuggle back into Blake as his arm draws me closer.

Coop chuckles low, and I open my eyes to his smiling face.

"Morning, sweetheart." His voice is low and gruff. "Heading off for my workout."

I nod and tip my chin up, hoping for a kiss. He doesn't disappoint, claiming my mouth in a deep and thorough kiss that makes me ache for more.

When he lifts his mouth from mine, he runs his thumb over my lip. "You tempt me."

"Same." I smile as he pulls away and climbs off the bed.

My heart feels like it's going to burst in my chest.

They love me.

Seth, Noah, and Coop love me. I don't know about Blake. He heard what Seth said . . . twice. Maybe he'll never say it. It doesn't matter, because I love him so much.

Things seem good. Finally.

I'm not sad over Valerie's passing, but I'm not happy about it either. She deserved to go to jail, but she didn't deserve to die. She and I didn't really have a relationship outside of sharing a living space and rent.

I was too busy with school. She barely acknowledged my existence. Until that night with Jeff. I shiver involuntarily. My fingers go to my throat and smooth over my skin.

"Sleep, tiger," Blake mumbles into my hair, squeezing me tight.

I close my eyes but it's no use. I'm awake. Even his heat surrounding me isn't enough to lull me back into sleep. My eyes open to see Seth sitting up.

He holds a hand out to me. His eyes silently ask me to come with him, but if I want to stay here in Blake's arms, he wouldn't be mad.

I roll and kiss Blake on the cheek. "I'll see you at breakfast."

He grumbles and snuggles down into his pillow. I run my fingers through his thick hair, and a smile brightens his face. I did that. My insides glow.

On the other side of Blake, Noah lies on his stomach with his head buried in the pillow. So not a morning person.

Reaching out, I take Seth's hand and follow him into the bathroom. He shuts the door behind us and turns on the shower. A little distance remains between us.

Not physically, but my heart still aches. He messed up last night. Let things go too far. But I believe him when he says he did it to protect me.

He's proven he'll do anything to protect me, even lose clients.

I pushed for him to go out with Elizabeth. I should have known it wouldn't go smoothly. That it would put him in impossible situations. He warned me, but I thought I could handle it.

This morning, his uneasiness makes my heart ache. It's just as much my fault as his. He didn't want to kiss her. I step into his arms and wrap mine around his waist.

"We're good, boss." I press my lips to his chest. "You and me are fine."

His arms wrap around me, and he holds me close with his chin resting on my head. My heart settles into a steady, warm beat.

"I love you, princess."

I tip my chin up to meet his eyes. They shine with love. Those eyes have captivated me from the beginning. "I love you."

He steps back and draws me into the shower with him. We take our time as we wash each other. Each touch, each caress, floods my veins with desire. When we rinse off the soap, he drags me into his arms. Our bodies, slick with water, slide against each other as he kisses me. His hard cock rests against my stomach, making need ache between my legs.

The shower door opens, and Blake steps in behind me. He kisses the nape of my neck. I suck in a breath from Seth's mouth. Blake's skin is hot. His hands curve around my ass.

"Good morning, tiger." His voice makes my knees weak with want.

When Seth lifts me against him, I wrap my legs around his waist. My hands go into his hair as we kiss, holding him, never wanting to let go. Blake angles my hips and eases his thick cock into my pussy. Each inch stretches me until I take him all.

I whimper into Seth's mouth at how good it feels. My walls flutter around Blake.

When he draws almost all the way out before thrusting in deep, a groan rumbles through me.

Blake pulls his cock out of my pussy. His cockhead nudges at my puckered hole before pushing through the tight ring of muscle. My breath catches as he works his way in, inch by inch, stretching me, filling me. Seth shifts suddenly before Blake is all the way in and thrusts his cock deep into my pussy.

I tear my mouth away from his as I cry out at the overwhelming feeling of them both inside me. Breathing and relaxing my muscles, I press my forehead against Seth's as I adjust to their size.

"You like that, princess?" Seth's gaze meets mine and all I can do is nod. My fingers clench Seth's hair as Blake pushes in the last few inches, filling me completely with both of them. I take in a breath, anticipation a hot drug flooding me.

"Good girl." Blake kisses my neck and tingles chase after his lips. I release my breath, my heart thundering. Waiting.

Seth draws out. When he slides back in, Blake draws out. The rhythm is slow, but with each thrust, my breath and pulse quicken. I tremble between them. Every brush of skin, every slide of their cocks within me, every kiss against my lips and neck fuel the fire building to my climax.

When they quicken their pace, I fall into the rhythm and let them take me. My release shatters through me. For a moment, I'm suspended in time. Mouth open. No breath. No pulse. Just pleasure exploding down to my fingertips and toes.

They bring me back to earth. As they continue to work me through my orgasm and chase their own, I cling to Seth and bite down on his shoulder. My body clutching at their cocks to keep them deep within. The orgasm never seems to end, just keeps crashing over me in waves.

Their groans join my moan as they release their hot cum deep inside me. Their cocks jerk against my walls as they fill me.

Seth captures my mouth while Blake sucks on my neck. The waves slow down, but I still tremble within their embrace. This is mine, and I'll do whatever it takes to keep it.

It's Friday, and we have a new client to meet for lunch today. I'm at my desk going through the files when my phone dings.

HOPE:
Thanks again for your help on Sunday.

She texted me earlier in the week to let me know her brother was okay. This week has been so hectic I haven't had time to check in with her. With everything that's been going on, it feels like forever since we found her brother unconscious.

ME:

I'm glad I could be there for you.

HOPE:

I'm going to my brother's bar for happy hour tonight. If you want to come?

He wants to thank you for helping me.

I glance at the doors behind me. We have about an hour until lunch time. I really want to go with Hope tonight and recapture that feeling I got when we went there the first time.

Everything was so shiny and new. It feels like a lifetime ago. I tap my pen on my desk. I want to go, but I don't think the guys will let me go to a busy bar on a Friday night with only Hope.

ME:

I really want to go, but I'll need to check with

My fingers almost type *the guys*, but that wouldn't make much sense to Hope. I'm only dating Coop in her mind.

ME:

Coop to make sure he doesn't have plans for us

HOPE:

He could come with. I know it's not his normal scene, but we missed our Sunday Witcher marathon. I don't know about you, but I could use some girl time.

ME:

Me too.

And I do. It's been a long time since I had a friend to just hang out with. Maybe as long ago as elementary school. Another idea pops into my head. What if our group was more than just Hope and me? The guys might be more amenable to that.

ME:

Let me check, but maybe I can get Sara to come with. She's dating Noah.

Somehow it doesn't burn as much to say that. But Sara knows the deal. At least with Coop and Noah. That makes it easier because she doesn't try to make something where there isn't anything like Elizabeth did.

HOPE:

The more the merrier. *smiley face emoji*

ME:

I'll get back to you after lunch.

I set my phone to the side and open the client file. The company is Cliodhna. As I read through the details, I get excited to meet the person behind the company, Deidre Byrne. She started the company forty years ago and has built it into a multi-million-dollar business.

The business is centered on feminine pleasure. Toys, lubes, self-care. The list of subsidiaries is impressive. I can't wait to learn more about her business.

"You ready to go, kitten?" Noah comes out of his office and holds out his hand.

I grab my purse and put my computer to sleep. When I stand, Blake, Seth, and Coop have all joined us. "Who am I riding with?"

Noah draws me into his arms. "We get you today."

A pulse of heat flows through me at the look in his dark eyes. Today is a business meeting day. I'm not sure how it will go, but I have high expectations given our other meetings. But I'm also looking forward to my ride with Coop and Noah.

Noah leads me into the elevator with all of them surrounding me. I run my hand over the skirt of my dress. It's loose, and Seth chose the prettiest bra and panty set in a light blue with garters and stockings. The outfit is feminine and soft and sexy as hell.

Coop's hand slides over the curve of my ass. When I glance at him, he winks. The elevator doors open, and Blake and Seth head to the lead car while I get in the other car between Noah and Coop. The privacy screen is already up, and I swear my panties get even wetter, like a Pavlovian response.

Noah's hand slides up my thigh. "What did you learn about the client?"

Tingles race to catch up with his touch.

"She's a self-made millionaire running a multi-million-dollar company. Her products are varied, but all are devoted to feminine pleasure. From clothing lines to bath products—"

"To sex toys." Coop draws my attention with a soft whir. In his hand vibrates a small egg-shaped toy. He arches a dark eyebrow. "We figure we should test the product to understand the business better."

"Of course." I bite my lip as Noah's hand inches closer to where I ache.

Coop bunches my skirt up around my waist. He slides a towel beneath me, making me lift my ass.

"Is that really necessary?" I ask. Noah draws my panties down my legs and slides them into his pocket.

"Yes, kitten." His fingers trail back up my thigh.

When I part my knees to give them better access, Noah lifts my leg and rests it over his. Coop does the same, spreading me wide open.

Coop turns the egg on and presses it against my clit. A breath rushes out of me as I squirm against the vibration. Noah takes the egg from Coop and slides it to my entrance, dipping the tip of it inside a few times before moving it back to my clit.

My breathing is heavy as the fire swells within. Coop shows me a beaded anal plug as he coats it in lube. My pussy gets even wetter in anticipation. After he slathers the plug in lube, he uses his hand to lube my puckered hole, thrusting his finger in deep a few times.

I clutch at his arm, feeling the familiar burn. Noah slips the egg back down to tease my entrance again, thrusting a little deeper each time. When Coop pulls his finger out, he eases the beads in one at a time.

"What do you think of the toys, my little whore?" Coop kisses my neck, and a full-body shiver rushes through me. He clicks on the beads, making them vibrate.

"Oh, fuck." I close my eyes as they play with my pussy and ass. Coop teases the beads in and out of my ass while Noah alternates between my clit and pussy with the egg. When fingers thrust deep into my pussy, I lose it.

My body arches as they fuck my pussy with their fingers and ass with the beads while holding the vibrator against my clit. I come all over their hands, unable to stop the rush of fluid at their stimulation.

Coop jerks the beads out all at once. I scream as a release shatters through me. He captures my mouth, swallowing my pants and cries as wave after wave hits me. Noah removes his fingers and the toy.

He rubs my clit as I come down, sending aftershocks crashing over me. Coop lifts his mouth, and when I open my eyes, his light blue eyes smile into mine.

"Good products?" His smile is devastating.

I cup his cheek and breathe out. "Good."

He kisses me before tipping my face toward Noah. His dark eyes search mine as he slips a finger inside me again. A tiny burst of release sweeps through me.

"So fucking responsive." Noah takes my mouth with his and pulls out his finger. While we kiss, Coop uses the towel to clean me up. When Noah leans his forehead against mine, I open my eyes to his dark ones.

"I love you, kitten."

I press my lips against his and say, "I love you."

He draws away to pull my panties back on. Coop sweeps his fingers over my lower lip.

"I love you, Coop."

His smile is surprised and genuine when he kisses me lightly. "I love you, sweetheart."

Chapter 126

Business Opportunities

"Deidre Byrne, but you can call me Dee. Everyone else does." Deidre gives me a wink while she shakes my hand. "I was a little worried about the boys' club, but they're the best in the business, so I knew I had to at least meet with them."

"They are the best at what they do," I assure her.

Deidre is a little taller than me with more sensible heels on. Her gray hair is swept into a bun low on her head. Her dark eyes have a spark of intelligence and kindness. The crinkles around her eyes dance when she smiles.

She leans in close to me. "It doesn't hurt that they're good looking too."

I can't help my smile. "Definitely."

Coop leads me to my chair and holds it out for me to sit. Seth does the same for Dee.

"And gentlemen too. My goodness. You'll have this old woman's heart all in a flutter." Dee sits and smiles at Seth.

"We aim to please, Ms. Byrne."

"Dee, please. I'm too young to be Ms. anything." She waves off the words like an unpleasant odor. "So are you just a pretty young thing to these guys or are you sharp too?"

My eyes widen at her directness. "Uh . . ."

"She's intelligent and working on learning the ropes so someday she can lead her own company." Seth's voice brims with pride as he looks at me.

My heart flutters and my cheeks grow warm.

"Working with all of us gives her experience with each of our different roles." Blake leans back in his chair. "She's a quick learner and an invaluable asset to the company."

"Beauty and brains and a group of men who know how to appreciate you. My word, you've got it made, young lady." Dee leans her elbows on the table and rests her chin on her hands. Her dark eyes take me all in. "Very interesting."

The waiter comes by with drinks and takes our orders.

"Let's talk business, gentlemen." Dee leans back in her chair and absorbs every word the guys have. Asking questions from time to time. Every now and then, her gaze falls on me with a thoughtful expression.

Coop tangles his fingers with mine below the table and squeezes them. This woman is exactly who I want to grow up to be. She's in charge of her company and doesn't care what people think about her product line as long as her customers are happy.

Dinner arrives, and the conversation revolves more around what Morrigan can do for her companies. When the check arrives, Dee sits back in her chair and eyes me again.

"What's your plan then, Madison?" Dee folds her hands on the table.

"Plan?" I ask, confused.

She leans forward, all her attention on me. "Your plan. You have this career path you want to pursue. You're training under some very brilliant minds, but you can't remain their assistant forever, so what's the plan? Five years? Two? Ten?"

My mouth opens and closes. Leave them? How could I ever leave them? But she's right, to pursue my dream, I'm here to learn and then move on. "At least two years, I think."

I don't look at any of them. We haven't really talked about a future together. Do I assume they'll still be in my life then? I want them to be, but I can't remain their assistant and be someone else's boss.

Will they want a new assistant? With the same contract? Or will we stay together?

Coop squeezes my hand. I meet his soft eyes full of encouragement. I take a breath.

"Ideally, I'll find something that I'm as passionate about as you are, Dee." I smile. "Being able to bring so many people joy would be amazing. I still need some actual experience to get me there. And time to pay off my college debt. But I'll find my niche."

"Good." Her smile grows. "Gentlemen, I have to get back to work. I'll expect your proposal next week sometime?"

"Of course." Seth stands and pulls her chair out.

She takes his hand and shakes it. "I think we'll do great things together."

"We'd be honored to help you out." Blake steps in to shake her hand.

Noah and Coop follow Blake before I step up.

She takes my hand between hers.

"Madison, I hope you get to achieve your dreams. You remind me a lot of myself at your age." She reaches into her purse and draws out a card. "Take this. If you have questions or need advice, you call me. Woman to woman. Sometimes we need to give a hand up to the next generation. Someone helped me a long time ago."

I slip her card into my purse, feeling like she just offered me a golden ticket. "Thank you. I'm honored."

She glances around at the guys waiting for me by the door. "Honestly, I don't know how you'll ever leave those guys."

I smile as my gaze meets each of theirs. "I know."

Blake

Coop and Noah take off with Madison, but Seth and I wait with Dee for her car to arrive.

"You know, I'm a grown woman and can wait for a car by myself." She arches an eyebrow at us.

"We're waiting for our car as well." Seth smiles, like he didn't tell the driver to wait around the block for us.

"Wherever did you find that young lady?" Dee gives us a searching look.

"She applied for the position out of college. Tons of internship experience. We thought she'd be a good fit." I can feel the tips of my ears burn, thinking of how perfectly Madison fits us. We needed a self-starter, but we got a lot more when we hired Madison.

"Hmm." Dee's gaze is sharp. "If I thought you were wasting her talent, I might try to poach her from you. I need someone young and hungry at my company."

"Madison is quite happy in her current position." Seth leans against the valet stand, but I can tell he's tense. Is he worried she'll take Madison away from us?

A black car pulls up. Her gaze takes our measure. "I'll be in touch."

Seth steps up to open her door for her. "We look forward to hearing from you."

We back up as the car drives away. That conversation with Madison about her future made my gut tighten. It's something that seems far off. But the more time we spend together, the tighter I want to hold on to her.

"Come on. Let's walk to the car." Seth gestures to where we told the driver to park.

I shrug. It's not far. As we walk by a passageway between buildings, I hear someone call out. Seth keeps walking while I pause and stare down the shadowed path behind a chain-link fence.

A large man steps into the light, and instantly, I recognize him. Jeff, Val's boyfriend. I pull out my phone readying to dial 9-1-1.

His hair is greasy and dark. His brown eyes are bloodshot. He's still a big motherfucker, but he's lost some weight. His clothes hang on him as if they aren't his. The only way around the fence is over.

"Yo, you're the guy who came for Madison?" Jeff holds up his hands as he comes up to the fence. "Hey, wait. Don't call the police. Dude, you gotta help me."

"I don't 'gotta' do anything but make sure you're arrested." I pause with my finger over the Call button though. That he sought me out over Madison makes me give him a chance. If he steps anywhere near her, I'll take him down however I can. I won't let him get his hands on her again.

"I don't know if you know Valerie OD'd. But she didn't OD on her own, man. She never took that much before. She wouldn't. She only used it to take the edge off." Jeff's hands shake as he reaches out for the fence. Obviously, it's been a while since he had his last hit. "You gotta help me, man. Whoever killed her is probably after me too. I need to get out of here."

I step closer. "What do you know?"

"Fuck, man, give me a couple hundred and I'll tell you." Jeff glances over his shoulder. His dark eyes are wide and paranoid. He scratches his neck. The couple hundred will probably go directly into his veins. It wouldn't be a bad thing if he overdosed too.

Glancing down at my phone, I have to decide whether his information is worth more than getting him thrown in prison. But with Valerie gone, we have no one else to clue us in on who Madison's stalker is.

"Did you know about the video cameras?" I lead with it, because if that wasn't Val, she probably didn't know anything useful.

"Yeah, I installed them for her." He smiles like he's got me now. Like he knows I want his information. "Dude, cash and I'll tell you everything I know."

I scan the area to make sure this isn't an ambush. The street is deserted except for our car parked a little down the block. Seth is already in the car, but I'm sure he's on the phone with the police as we speak.

The longer I keep Jeff talking, the better chance the police have of catching him. Setting my phone to record, I slide it into my pocket and pull out my money clip.

I peel off a couple hundred-dollar bills and hold them out to Jeff. When he reaches out, I snatch them back.

"Information first." I'm not an idiot.

"Val met this guy. Nice guy, rich. He wanted access to her apartment. She didn't give a shit and he paid her money. He paid her a lot of money. So when he gave her cameras to put in her place, she thought, Why the fuck not? He told her how to install them. I came over and put one in the bathroom and one in Madison's bedroom. One in the kitchen and one in the living room."

Fuck. Only the bathroom was still drawing power when I went through her apartment.

"What else?" I keep the anger out of my voice.

"He was a real piece of work." Jeff smiles and leans forward. "He wanted her panties. Not fresh ones, if you know what I mean."

Angry bees swarm inside me. "What else?"

"He paid Val to keep him up-to-date on her movements. Gave her this fancy phone to take pictures of her." Jeff's hands shake against the chain-link fence. "I think Val gave him a spare key, but I'm not sure."

"Why did you attack Madison?" I narrow my eyes.

"Asshole stopped paying Val. Said he wouldn't be needing us anymore. Said he had another way to get access. Man, we needed that cash, and then Madison paid the rent, the full rent, and we knew the bitch came into money." Jeff laughs. "Val figured the chick started hooking to make ends meet."

Restraining my anger, I clip out, "What else do you know about the guy? Age, height, weight, anything?"

"He only met with Val. She knew him, but there might be a pic of him on the phone he gave her. She said it was her insurance if he ever came after her." He rubs the back of his neck. "I can't get to it though."

This is the first thing he said that might be useful. "Where is it?"

"The money first." He wiggles his fingers.

I'm tempted to not give it to him at all, but he presses his lips together. He's not going to give me more until I give him the money.

Fuck. I step closer and hand him the money. "Where's the phone?"

"Val hid it in the apartment. Said if she ever went missing to find it." He backs away as he talks, until he becomes one with the shadows.

Sounds like another trip to Madison's apartment is in my future. And soon. We need to find it before anyone else does.

Find out what happens next in PRIVATE LISTING: TEASE ME.

Meet C.S. Berry

C.S. Berry is a combination of my love for writing and my love for reading. She began as an experiment and took off into something I absolutely adore. It's not often you can do what you love and it works as a career. As for me, I love reading and romance and heroines seriously getting railed. I assume since you've read my books that you do too.

If you want to discuss books or anything with me, come join my Facebook group, C.S. Berry's Spicy Executive Suite. And you can always catch me on Instagram @csberry.

Oh and me, I have a lovely family who aren't allowed to read my books. But are so proud, they keep leaking my pen name. My dog and cats don't care about my writing as long as I sit still long enough for them to snuggle. For more of my books and to join my newsletter, visit my website csberry.com.

XOXOXO,
C.S. Berry

For more stories and updates:
csberry.com
Join my Newsletter

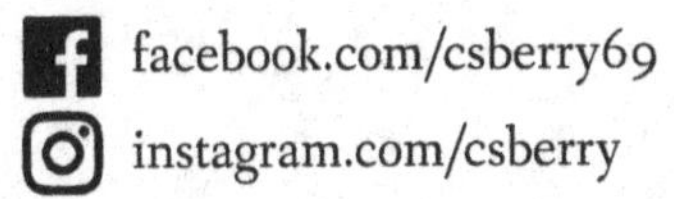

facebook.com/csberry69
instagram.com/csberry